EYEWITNESS ⬤ *HANDBOOKS*

CATS

DAVID ALDERTON

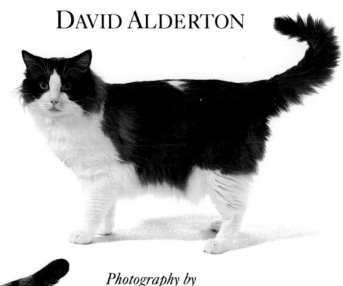

Photography by
MARC HENRIE

US Consulting Editor
DAPHNE NEGUS

A DK PUBLISHING BOOK

Important Notice
The publisher has made every effort to ensure that the color of the
cats' fur has been reproduced precisely but, because of the technical difficulties
inherent in color reproduction, this may not have been achieved in every case.

Editor Irene Lyford
Art Editor Colin Walton
Production Controller Caroline Webber
US Editor Charles A. Wills
US Consulting Editor Daphne Negus

First American Edition, 1992
10 9 8 7

Published in the United States by DK Publishing, Inc.
95 Madison Avenue, New York, NY 10016

Library of Congress Cataloging-in-Publication Data
Alderton, David, 1956-
The eyewitness handbook of cats / David Alderton; with an introduction by Daphne Negus.
–1st American ed.
p. cm.- (Eyewitness handbooks)
Includes index.
ISBN 1-56458-073-3 – ISBN 1-56458-070-9 (flexibinding)
1. Cats. 2. Cat breeds. 3. Cat breeds–pictorial works.
I. Title. II. Series
SF442.A44 1992
636.8–dc20
92-7611 CIP

Computer page make up by Colin Walton Graphic Design, Great Britain
Text film output by The Right Type, Great Britain
Reproduced by Colourscan, Singapore
Printed and bound in Singapore by Kyodo Printing Co.

EYEWITNESS ● HANDBOOKS

CATS

CONTENTS

Introduction 6
The Cat Family 10
What is a Cat? 12
Senses and Instincts 14
Cats and Kittens 16
Breed / Color
Development 18
Choosing a Cat 20
Grooming for Showing 22
Showing 24
Fur Types 26
Fur Colors 28
Coat Patterns 30
Identification Key 32

SHORT-HAIRED CATS
British Shorthair 118
Color Pointed British
Shorthair 132
Exotic 136
Manx 140
Japanese Bobtail 143
Scottish Fold 144
Snowshoe 147
American Shorthair 148
American Wirehair 156
American Curl 158
European
Shorthair 160
Color Pointed
European
Shorthair 164
Chartreux 165
Cornish Rex 166
Devon Rex 172
Sphynx 178
Selkirk Rex 180
Russian Shorthair 182
Korat 183
Siamese / Colorpoint
Shorthair 184

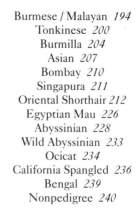

Burmese / Malayan 194
Tonkinese 200
Burmilla 204
Asian 207
Bombay 210
Singapura 211
Oriental Shorthair 212
Egyptian Mau 226
Abyssinian 228
Wild Abyssinian 233
Ocicat 234
California Spangled 236
Bengal 239
Nonpedigree 240

— 🐈 —

Cat Credits 246
Glossary 250
Index 252
Useful Addresses and
Acknowledgments 256

LONG-HAIRED CATS
Persian 40
Himalayan 62
Birman 68
Turkish Angora 74
Turkish Van 78
Angora 80
Javanese (UK) 83
Maine Coon 84
Norwegian Forest 90
Siberian Cat 93
Ragdoll 94
Somali 96
Balinese / Javanese 102
Tiffany 108
Cymric 110
Scottish Fold 111
American Curl 112
Nonpedigree 114

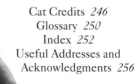

INTRODUCTION

During the 9,000 years or so since the domestication of the cat began in the Middle East, these remarkable creatures have provoked a mixed reception. Although worshipped in ancient Egypt, and treasured in the Far East, they suffered undeserved persecution in Europe during the early Christian era because of their associations with the old pagan religions. However, the role of cats in destroying the rats that carried the Black Death across Europe regained them some status.

BASTET
The focus of cat worship in Egypt was Bubastis, site of the temple of the goddess Bastet, shown here in the form of a woman with a cat's head.

Victorian Great Britain was a prime spot for nurturing feline popularity, the first cat shows being organized there by the famed author and illustrator Harrison Weir. The cat fancy soon spread to the United States, and on May 8, 1895, the first American all-breed cat show took place at Madison Square Garden. The Chicago Cat Club and the Beresford Club were formed four years later. In 1904 the task of registering cat breeds was taken on by the American Cat Club (ACA), which is now the oldest registration body in North America. In 1906, some ACA members set up the Cat Fanciers' Association (CFA) which has since grown into the largest cat association in the world. The next offshoot was the Cat Fanciers' Federation, founded in 1919, followed by the American Cat

HARRISON WEIR
First president of the National Cat Club, organizer of the first cat show, and notable cat illustrator.

FIRST CAT SHOW AT CRYSTAL PALACE
The first major cat show took place at Crystal Palace, London, on July 13, 1871. Organized by Harrison Weir, the show was comprised largely of British Shorthairs and Persians.

Fanciers' Association (ACFA) in 1954. The Canadian Cat Association was formed in 1960, and is still in existence.

In 1979, a large number of ACFA members decided to form a new registry with fresh rules, including registrations based on genetics, and with the express intention of improving the equality in judging. This new registry, known as The International Cat Association (TICA), is currently the second largest registration body in the United States.

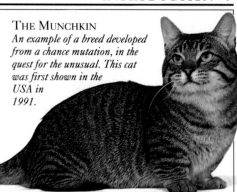

THE MUNCHKIN
An example of a breed developed from a chance mutation, in the quest for the unusual. This cat was first shown in the USA in 1991.

INTERNATIONAL SCENE

Clubs with affiliation to US associations have been organized in many countries, including Japan, Germany, Australia, and South America, and entries to US shows come from many countries not restricted by quarantine laws.

As cats have gained in popularity and importance, the cat fancy has become more global in scope. Export and import is commonplace, as ever more native breeds and newly discovered mutations depart for foreign show benches.

ROLE OF CAT ASSOCIATIONS

Cat associations are responsible for the proper recognition of breeds and for their accurate registration. They must also ensure

CAT ARTIST
Louis Wain, another President of the NCC, was famed for his whimsical cat illustrations.

CAT SHOW WINNERS
Winning at shows confers status and value on the cat concerned. The thousands of cat shows, of varying degrees of formality, that take place throughout the world every year play a crucial role in maintaining standards.

that their rules are based on a genuine commitment to both the welfare and the protection of cats. Breed standards are discussed, and rejected or accepted, by association board members who also give recognition to new breeds and varieties.

AIM OF THIS BOOK

This book is intended primarily as an identification guide to cats. However, with so many registries, both nationally and internationally, there are bound to be differing standards and classifications. In the United States, for example, the name Siamese is applied only to the four "pure" or traditional colors, other colors being known as Colorpoint Shorthairs.

In the United Kingdom, on the other hand, all of these colors are grouped as Siamese. Similar differences arise with the long-haired versions of these cats, known in the United States as Balinese (the four traditional colors) or Javanese. In the United Kingdom, on the other hand, all of the colors are known as Balinese – and the name Javanese is applied to a completely different group of cats – one that emerged from a breeding program that was aimed at recreating the Angora. As well as such variations in standards and groupings, differences in the names given to colors also occur. All of these differences are discussed throughout the book.

NEW COLORS
The Oriental group is growing rapidly in terms of colors and patterns, such as this individual. Development is progressing on a long-haired form.

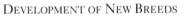

DNA TESTING

All the features of each cat are encoded on genes. DNA is the genetic material used to carry the information. It occurs in chains, and scientists are now using the sequencing within these chains to study cat evolution. Closely related species show less variance in their DNA sequencing than those that are more widely separated in evolutionary terms.

This method has also enabled scientists to assess when major changes occurred in the evolution of the cat family.

intervals over the decades. By this means, small wild cats have been used to contribute their markings to domestic cat bloodlines. A recent example of a breed obtained by this method is the Bengal. Breeders who show proper respect for such hybrids put great emphasis on breeding for sound temperament.

DEVELOPMENT OF NEW BREEDS

Some of today's breeds have been produced by the selective crossing of two established breeds. Most, however, are actually refined variants of cats that have arisen naturally in various parts of the world, outcrossings to other breeds then being used to increase the available range of coat lengths and colors.

HYBRIDIZATION

Obtaining new breeds by a process known as hybridization has occurred at

BENGAL
The Bengal is the result of hybridization – mating a wild Asiatic leopard cat with a domestic cat.

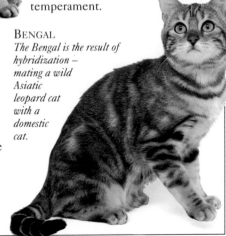

HOW THIS BOOK WORKS

FOLLOWING the Introduction and the Identification Key, the main breed section of the book is divided into two parts: Long-haired Cats on *pp.40–117* and Short-haired Cats on *pp.118–245*. As conventional classifications of pedigree cat breeds presuppose a fairly extensive knowledge of the subject, this straightforward division is intended to simplify the subject for newcomers, as well as to enhance the book's usefulness as a recognition guide. The annotated example below shows how a typical breed entry is organized.

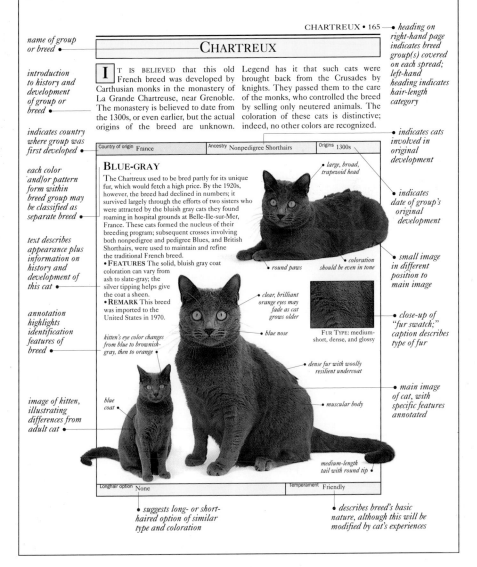

name of group or breed •

CHARTREUX • 165 —• *heading on right-hand page indicates breed group(s) covered on each spread; left-hand heading indicates hair-length category*

CHARTREUX

introduction to history and development of group or breed •

I T IS BELIEVED that this old French breed was developed by Carthusian monks in the monastery of La Grande Chartreuse, near Grenoble. The monastery is believed to date from the 1300s, or even earlier, but the actual origins of the breed are unknown.

Legend has it that such cats were brought back from the Crusades by knights. They passed them to the care of the monks, who controlled the breed by selling only neutered animals. The coloration of these cats is distinctive; indeed, no other colors are recognized.

indicates country where group was first developed •

| Country of origin | France | Ancestry Nonpedigree Shorthairs | Origins 1300s |

•—• *indicates cats involved in original development*

each color and/or pattern form within breed group may be classified as separate breed •

BLUE-GRAY
The Chartreux used to be bred partly for its unique fur, which would fetch a high price. By the 1920s, however, the breed had declined in numbers; it survived largely through the efforts of two sisters who were attracted by the bluish gray cats they found roaming in hospital grounds at Belle-Ile-sur-Mer, France. These cats formed the nucleus of their breeding program; subsequent crosses involving both nonpedigree and pedigree Blues, and British Shorthairs, were used to maintain and refine the traditional French breed.

large, broad, trapezoid head •

•—• *indicates date of group's original development*

text describes appearance plus information on history and development of this cat •

• **FEATURES** The solid, bluish gray coat coloration can vary from ash to slate-gray; the silver tipping helps give the coat a sheen.
• **REMARK** This breed was imported to the United States in 1970.

round paws •

• *coloration should be even in tone*

•—• *small image in different position to main image*

annotation highlights identification features of breed •

kitten's eye color changes from blue to brownish-gray, then to orange •

• *clear, brilliant orange eyes may fade as cat grows older*

• *blue nose*

FUR TYPE: medium-short, dense, and glossy

•—• *close-up of "fur swatch;" caption describes type of fur*

• *dense fur with woolly resilient undercoat*

•—• *main image of cat, with specific features annotated*

image of kitten, illustrating differences from adult cat •

blue coat •

• *muscular body*

medium-length tail with round tip •

| Longhair option | None | Temperament | Friendly |

• *suggests long- or short-haired option of similar type and coloration*

• *describes breed's basic nature, although this will be modified by cat's experiences*

THE CAT FAMILY

WILD CATS are widely distributed around the world, in all inhabited continents except Australia. They tend to live on their own (with the exception of the lion, which lives in groups called prides) and are predatory by nature, hunting a wide variety of prey. Several species have been adversely affected by furhunters, but international resolve to regulate this illegal trade has increased

UNDETERMINED TAXONOMY

SUBFAMILY PANTHERINAE

CHEETAHS

Cheetahs are the fastest land mammals in the world. They are capable of achieving speeds of up to 56 mph/h (90 km). They live in open areas, where there is very little cover, so pace is vital.

PANTHERA LINEAGE

Recent work, involving the use of DNA testing, compared the genetic similarities between different species in the cat family. The results suggest that there are actually three main lineages that cut across existing classificatory divisions. These are the Ocelots from South America; the Wild Cats, including the ancestor of the domestic cat; and the Panthera group, which is made up of the remaining members of the sub-families Pantherinae and Felinae.

PANTHERA GROUP
Lion
Tiger
Leopard
Jaguar
Snow Leopard
Clouded Leopard
Marbled Cat
Caracal
Bobcat
North American Lynx
Eurasian Lynx
Spanish Lynx
Serval
African Golden Cat
Asian Golden Cat
Leopard Cat
Fishing Cat
Flat-headed Cat
Rusty Spotted Cat
Bay Cat
Iriomote Cat
Jaguarundi
Puma
Onza

TIGER
Instantly recognizable by its striped patterning, the tiger is the biggest of all wild cats, with Siberian Tigers weighing up to 705 lb (320 kg).

during recent years, and the future of these cats now seems more secure.

Most species are well camouflaged by their coloring and the patterning of spots or bars on their coats and this, along with their slow, quiet movements, enables them to get close to prey for a successful kill. The coloration of their coats can be directly influenced by local factors. For example, leopards in Asia, which inhabit forested areas to a greater extent than do their African cousins, show an increased tendency towards melanism; this means that their coats become black, thus helping to conceal more effectively their presence in the darkness of the forests.

FELIDAE

SUBFAMILY FELINAE

NEW CATS

Scientists had always been reluctant to accept rumors of a pumalike cat that was said to exist in Mexico – although the cat was known to the Aztecs and to the early Spanish explorers. On January 1st, 1986, however, one of these cats was shot; they are now known by the traditional name, the Onza.

OCELOTS

These small cats, some almost unknown because of their shy natures and remote territories, are to be found in a wide range of New World habitats.

OCELOT FAMILY
Ocelot
Geoffroy's Cat
Pampas Cat
Andean Mountain Cat
Margay
Kod Kod
Oncilla

WILD CATS

This Old World group consists of cats living in parts of Europe, Africa, and Asia. The largest member is the Jungle Cat, which can weigh up to 35 lb (16 kg). Most hunt small mammals.

Pallas's Cat
Jungle Cat
Black-footed Cat
Sand Cat
Chinese Desert Cat
Wild Cat
Domestic Cat

OCELOT
In the United States these cats are now found in only a restricted area, but range as far south as Argentina.

WILD CAT
The most widely distributed member of the group, the Wild Cat varies throughout its range in appearance.

DOMESTIC CAT
The domestic cat is thought to be descended from the African Wild Cat. The tabby markings seen on Wild Cats also occur frequently in the domestic form.

WHAT IS A CAT?

DOMESTIC BREEDS of cat show very little variation in appearance, all being of relatively similar size. Precise features, such as the head shape and coat length, may well differ, however, particularly in the case of pedigree cats that have been modified by selective breeding over generations in order to conform to the standards laid down by breeders and cat assocations. In many ways, though, domestic cats are still very similar to their wild ancestors and possess the same athleticism and hunting skills. These features are vividly demonstrated by feral cats – cats that have reverted back to nature, living wild wherever they find suitable cover.

• upright carriage

medium-length tail •

• PERSIAN
The short, bushy tails should be in proportion to the body length; they are often carried low.

• MANX
This breed shows a variable absence of tail. In the Rumpy, the tail is entirely missing.

TAILS
Tails, in a variety of shapes and sizes, play a vital part in the cat's balance and in the "righting reflex" that allows it to land on its feet after falling from a height.

• TAIL
helps cat keep balance as it climbs and walks; held upright here

BODY •
cats are not generally prone to obesity

RIB CAGE •
protects the body organs, such as the heart and lungs, and moves as the cat breathes

• THIGHS
thigh muscles provide the thrust that enables the cat to jump effectively

• REAR PAWS
usually four toes on each of the hind feet

BODY SHAPES

PERSIAN

BRITISH SHORTHAIR

BURMESE

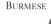

SIAMESE

The outline of a cat's body usually gives a clear indication of the group to which it belongs. Persians, and their relatives, and the British, American, and European Shorthairs, have cobby bodies, set low on the legs. Burmese and Asian cats are of medium size with slender legs, whereas Orientals and Siamese have a slender, svelte body shape.

broad skull

small ears

broad skull

round eyes

large ears

long, tapering wedge

flat skull

large ears

round face

round eyes

round face

short nose

long face

slanting eyes

wedge-shaped head

oval eyes

PERSIAN

BRITISH SHORTHAIR

SIAMESE

DEVON REX

EARS
usually erect, but may
be folded or curled in
some breeds

EYES
shape and coloration
vary, but all cats are
well-equipped to see in
the dark

FURNISHINGS
the hair in the ears is
more profuse in some
cases than in others

EYELIDS
serve to protect the
eyes from injury, with
the color sometimes
contrasting with that
of the eyes

NOSE LEATHER
the hairless area,
incorporating the two
nostrils

WHISKERS
an important part of the
cat's sensory system,
enabling it to assess width

NECK
the neck contributes to
the overall impression
of the body shape

CHEST
size varies according to
breed; in this case it is of
medium, semicobby type

HEAD
The shape of the cat's
head is an important
identification feature;
some, such as the
British Shorthair, are
rounded, whereas
others, such as the
Oriental, are of a
triangular shape when
viewed from the front.

RUFF
Some breeds have longer
fur around the neck and
chest, described as a ruff

ruff may be
less distinctive
in summer

FEET
Cats' paws are important,
both for climbing and for
catching prey in the wild.
Many breeds of domestic
cat, such as the Persians,
have large, rounded paws,
but in Orientals the paws
are much smaller and
oval in shape.

FRONT PAWS
normally five toes, with
the dewclaw not in
contact with the ground

carpal pad (front paws only)
helps prevent cat from sliding
on slippery surface when
jumping

sharp
claws

toe
pads

metacarpal
pads

dewclaw

SENSES AND INSTINCTS

CAT NAPPING
Cats may sleep for up to three quarters of the day, especially when they are young.

ALTHOUGH THE DOMESTIC CAT retains many of the behavioral traits associated with its wild relatives, adaptations to domestic living have occurred, most noticeably in territorial matters. Cats in urban areas inevitably have to share space, rather than maintain large territories, but as they are fed by their owners and do not have to fend for themselves, this does not cause great problems.

WEANING
Kittens may start feeding on their own when they are about three weeks old but will not be fully weaned from the mother until they are at least two months of age.

ESCAPING
Most female cats are very diligent mothers and keep a close watch on their kittens; any that stray too far (left) are likely to be carried back, held in the mother's mouth, as shown above.

FIRST MEETING
Cats tend to be cautious when they first meet (left), males being most likely to show aggression.

MAKING FRIENDS
Kittens reared together become close companions, spending most of their time together (right).

HUNTING
Although cats are born with a natural hunting instinct, they have to learn the specific skills required. They do this in early kittenhood by observing their mother and other cats. The skills then have to be practiced repeatedly in order to become perfected.

CATCHING
The games that kittens love to play enable them to practise specific hunting skills, such as stalking and catching, as seen here.

CLIMBING
Cats are extremely agile climbers, using both their legs and claws to anchor themselves firmly on a branch. Kittens have to learn these skills by trial and error.

BALANCING
Balance is maintained by the semi-circular canals in the ears. If the cat begins to fall, its body will swing round so that it will land on its feet.

CLEANING
Cats spend time grooming themselves every day. The rough surface of their tongues helps remove loose hairs as they lick their fur but, if swallowed, these may form a mat, or hairball, in the stomach.

SCENT MARKING
Male cats who have not been neutered tend to spray their pungent urine both inside and outside the home as a means of staking out their territory. Scratching and rubbing against objects, as well as against people, also serves to mark out territory by scent.

SEEING IN THE DARK
As night hunters, cats rely on a special layer of cells (tapetum lucidum) behind the retina, at the back of their eyes, which reflects light back, increasing its intensity. This causes the cat's eyes to glow in the dark.

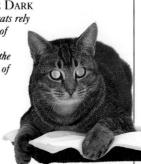

CATS AND KITTENS

T HE APPEARANCE of kittens is often different from that of adult cats. It can take several years for a kitten to develop its full coat and coloring, and this makes it difficult to assess the show potential of a litter of kittens at the stage (from twelve weeks of age) at which they are ready to go to new homes. In the case of pedigree kittens, however, it is very important to ensure that they are correctly registered with the appropriate associations at this early stage.

COAT LENGTH
The Cinnamon Angora and her four kittens on the right are of similar coloring, but the silky coats of the kittens are somewhat shorter than that of their mother.

MALE CATS
The Lilac and Chocolate British Shorthairs (left) both show the well-developed jowls of entire, adult males; these are missing from the male kittens (below), as well as from neutered adult males.

PATTERNS AND MARKINGS
These young British Shorthairs show signs of tabby markings. While their coloration may well darken over successive molts, their colored pattern will not change; the white areas will also remain constant in both their size and shape.

CHANGING COLORATION
The adult cat (left) is much darker than the kitten. Tabby markings in young Blue-creams should disappear as they mature, but the actual pattern of the colors will not alter later.

POINTED COLORS
The points become visible gradually in kittens, more rapidly in some cases than in others. They appear first on the tips of the ears and on the tail. Siamese kittens lack the "tracings" that connect the mask to the ears in adults.

SPOTTED PATTERNING
The difference in the depth of coloration between kitten and adult is clear here, although the kitten is now showing signs of its adult eye coloration. Its blue spotted patterning will not change, but it should become more distinctive.

TABBY PERSIANS
The tabby patterning can become blurred in later life as the coat grows.

It is believed that kittens showing the darkest markings are likely to develop the best adult coats.

BREED DEVELOPMENT

THE SELECTIVE breeding of cats has been taking place for just over a century; prior to this, no attempt had been made to lay down standards by which entries to cat shows could be judged. Although the standard today is open to interpretation, and may differ from one association to another, two aspects are traditionally included. The first is an attempt to describe what should be the ideal appearance (or "type") of the breed. The second gives guidance on coloration and patterning, depending on the breed concerned. Only recently, in some associations, has temperament come under scrutiny.

SIAMESE DEVELOPMENT

Since the first Siamese cats were imported to Britain in the 1880s, the type of this breed has altered greatly. Below is a prize-winning Siamese of the early 1900s, with its modern counterpart on the right.

as well as the original Seal Point coloration, shown here, other color forms are now available •

difference most noticeable on head; now distinctly triangular in shape •

body shape now longer and more lithe •

• selective breeding has eliminated kinks in tail

• today's cat has longer legs

PERSIAN DEVELOPMENT

The typical Persian features shown in the cat below, dating from the early 1900s, can also be seen in the contemporary cat on the right, but these have become more exaggerated over the years.

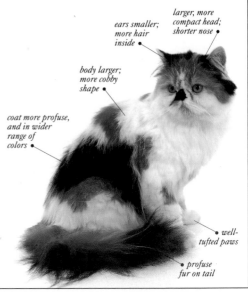

larger, more compact head; shorter nose

ears smaller; more hair inside •

body larger; more cobby shape •

coat more profuse, and in wider range of colors •

• well-tufted paws

• profuse fur on tail

COLOR DEVELOPMENT

FELINE GENETICS are now more clearly understood than in the early days of the cat fancy, and this has enabled breeders to develop programs that are more specifically aimed at producing new colors or patterned forms. Because of the random way in which chromosomes carrying the genes combine, however, there is no guarantee of the color of kittens resulting from a given mating.

round face •

thick tail, with rounded tip •

THE MOTHER
This Blue-cream British Shorthair female can produce Blue-cream kittens as well as Creams. She is also highly valued for producing good-quality Blue offspring.

• firm body

good coat quality in this British cat

THE FATHER
Choosing the stud carefully to compensate for any weaknesses in the type of the female should help ensure that the kittens will be of merit equal to the parents, and may be of even better type.

• cheek folds or jowls

• muscular, cobby body

deep, broad chest •

• good, even depth of blue coloration

THE KITTENS
It is difficult to predict the show potential of these kittens with certainty, as their adult coloration, including eye color and type, will develop as they mature.

• body low on legs

traces of silver tipping, not permitted in adults, may be seen here •

BLUE KITTEN

being a tortie, this kitten is almost certainly female •

BLUE-CREAM KITTEN

unwanted tabby markings are often seen in Cream kittens •

CREAM KITTEN

CHOOSING A CAT

HAVING DECIDED that you want to acquire a cat, the next question is whether you should choose a non-pedigree or a purebred specimen. Non-pedigrees are always easier to find – try looking through advertisements in local newspapers, or in pet stores, or contact an animal rescue organization.

If you are seeking a purebred cat, it may be more difficult to obtain the kitten of your choice, especially one of the rarer breeds. Bear in mind, also, the differences between the various breeds: Persians are much more placid than Orientals, and long-haired cats always require more grooming than do their short-coated relatives. There are no serious breed weaknesses in cats, however, and both pedigree and non-pedigree animals have a similar life span, which can be fifteen years or more.

NONPEDIGREE CAT
The result of a random mating, such cats show great variation in appearance; like all cats, they are also highly individual in temperament.

If you are hoping to exhibit in the future, it is important to select a kitten that has show potential. Breeders are usually able to assess this by the time that kittens are ready to go to a new home (three months of age). These are likely to be more expensive than kittens with faults, such as obviously poor type or patterning, that would impair their show chances. Such faults, however, will be of little concern if you are simply looking for a healthy and appealing pet.

WHERE TO BUY

If you decide to get a pedigree cat, the advertisement columns of the various cat magazines may help you to find a breeder with kittens available; alternatively, contact one of the cat associations or a specialist breed society. Visiting shows is another way to make contacts if you are searching for a particular breed; you may have to go on a waiting list, as demand for some breeds can outstrip supply.

PEDIGREE (PUREBRED) CAT
The result of careful selective breeding, this cat has been bred to conform as closely as possible to the recognized "type" specified in the breed standard.

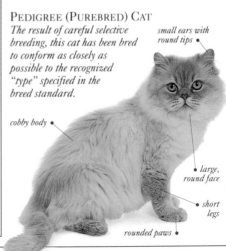

small ears with round tips

cobby body

large, round face

short legs

rounded paws

TAKE YOUR PICK

Choosing a kitten is never easy, as all young cats are so appealing. Decide in advance whether you want a male or a female. In many breeds, males are slightly larger when mature and should always be neutered, unless required for breeding purposes. This will prevent them from straying from home, and lessen the risk of injuries from fighting. Females will also need to be spayed, at around six months of age, if you wish to avoid unwanted pregnancies.

1 OBSERVE THE KITTENS
Spend a few minutes simply observing the kittens: look for an alert, playful, inquisitive individual who does not appear reluctant to be handled.

watchful mother •
• ready to play
interested •
• mischievous

2 CHECK THE COAT
Part the fur and look for any dark specks that are likely to indicate the presence of fleas: these can act as intermediate hosts for tapeworms.

3 CHECK EARS AND EYES
Ears should be clean and free of wax. The third eyelid, or nictitating membrane, should not extend across the eye, nor should there be any discharge from here.

4 CHECK THE MOUTH
Look inside the mouth after prizing the jaws apart. This is vital with older cats, which may have broken teeth, gum disease, or show signs of dental decay.

5 CHECK THE ANAL AREA
Lift the tail and check that the kitten is not suffering from diarrhea; there should be no signs of staining here. At the same time check the gender of the kitten: in a female (right), the two openings are close together; in a male they are farther apart.

clean ears •
alert demeanor •
• round, firm chest

6 MAKING YOUR CHOICE
It is advisable to arrange a veterinary check up for your kitten, either before or soon after purchase. You should also obtain certified proof from the owner or breeder that the kitten has been inoculated, as well as a copy of its pedigree.

GROOMING FOR SHOWING

ALL CATS require grooming. Under normal circumstances, they lick their coat, removing dead hairs with the rough surface of the tongue; but the hairs may form a hairball in the stomach, which can affect the cat's appetite and its health. Although this is most likely to occur during the shedding period, regular grooming is useful at all times for revealing the presence of parasites such as fleas, ticks, and lice, which will cause the cat to scratch excessively.

On these pages we show just a small selection from the huge range of equipment that is available. A slicker brush is handy for removing dead hair from long-haired cats, but it must be used with caution to avoid pulling out other hairs. Bristle brushes are useful for shorthairs, and some owners like to give their cats a final polish with a chamois cloth or with a piece of silk or velvet before a show. You will need a supply of cotton-tipped swabs for cleaning around the eyes, ears, and nose, as well as talcum or grooming powder, shampoo, and conditioner.

GROOMING PERSIANS

Long-haired cats need daily grooming in order to prevent their coats from becoming matted and tangled.

wide-toothed comb

metal comb with rotating teeth

wire- and nylon-bristled brushes

dual-toothed metal comb

guillotine-type clippers

slicker brushes for removing dead hair

pure bristle brushes

1 APPLYING POWDER
Apply nontoxic baby powder, corn starch, or grooming powder to the coat, section by section. Work the powder well into the coat by hand, ensuring that it is evenly powdered all over.

2 REMOVING POWDER
Using a bristle brush, brush out the coat carefully and thoroughly. The powder adds body to the coat, but no traces must remain on the day of the show.

3 BRUSHING OUT
Brush or comb coat until it stands up all over the body.

4 GROOMING FACE
With a toothbrush, brush the hair on the face, being careful not to get too close to the eyes. Brush or comb the fur around the neck until it forms a ruff.

CLEANING THE COAT

For short-haired cats, a bran bath is an effective means of removing excess grease and dirt from the coat without using water and shampoo, which many cats dislike. If you do bathe your cat with water, use a shampoo that is specifically formulated for cats. Some owners use a cloth soaked in witch hazel to wipe dirt and grease from the coat. Have everything ready before you start: combs and brushes, towels, and a velvet or chamois polishing cloth.

1 RUBBING IN BRAN
Stand the cat on a towel. Massage warm bran into coat, avoiding eyes and nose. Some owners wrap the cat in a towel before brushing out the bran.

2 BRUSHING OUT BRAN
Brush out the bran thoroughly and systematically. This method is not suitable for long-haired cats, as any particles left in the coat could cause matting.

GROOMING SHORTHAIRS

Shorthairs should generally be combed or brushed in the direction of the fur, from head to tail. Use a fine-toothed comb to smooth the coat and help spot fleas.

rubber brushes

nail clippers

bristle brush for general grooming

metal comb, useful for detecting fleas

chamois / velvet polishing glove

1 CLEANING THE FACE
With a cotton-wool swab and weak salt solution, gently clean around the nose, eyes, and ears.

2 CLIPPING THE CLAWS
If in doubt, ask your vet to show you how to do this without causing injury. Use veterinary clippers that are designed to prevent splitting of the claws.

3 USING A RUBBER BRUSH
This is useful for shorthairs, but must be used gently to avoid removing too much of the undercoat. It is particularly good for rexes, as it won't scratch the skin.

4 POLISHING THE COAT
For a finishing touch to grooming, polish the coat with a polishing mitt that has velvet on one side and chamois leather on the other, or with a piece of silk.

SHOWING

IT IS OFTEN THOUGHT that only pedigree cats can be shown but, in fact, there are also classes for non-pedigrees, or "household pets," at most shows. Cat shows are usually advertised in the specialist magazines or you may hear about an event from a fellow enthusiast. In either case you will need to obtain an official entry form. Some cat associations also produce a calendar of shows for the entire year, and there you will find the addresses of the show secretaries. When requesting information about a show, remember to enclose a stamped, self-addressed envelope of legal size, or else you may not receive a reply. Send for entry details as soon as possible, so that you will have enough time to enter your cat for the show.

APPLYING FOR ENTRY

Always be sure to read the schedule carefully, so that you can complete the entry form correctly. If you are in any doubt, the show secretary will usually be very pleased to advise you. You should also send for a copy of the association's official rules and study them. The entry form must then be sent back well in advance of the closing date, along with the appropriate entry fee.

It is vital that your cat is properly vaccinated before taking part in a show, so check that its inoculations are up to date, especially if you are not a regular exhibitor. Should your cat appear unwell for any reason before a show, consult

---

WHEN YOU GET TO THE SHOW

• Upon checking in, your cat will receive a number that corresponds with its number in the show catalog. It is also the same number as the one attached to the cage in the judging ring when your cat is called to be judged.

• Be sure to give your cat enough time for it to settle in its cage before judging begins.
Put a litter tray with clean litter, and a water bowl with fresh water, in the cage.
• Give your cat a final grooming, and check its eyes, ears, and tail for dirt.
• When your cat is called for judging, take it to the judging ring and place it in the cage on which the appropriate number has been put by the ring clerk.

TRANSPORTING YOUR CAT
The carrier (left) provides a secure means of transporting your cat. The top-opening carrier (right) is easily cleaned, with removable lining.

BRITISH SHOW
British cat shows vary in size, from the smaller exemption shows, up to national events.

AMERICAN SHOW
In the United States, owners may enter more shows by registering with several bodies.

your vet without delay, although you will probably have to withdraw from the event. This is clearly in the interests of all exhibitors, in order to prevent the possible spread of illness. Similarly, if your cat becomes pregnant, you will not be able to exhibit it. Pregnant and lactating cats are disqualified.

PREPARING FOR THE SHOW

The regulations concerning equipment vary according to the event. If you are in doubt about this aspect, check beforehand. Careful grooming in the period leading up to the show is essential to ensure that your cat looks its best. Good show cats must also accept handling by strangers, without resentment, and this is why it is so important for kittens to be handled regularly as they grow. You should also get your cat used to traveling from an early age. Check all equipment before leaving, packing the night before, if possible. To avoid last-minute panic, be sure you take instructions on how to get to the show, leave in plenty of time to get there, and don't let your cat out of the house just before you plan to leave!

SHOW EQUIPMENT
Exhibitors should bring all required cage furnishings. Litter trays, litter cardboard, and food (if announced in the entry form) are usually provided.

A WINNER!
A winning cat can accumulate an impressive collection of rosettes. An outstanding purebred cat can be named champion after a single show, whereas registered household cats can compete for titles like Master and Grand Master.

FUR TYPES

Nᴜᴍᴇʀᴏᴜs ᴠᴀʀɪᴀᴛɪᴏɴs have occurred in the fur types of domestic cats, some having evolved naturally, while others have been produced by selective breeding. Fur type is an individual feature of each breed, independent of color, and is determined by the specific combination of down, awn, and guard hairs in the fur (*see right*). Close-up photographs of fur are shown throughout this book to help distinguish between the coats of cats of the same color.

relatively coarse guard hairs

soft, woolly down

thick tips to awn

GUARD
Otherwise known as primary hairs, these constitute the longest and the most visible part of the coat.

DOWN
Short and soft, the down hairs help provide body insulation. Some breeds, however, lack down hairs.

AWN
Slightly longer, bristly hairs that, together with the soft down hairs, constitute the secondary hairs.

LONG-HAIRED CATS

Coat length can be variable, depending on the breed and the season; the density of the coat results largely from the down hair, which also provides the greatest insulation. The Persian Longhair has long guard hairs protruding through the thick down hairs, creating a very dense coat. The hairs of the Angora are finer and less profuse, while the shaggy appearance of the Maine Coon results from the uneven lengths of the individual guard hairs.

Fᴜʀ Tʏᴘᴇ: fine; silky; no woolly undercoat

ANGORA
Sometimes described as semilonghair, the Angora's coat lies close to the body, especially in summer.

Fᴜʀ Tʏᴘᴇ: long, thick, silky, and fine

PERSIAN
These cats have the longest and densest fur of all domestic cats. The topcoat may be up to 5 in long.

Fᴜʀ Tʏᴘᴇ: thick, silky, and of variable length

MAINE COON
Adapted to living outdoors, these cats have a dense undercoat and a glossy, waterproof topcoat.

SHORT-HAIRED CATS

There is considerable variation in both the appearance and texture of the coats of this group of cats. The Siamese and Orientals have sleek, soft coats with very short, fine-textured hair. By contrast, the Manx has a pronounced double coat – a vital feature of the breed – which serves to emphasize the size of the cat; the undercoat is short and very thick, the guard hairs being just slightly longer. The Russian Blue is another breed that has a very distinctive double coat; this stands up, away from the body, and is soft and silky in texture, as well as being short and thick.

FUR TYPE: short, fine, soft, wavy, and curly

DEVON REX
All three hair types are present, but guard and awn hairs are modified to resemble down hairs, giving a wavy appearance.

FUR TYPE: medium, crimped, and coarse

AMERICAN WIREHAIR
The hairs are crimped into waves, giving the coat a springy, wiry texture.

FUR TYPE: short, dense, and crisp

BRITISH SHORTHAIR
In this case, the coat stands out from the body, giving a rug-like texture, but it must not be too long.

THE "HAIRLESS" SPHYNX

In spite of the name, the Sphynx does have some hair, most conspicuously on the extremities. It also has eyebrows and whiskers, but these are usually shorter than normal. Most of the body has a light covering of down hairs.

FUR TYPE: sparse, very short, and downy

SPHYNX
This highly distinctive breed has not found favor with all cat-lovers.

SEMILONGHAIR

This description is used for cats that have a fairly long topcoat and a greatly reduced undercoat, compared with either Persians or Himalayans. Included in the semilonghair group are breeds like the Maine Coon that have evolved naturally. These breeds usually show a difference in coat length between winter and summer.

FUR COLORS

ALTHOUGH a number of pure colors are now well established within the cat fancy, the basic underlying coloration of the domestic cat is tabby. Actual coloration results from the presence of color pigments in the hairs, but it is also influenced by light, which may act to dilute the color of the hairs, so that they appear lighter than usual. There are also natural variations of the same color, so that even littermates may differ in the exact depth of their coloration. In particular, some creams may appear much redder than others.

SELF COLORS

In selfcolored cats, the coloration should be solid from the tips to the roots. Even so, realignment of color pigment does cause

- solid color
- standard depth
- no variation in coloration

dilution, and this has increased the range of self colors. None of the striping that occurs in tabbies, however, is discernible along the length of the individual hairs of a self-colored cat. In the case of white selfs, there is no pigment present in the coat, but these are usually not pure albinos.

NEW COLORS

FAWN
This is the dilute form of cinnamon and resembles pale shades of lilac.

CINNAMON
This form of brown is produced by another mutation of the "black" gene.

DILUTE COLORS

The dilution effect is illustrated here, with dilute colors shown in the upper band above the related dense color. In the dilute colors, some areas have less pigment than others; these reflect white light and create a paler impression.

CREAM
This is the dilute form of red; it tends to be variable in depth of color, often with traces of tabby markings.

LAVENDER
Variations in the precise shade are also common in this color, some cats being of a lighter shade than others.

BLUE
This color approximates more closely to gray than to pure blue because it is, in fact, a dilute form of black.

WHITE
Caused by a dominant gene, which means that white kittens are likely to occur even if just one of the parents is white.

RED
Sometimes known as Yellow but breeders have, in fact, tried to produce a red rather than an orange shade.

CHESTNUT
This is a dense color that is now being developed in various breeds, including the Oriental group.

BLACK
Well known and widely represented in the cat fancy, black should be a pure shade, with no trace of white hairs.

TIPPED

The extent of the tipping on the guard hairs, and also on the awn hairs in some cases, will have a significant effect on

colored tip

hairs mainly white

near-white bases

the overall appearance of the coat. In the case of the Cream Shell Cameo Persian seen here, the undercoat is almost pure white, while the coloration is confined almost exclusively to the tip of the guard hairs.

CHINCHILLA PERSIAN
The lightest of the silver forms, with the trace of black tipping creating a sparkling effect.

CREAM SHELL CAMEO PERSIAN
The equivalent in the cream series, with white undercoat and cream tipping.

SHADED

In this case, although the undercoat is hardly affected, being largely white, the tipping extends much

more pigment

darker appearance

whitish bases

farther down the length of the guard hairs from their tips, creating a noticeably darker appearance. It is possible to see the lighter undercoat when the cat is moving, or simply by parting the fur to reveal the underlying contrasting color.

CREAM SHADED PERSIAN
Here the cream tipping is more pronounced, leading to a more definite coloration.

RED SHADED PERSIAN
Identical to the Cream except that, in this case, darker red coloration replaces cream.

SMOKE

This is the darkest form of tipping, most of the guard hair being pigmented. The undercoat still remains lighter,

dark coloration

hairs mainly colored

dense pigmentation

however, and the contrast is most apparent when the cat walks. The Smoke characteristic is now widely distributed, although the darker forms, in which the distinctive contrast is pronounced, are most popular.

BLUE SMOKE PERSIAN
Pigmentation is most pronounced in the Smokes, so that these cats can resemble selfs.

BLACK SMOKE PERSIAN
Smoke coloration is variable, and some cats will therefore appear lighter than others.

TICKED

Ticking provides a useful means of camouflage for cats. With the coloration broken into bands

tips colored

variable pigment

lighter banding

along the length of the individual hairs, the cat's coat becomes less conspicuous. Where the tabby markings are solid, there are hairs with no banding, and this creates further contrast in the coat, sometimes known as disruptive coloration.

SILVER SORREL SOMALI
Here the white hair is ticked with chocolate, creating an impression of silvery peach..

RUDDY ABYSSINIAN
The effect of ticking is to create a distinctive coloration that may be variable in depth over the cat's body.

COAT PATTERNS

MOST CATS have a coat patterning that reflects to some extent the natural tabby markings of their wild ancestors. Breeders have refined these markings, developing them to conform to precise standards. Gradually, by the careful selection of breeding stock, and over successive generations, patterning has been altered in line with the requirements of breeders. An element of luck is required to produce a cat with an ideal coat patterning, but the probability can be greatly increased by following a well-designed breeding program.

Undesirable features can also be bred out from the cat, as has occurred in the case of the Abyssinian. Its tabby barring has now virtually disappeared, creating the so-called "ticked tabby" pattern.

With few exceptions, a cat's patterning does not change after birth, although the markings may become more distinctive.

PARTICOLORS
Many cats have areas of white fur alongside colored areas. This can vary from the "magpie" appearance of black and white cats, to the Calico with its combination of white, cream, black, and red patches.

CALICO
Clearly defined patches of black, cream, red, and white are all visible in this particolored individual •

• BICOLORED
It has been possible, by a process of selective breeding, to restrict the proportion of white fur, so that it should cover no more than one half of the entire body area

TORTOISESHELL
In the tortoiseshell, the black, cream, and red coloration should be evenly intermingled and distributed over the body; a facial blaze of cream or red is desirable in torties.

BLUE-CREAM
In these cats, otherwise known as Dilute Torties, blue replaces black, and cream replaces red, giving them a distinctive coloration •

TORTOISESHELL •
For genetic reasons, almost all cats showing the tortoiseshell patterning are female

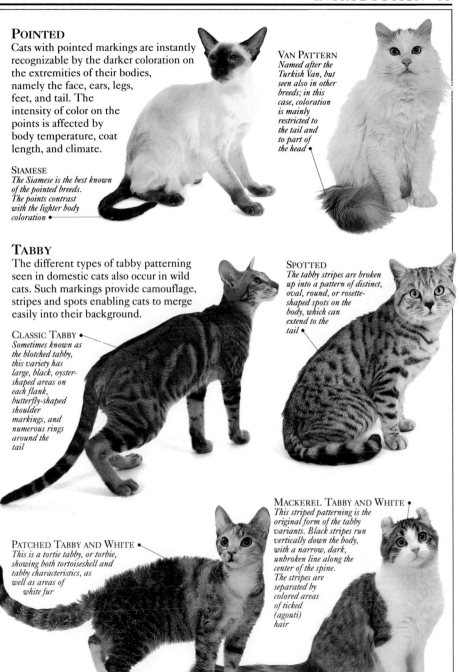

POINTED

Cats with pointed markings are instantly recognizable by the darker coloration on the extremities of their bodies, namely the face, ears, legs, feet, and tail. The intensity of color on the points is affected by body temperature, coat length, and climate.

SIAMESE
The Siamese is the best known of the pointed breeds. The points contrast with the lighter body coloration •

VAN PATTERN
Named after the Turkish Van, but seen also in other breeds; in this case, coloration is mainly restricted to the tail and to part of the head •

TABBY

The different types of tabby patterning seen in domestic cats also occur in wild cats. Such markings provide camouflage, stripes and spots enabling cats to merge easily into their background.

CLASSIC TABBY •
Sometimes known as the blotched tabby, this variety has large, black, oyster-shaped areas on each flank, butterfly-shaped shoulder markings, and numerous rings around the tail

SPOTTED
The tabby stripes are broken up into a pattern of distinct, oval, round, or rosette-shaped spots on the body, which can extend to the tail •

PATCHED TABBY AND WHITE •
This is a tortie tabby, or torbie, showing both tortoiseshell and tabby characteristics, as well as areas of white fur

MACKEREL TABBY AND WHITE •
This striped patterning is the original form of the tabby variants. Black stripes run vertically down the body, with a narrow, dark, unbroken line along the center of the spine. The stripes are separated by colored areas of ticked (agouti) hair

IDENTIFICATION KEY

THIS IDENTIFICATION KEY has been designed to help you identify both pedigree and nonpedigree cats. The Key is in four stages. In Stage 1, cats are classified according to their coat length; in Stage 2, these categories are broken down further according to face shape; in Stage 3, photographs of one individual from each breed group, with page references, guide you to the appropriate section of the book. Stage 4 covers non-pedigree cats and, as before, photographs of individual cats, with page references, guide you directly to the relevant section.

STAGE 1: LENGTH OF HAIR

A cat's coat is its most striking feature, not just in terms of coloration and pattern, but also in the way that it affects the overall impression of the cat's shape and size. It is for this reason that the classificatory groupings applied to pedigree cats rely in the first instance on coat length. There are, of course, differences in the texture of the coat as well. This information is covered fully in in the appropriate breed section entries, in the main part of the book.

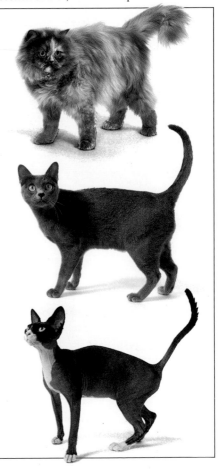

LONG-HAIRED CATS
The coat of a long-haired cat is often so profuse that it may appear to double the cat's size. This is particularly true of the classic Persian whose coat can be up to 5 in (12.5 cm) in length, and can come in three types, commonly called wool, cotton, and silk. Like all cats, longhairs may shed a substantial amount of hair during the warmer months, and this can have the effect of altering their appearance considerably.

SHORT-HAIRED CATS
The coat of a short-haired cat allows you to see the underlying body shape more clearly. It may be sturdy and muscular, or lithe and sleek. The coats of shorthairs can vary in appearance and texture; it may be very short, sleek, and close-lying, or the fur may vary in length on different areas of the body. The texture may be fine or coarse, dense, or plush, and the hairs may be straight, crinkled, curly, or wavy.

"HAIRLESS" CATS
Hairlessness, or relative lack of hair, in pedigree cats is the result of a spontaneous mutation that has subsequently been developed by selective breeding. Although such mutations have been recorded in the past, only one pedigree breed has been developed – the Sphynx – which does, in fact, have a fine covering of down, especially on the face, ears, feet, and tail. For further details of this rather controversial breed, turn to p.178.

STAGE 2: FACE SHAPE

The face shapes of both long-haired and short-haired cats fall into three broad categories, and at this stage you must decide whether the face of the cat you are trying to identify is round, or angular and wedge shaped, or whether it belongs in the middle category of shapes that falls between these two extremes. Face shape can usually be related also to body shape; cats with a round face tend to have cobby bodies, whereas those with wedge-shaped faces typically have a lithe and svelte outline.

It is worth noting that facial characteristics may vary slightly between the sexes, in that unneutered male cats are likely to develop jowls once they mature: jowls are a secondary sexual characteristic, however, and if male cats are neutered before puberty the jowls will not develop. The shape of the face will also vary at different times of the year, according to whether the cat is shedding or in full coat.

LONG-HAIRED CATS

ROUND-FACED
In this case the head is massive and round, with a broad skull and small, round-tipped ears that are set wide apart and low on the head. The face has full, rounded cheeks, and a short, broad nose with a stop.

INTERMEDIATE-FACED
In this group, the head is of medium length. It is well proportioned, with a straight profile, or with a slight break. The ears are usually large, pointed, set well apart, and positioned high on the head.

WEDGE-FACED
This face narrows in straight lines from the widely spaced ears to the muzzle, forming a perfect wedge. The profile is slightly convex, and the nose is long and straight. The ears are large and pointed.

SHORT-HAIRED CATS

ROUND-FACED
This face is round with full cheeks and good breadth of skull. The broad, short nose is straight, and the profile shows a rounded forehead and a slight break. The small, round-tipped ears are set wide apart.

INTERMEDIATE-FACED
The head in this case is of medium proportions, slightly broader at the top, tapering to a soft, rounded triangle. The nose can show a shallow indentation, while the ears are medium to large, and broad at the base.

WEDGE-FACED
This is an elegant, elongated face that narrows in perfectly straight lines to the noticeably fine muzzle. The profile is straight, with no break in the long nose. The ears are large, pointed, and wide at the base.

STAGE 3: IDENTIFY YOUR CAT

Having made your decisions about coat length and face shape at Stages 1 and 2, now refer to the appropriate section below where all the pedigree breeds featured in the book can be found. The silhouettes of body shapes that accompany each face are given as an additional identification aid, while the adjacent numbers are page references. Where there are many different color forms of a breed (such as the Persian Longhairs) we have selected just one representative example for the Key; the cat chosen illustrates the typical features of the breed, differing from the others only in color. It is important to bear in mind that coloration is not necessarily a significant feature in the identification of breeds, and that many breeds can be of similar coloration. However, color is a guide in the identification of pointed breeds that display darker markings on their body extremities, such as the ears, feet, and tail.

LONG-HAIRED CATS WITH ROUND FACES

Persian *40*

Tabby Persian *54*

Chinchilla *55*

Himalayan *62*

Birman *68*

Cymric *110*

Scottish Fold *111*

American Curl *112*

LONG-HAIRED CATS WITH INTERMEDIATE-SHAPED FACES

Turkish Angora *74*

Turkish Van *78*

Maine Coon *84*

Norwegian Forest *90*

Siberian Cat *93*

Ragdoll *94*

Somali *96*

Tiffany *108*

LONG-HAIRED CATS WITH WEDGE-SHAPED FACES

Angora *80*

Javanese (UK) *83*

Balinese / Javanese *102*

SHORT-HAIRED CATS WITH ROUND FACES

British Shorthair *118*

Color Pointed British Shorthair *132*

Exotic *136*

Manx *140*

Scottish Fold *144*

American Shorthair *148*

American Wirehair *156*

American Curl *158*

European Shorthair *160*

Color Pointed European Shorthair *164*

Chartreux *165*

Bengal *239*

SHORT-HAIRED CATS WITH INTERMEDIATE-SHAPED FACES

Japanese Bobtail *143*

Russian Shorthair *182*

Korat *183*

Burmese / Malayan *194*

Burmilla *204*

Asian *207*

Bombay *210*

Singapura *211*

Abyssinian *228*

Wild Abyssinian *233*

Ocicat *234*

California Spangled *236*

SHORT-HAIRED CATS WITH WEDGE-SHAPED FACES

Snowshoe *147*

Cornish Rex *166*

Devon Rex *172*

Sphynx *178*

Selkirk Rex *180*

Siamese / Colorpoint Shorthair *184*

Tonkinese *200*

Oriental Shorthair *212*

Havana Brown *216*

Oriental Tabby *220*

Egyptian Mau *226*

STAGE 4: NON-PEDIGREE CATS

Non-pedigree cats, by their nature, tend not to be of a recognizable type, and there can be wide variation in their appearance, as the examples below illustrate. The range of coat patterns is very variable in non-pedigrees, where there are no restrictions on their breeding. It is not possible to group them meaningfully on the basis of their facial characteristics, either, although there may well be local similarities within a particular area where some in-breeding of related non-pedigree cats has occurred. Selective breeding can then serve to reinforce such natural features and a new breed can evolve, as happened recently with the Singapura. A similar process took place on the Isle of Man, where the gene for taillessness arose, breeders carrying on the process begun by nature. Many of today's breeds have been developed from spontaneous mutations in non-pedigree stock.

LONG-HAIRED NON-PEDIGREE CATS

Blue *114*

Cream and White *115*

Silver and White *117*

SHORT-HAIRED NON-PEDIGREE CATS

Black and White *241*

White and Tortie *241*

Blue-cream *242*

Red Tabby and White *243*

Blue Tabby and White *243*

Brown Tabby and White *244*

LONG-HAIRED CATS

PERSIAN

T HESE ELEGANT and graceful cats, known as Persian in the US and as Persian Longhairs in the UK, have been popular since Victorian times. They have been bred in an ever-increasing range of colors, but their appearance has changed considerably since the early days. They now have a flatter, more rounded face and the ears are smaller; the coats have also become more profuse, and these require daily grooming in order to prevent matting.

Country of origin Great Britain	Ancestry Angoras x Persians	Origins 1880s

ORANGE-EYED WHITE

Some of the earliest Persians in Europe and in the United States were white. These cats usually had blue eyes, and this orange-eyed form resulted from subsequent crossings involving Blue, Cream, and Black Persians.
• FEATURES Pure white, with a long, thick coat, these are quite large cats, with a distinctly cobby profile. On occasion, kittens may show traces of dark markings on the head, but these usually disappear later in life.
• REMARK It was only in 1938 that the Blue-eyed and the Orange-eyed White Persians were divided into separate categories in Great Britain.

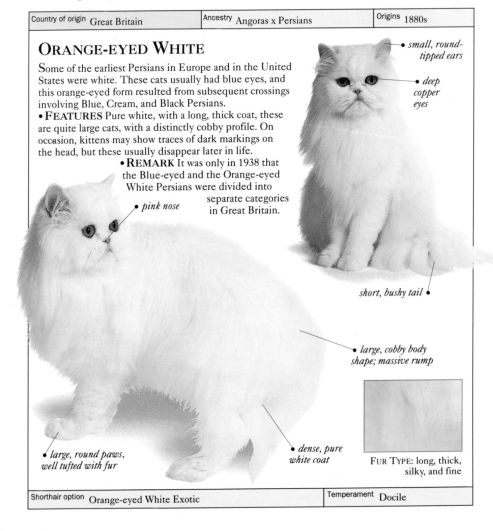

small, round-tipped ears

deep copper eyes

pink nose

short, bushy tail •

• large, cobby body shape; massive rump

• large, round paws, well tufted with fur

• dense, pure white coat

FUR TYPE: long, thick, silky, and fine

Shorthair option Orange-eyed White Exotic	Temperament Docile

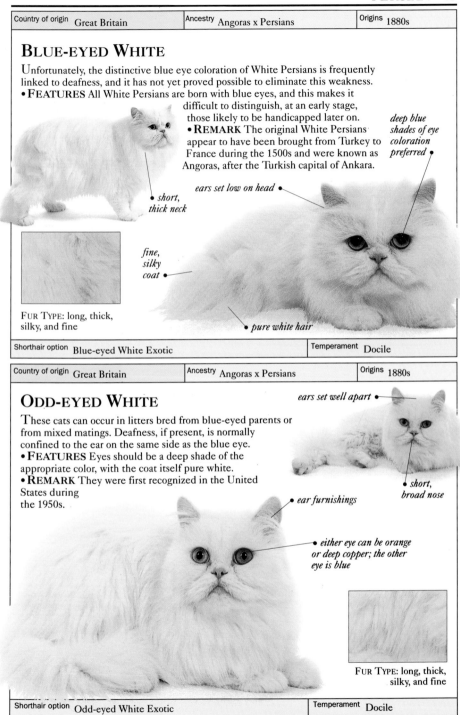

Country of origin		Ancestry		Origins	
Great Britain		Angoras x Persians		1880s	

BLUE-EYED WHITE

Unfortunately, the distinctive blue eye coloration of White Persians is frequently linked to deafness, and it has not yet proved possible to eliminate this weakness.
• FEATURES All White Persians are born with blue eyes, and this makes it difficult to distinguish, at an early stage, those likely to be handicapped later on.
• REMARK The original White Persians appear to have been brought from Turkey to France during the 1500s and were known as Angoras, after the Turkish capital of Ankara.

deep blue shades of eye coloration preferred •

• ears set low on head

• short, thick neck

fine, silky coat •

FUR TYPE: long, thick, silky, and fine

• pure white hair

Shorthair option		Temperament	
Blue-eyed White Exotic		Docile	

Country of origin		Ancestry		Origins	
Great Britain		Angoras x Persians		1880s	

ODD-EYED WHITE

ears set well apart •

These cats can occur in litters bred from blue-eyed parents or from mixed matings. Deafness, if present, is normally confined to the ear on the same side as the blue eye.
• FEATURES Eyes should be a deep shade of the appropriate color, with the coat itself pure white.
• REMARK They were first recognized in the United States during the 1950s.

• short, broad nose

• ear furnishings

• either eye can be orange or deep copper; the other eye is blue

FUR TYPE: long, thick, silky, and fine

Shorthair option		Temperament	
Odd-eyed White Exotic		Docile	

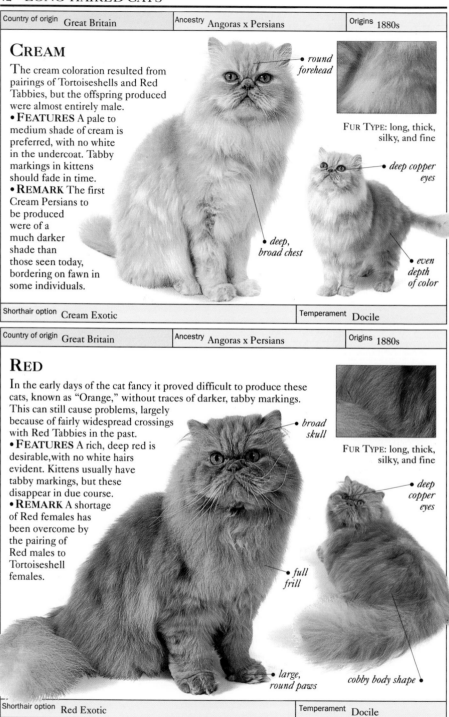

| Country of origin | Great Britain | Ancestry | Angoras x Persians | Origins | 1880s |

CREAM

The cream coloration resulted from pairings of Tortoiseshells and Red Tabbies, but the offspring produced were almost entirely male.
• **FEATURES** A pale to medium shade of cream is preferred, with no white in the undercoat. Tabby markings in kittens should fade in time.
• **REMARK** The first Cream Persians to be produced were of a much darker shade than those seen today, bordering on fawn in some individuals.

round forehead

FUR TYPE: long, thick, silky, and fine

deep copper eyes

deep, broad chest

even depth of color

| Shorthair option | Cream Exotic | Temperament | Docile |

| Country of origin | Great Britain | Ancestry | Angoras x Persians | Origins | 1880s |

RED

In the early days of the cat fancy it proved difficult to produce these cats, known as "Orange," without traces of darker, tabby markings. This can still cause problems, largely because of fairly widespread crossings with Red Tabbies in the past.
• **FEATURES** A rich, deep red is desirable, with no white hairs evident. Kittens usually have tabby markings, but these disappear in due course.
• **REMARK** A shortage of Red females has been overcome by the pairing of Red males to Tortoiseshell females.

broad skull

FUR TYPE: long, thick, silky, and fine

deep copper eyes

full frill

large, round paws

cobby body shape

| Shorthair option | Red Exotic | Temperament | Docile |

Country of origin Great Britain	Ancestry Angoras x Persians	Origins 1880s

LAVENDER

The Lavender is a dilute form of the Chocolate Persian, and the two breeds have been developed along similar lines. Further refinement to the type of these cats is continuing.
• **FEATURES** It has been difficult to create the desired shade of pinkish dove-gray, which must be of an even depth of color throughout the coat.
• **REMARK** This is one of the newer additions to the Persian group, dating back only to the 1960s. It is not yet very numerous.

massive rump

FUR TYPE: long, thick, silky, and fine

short, thick neck   *pure, even depth of color*

Shorthair option Lavender Exotic	Temperament Docile

Country of origin Great Britain	Ancestry Angoras x Persians	Origins 1880s

BLUE

The earliest Blues were bred from Black and White Persian crosses, selective breeding eliminating white blemishes from the coat. Queen Victoria kept this breed, thus ensuring its popularity in Great Britain.
• **FEATURES** Kittens often show tabby patterning but, oddly enough, those with the most pronounced markings often develop into the best adults.
• **REMARK** Blue cats originated in Russia, Persia (now Iran), and in the neighboring countries.

FUR TYPE: long, thick, silky, and fine

large orange or copper eyes

ears widely spaced and low on head

broad shoulders

short legs

paws tufted with fur

short, bushy tail

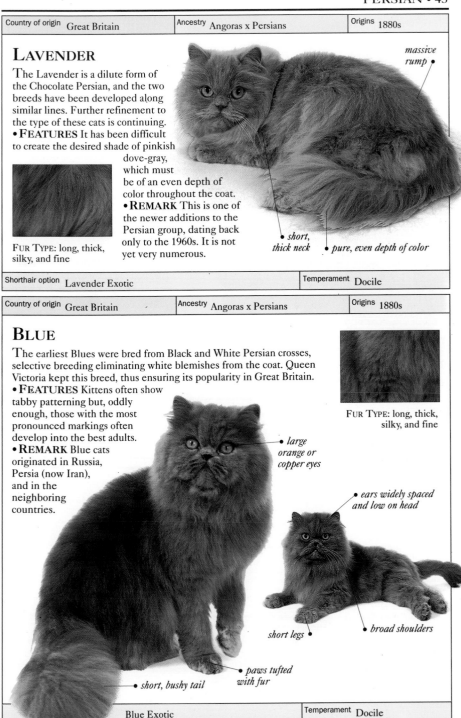

Blue Exotic	Temperament Docile

Country of origin Great Britain	Ancestry Angoras x Persians	Origins 1880s

CHOCOLATE

The Chocolate Persian originated with the crossing of a Havana and a Blue Persian. The first example of this color was exhibited in 1961.
• **FEATURES** The aim has been to produce cats with solid chocolate-brown coloration, and with no other markings of any kind.
• **REMARK** These cats are sometimes referred to as Kashmirs, being a self-colored form of the Himalayan, but this division is not widely recognized.

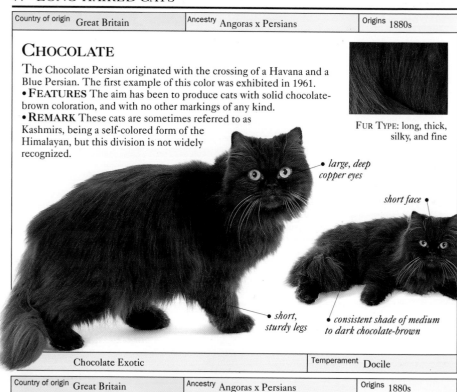

FUR TYPE: long, thick, silky, and fine

• *large, deep copper eyes*

short face •

• *short, sturdy legs*

• *consistent shade of medium to dark chocolate-brown*

Chocolate Exotic	Temperament Docile

Country of origin Great Britain	Ancestry Angoras x Persians	Origins 1880s

BLACK

First on the list of recognized breeds in Great Britain, these cats were exhibited at the first British cat show in 1871. They were equally popular in the United States at this early stage.
• **FEATURES** Good coloration is vital in this breed, with no shading, markings, or white hairs. Kittens may show a gray or rusty hue, but this should fade by about eight months of age.
• **REMARK** The early Black Persians had a more foreign type than do those seen today.

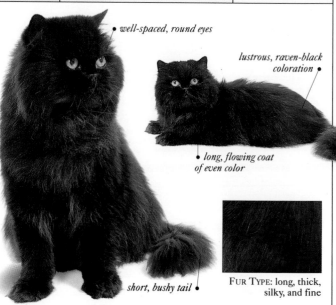

well-spaced, round eyes •

lustrous, raven-black coloration •

• *long, flowing coat of even color*

short, bushy tail •

FUR TYPE: long, thick, silky, and fine

Shorthair option Black Exotic	Temperament Docile

Country of origin Great Britain	Ancestry Angoras x Persians	Origins 1880s

CREAM AND WHITE

Originally, the aim with bicolors was to
breed them to resemble Dutch
rabbits, showing clear, encircling
bands of colored and white fur.
However, this proved
impossible to achieve.
• FEATURES A pale to
medium shade of cream is
required, with white
areas constituting
between one third and
one half of the coat.
• REMARK The bi-
colored form has a
long history in the
cat world but
never achieved
great popularity
in the early days.

small ears

FUR TYPE: long, thick,
silky, and fine

some white on tail permitted

large paws

Shorthair option Cream and White Exotic	Temperament Docile

Country of origin Great Britain	Ancestry Angoras x Persians	Origins 1880s

RED AND WHITE

This form of the bicolor is particularly difficult to breed successfully, as any
tabby markings apparent in the red areas of fur are deemed a fault.
• FEATURES A deep, rich shade of red is required, and the white areas must
be pure rather than off-white. These cats should not
differ from other Persians in terms of their type.
• REMARK The change of the standard for bicolors in Britain in 1971 led to greater interest in
the breed. Prior to this, it had been exceedingly
difficult to produce the desired symmetrical
pattern of markings.

slight shading in red on forehead

face shows both red and white

FUR TYPE: long, thick,
silky, and fine

colored fur on tail essential

definition between colored and white areas

Shorthair option Red and White Exotic	Temperament Docile

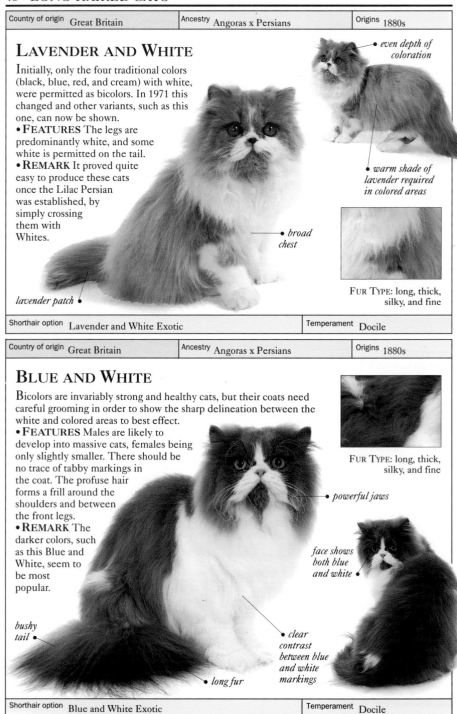

| Country of origin | Great Britain | Ancestry | Angoras x Persians | Origins | 1880s |

LAVENDER AND WHITE

Initially, only the four traditional colors
(black, blue, red, and cream) with white,
were permitted as bicolors. In 1971 this
changed and other variants, such as this
one, can now be shown.

• **FEATURES** The legs are
predominantly white, and some
white is permitted on the tail.

• **REMARK** It proved quite
easy to produce these cats
once the Lilac Persian
was established, by
simply crossing
them with
Whites.

even depth of coloration

warm shade of lavender required in colored areas

broad chest

lavender patch

FUR TYPE: long, thick, silky, and fine

| Shorthair option | Lavender and White Exotic | Temperament | Docile |

| Country of origin | Great Britain | Ancestry | Angoras x Persians | Origins | 1880s |

BLUE AND WHITE

Bicolors are invariably strong and healthy cats, but their coats need
careful grooming in order to show the sharp delineation between the
white and colored areas to best effect.

• **FEATURES** Males are likely to
develop into massive cats, females being
only slightly smaller. There should be
no trace of tabby markings in
the coat. The profuse hair
forms a frill around the
shoulders and between
the front legs.

• **REMARK** The
darker colors, such
as this Blue and
White, seem to
be most
popular.

FUR TYPE: long, thick, silky, and fine

powerful jaws

face shows both blue and white

bushy tail

clear contrast between blue and white markings

long fur

| Shorthair option | Blue and White Exotic | Temperament | Docile |

Country of origin Great Britain	Ancestry Angoras x Persians	Origins 1880s

CHOCOLATE AND WHITE

The Chocolate and White variety
followed on the development of
the Chocolate, the latter being
crossed with White Persians.
• **FEATURES** The colored
areas should cover between one
half and two thirds of the coat.
• **REMARK** The development of
this variety was encouraged by the
change in the British standard in
1971.

*• round, broad head
with good width
between ears*

FUR TYPE: long, thick,
silky, and fine

*• clear
delineation
between white
and chocolate
areas essential*

*• strong
chin*

Shorthair option Chocolate and White Exotic	Temperament Docile

Country of origin Great Britain	Ancestry Angoras x Persians	Origins 1880s

BLACK AND WHITE

These bicolors can be traced back to the early days of the cat fancy
when, because of their coloration, they were described as "magpie."
• **FEATURES** As in other bicolors, a symmetrical pattern of markings is
preferred, along with a facial blaze as shown here. The type of these cats
should not differ from that of other Persians.
• **REMARK** Bicolored Persians
were not recognized for
championship status in
Britain until 1966, and
little progress took place
before 1971 when the
more realistic standard for
markings was introduced.

FUR TYPE: long, thick,
silky, and fine

*• lustrous black coloration,
with no odd white hairs*

*temporary
rusty hue in
kitten's coat •*

*• white collar encircling
neck desirable*

Shorthair option Black and White Exotic	Temperament Docile

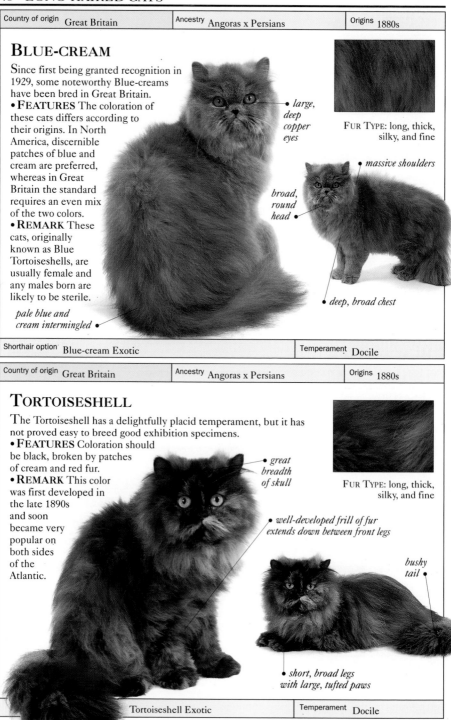

Country of origin Great Britain	Ancestry Angoras x Persians	Origins 1880s

BLUE-CREAM

Since first being granted recognition in 1929, some noteworthy Blue-creams have been bred in Great Britain.
• **FEATURES** The coloration of these cats differs according to their origins. In North America, discernible patches of blue and cream are preferred, whereas in Great Britain the standard requires an even mix of the two colors.
• **REMARK** These cats, originally known as Blue Tortoiseshells, are usually female and any males born are likely to be sterile.

large, deep copper eyes

FUR TYPE: long, thick, silky, and fine

massive shoulders

broad, round head

deep, broad chest

pale blue and cream intermingled

Shorthair option Blue-cream Exotic	Temperament Docile

Country of origin Great Britain	Ancestry Angoras x Persians	Origins 1880s

TORTOISESHELL

The Tortoiseshell has a delightfully placid temperament, but it has not proved easy to breed good exhibition specimens.
• **FEATURES** Coloration should be black, broken by patches of cream and red fur.
• **REMARK** This color was first developed in the late 1890s and soon became very popular on both sides of the Atlantic.

great breadth of skull

FUR TYPE: long, thick, silky, and fine

well-developed frill of fur extends down between front legs

bushy tail

short, broad legs with large, tufted paws

Tortoiseshell Exotic	Temperament Docile

Country of origin Great Britain	Ancestry Angoras x Persians	Origins 1880s

DILUTE CALICO

large, round eyes •

These Blue-cream and White cats must have white bellies, with clear white areas on the remaining lower parts of the body, and the face.
- **FEATURES** These areas must be clearly defined, with no white hairs mixed in with the blue-cream.
- **REMARK** Powdering the coat of a Dilute Calico Persian before a show helps increase the definition of each color.

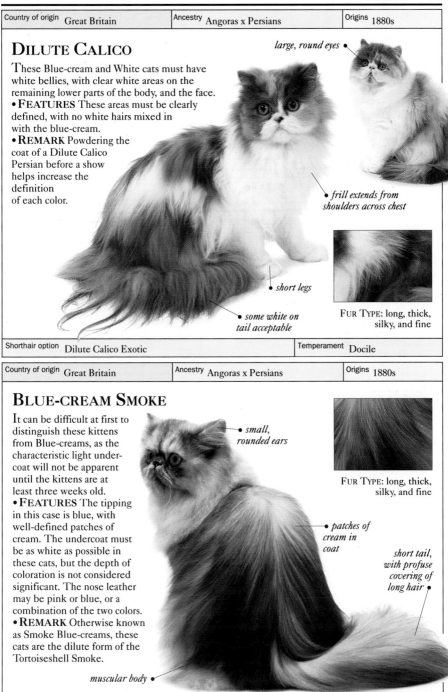

• frill extends from shoulders across chest

• short legs

• some white on tail acceptable

FUR TYPE: long, thick, silky, and fine

Shorthair option Dilute Calico Exotic	Temperament Docile

Country of origin Great Britain	Ancestry Angoras x Persians	Origins 1880s

BLUE-CREAM SMOKE

It can be difficult at first to distinguish these kittens from Blue-creams, as the characteristic light undercoat will not be apparent until the kittens are at least three weeks old.
- **FEATURES** The tipping in this case is blue, with well-defined patches of cream. The undercoat must be as white as possible in these cats, but the depth of coloration is not considered significant. The nose leather may be pink or blue, or a combination of the two colors.
- **REMARK** Otherwise known as Smoke Blue-creams, these cats are the dilute form of the Tortoiseshell Smoke.

• small, rounded ears

FUR TYPE: long, thick, silky, and fine

• patches of cream in coat

short tail, with profuse covering of long hair •

muscular body •

Shorthair option Blue-cream Smoke Exotic	Temperament Docile

Country of origin Great Britain	Ancestry Angoras x Persians	Origins 1880s

CALICO

Known in Britain as the Tortie and
White, these cats were rare before
being recognized in 1950. The name
"Calico" implies a resemblance of
the coat to the colorful cotton.
• **FEATURES** Between one third
and one half of the coat, in the
case of this UK cat, should show
clearly defined white patches,
with no white in the colored areas.
• **REMARK** A slightly different
standard for this breed has evolved in
North America, where white coloration
on the underparts is favored.

• *colored
and white
areas on
the head*

FUR TYPE: long, thick,
silky, and fine

• *clearly
defined
patches
of color*

• *cobby
body shape*

• *large, flattened face*

tail must show color •

Shorthair option Calico Exotic	Temperament Docile

Country of origin Great Britain	Ancestry Angoras x Persians	Origins 1880s

CALICO VAN (HARLEQUIN)

This variant of the Calico Persian is based on the Turkish Van, being a
predominantly white cat with restricted colored markings on the head,
ears, and tail. A range of colors has now been developed.
• **FEATURES** The Calico Pattern is a tricolored form of the breed, and
in this individual the
tortie base color is
black, cream, and
red. Bicolored
forms of Van
Persians are now
becoming more
numerous.
• **REMARK**
FiFe, the
international feline
body, granted
recognition to
these cats in 1986,
under the name of
"Harlequin."

• *color on head and ears*

FUR TYPE: long, thick,
silky, and fine

• *white
body*

*colored
tail* •

*up to three small spots
of color allowed on body* •

Shorthair option Calico Van (Harlequin) Exotic	Temperament Docile

Country of origin Great Britain	Ancestry Angoras x Persians	Origins 1880s

CHOCOLATE TORTIE

One of the newer color combinations to be developed, the
Chocolate Tortoiseshell shows to best effect in
winter when its coat is most profuse.
• **FEATURES** The basic color here is
chocolate, offset by light and dark red
patches. In type, these cats are typical
Persians, with large heads.
• **REMARK** After the development
of the Chocolate Persian, Chocolate
combinations, such as this
essentially female-only tortie
variety, could be produced.

*deep
copper
eyes*

*clear stop
between
forehead
and nose*

*fur may be up to
6 in (15 cm) long*

*short,
thick neck*

rounded rump

large, tufted paws

FUR TYPE: long, thick,
silky, and fine

Shorthair option Chocolate Tortie Exotic	Temperament Docile

Country of origin Great Britain	Ancestry Angoras x Persians	Origins 1880s

CHOCOLATE TORBIE

Most long-haired tabbies show classic patterning, as in this
case; the Mackerel form is quite scarce. Tabby markings
are often less distinctive in Persians than in shorthairs.
• **FEATURES** In this case, chocolate tabby markings
are combined with the tortoiseshell colors of cream
and red. The basic tabby patterning itself consists
of a bronze agouti ground color, with rich,
chocolate-colored markings. Paw pads can be
chocolate, pink, or a combination of both.
• **REMARK** These cats are sometimes known,
in other parts of the world, as "patched" or
"tortie" tabbies.

*broad,
round head
with short,
wide muzzle*

*strong
chin*

*pads may
be either
chocolate or
pink, depending
on distribution
of red*

FUR TYPE: long, thick,
silky, and fine

*short,
full tail*

Shorthair option Chocolate Torbie Exotic	Temperament Docile

Country of origin Great Britain	Ancestry Angoras x Persians	Origins 1880s

LAVENDER TABBY

Although bred from Lilac Persians, which date back to the 1960s, these tabbies are one of the more recent additions to the Persian category.
• **FEATURES** The ground color should be a beige agouti shade, offset by dense, clearly defined lilac markings, with no brindling. Markings should be evident on the sides of the body and running down the back in stripes.
• **REMARK** Tabby markings, long evident in Persians, have been introduced in association with the new colors as they have become available.

clear M-shaped marking on forehead •

• *lilac "necklaces" present on neck and chest*

• *lilac spotting on underparts*

FUR TYPE: long, thick, silky, and fine

Shorthair option Lavender Tabby Exotic	Temperament Docile

Country of origin Great Britain	Ancestry Angoras x Persians	Origins 1880s

BLUE TABBY

The earliest Blue Tabbies occurred in litters of Brown Tabby Persians, but they can also be bred by crossing a Blue self with a Brown Tabby.
• **FEATURES** There is good contrast in these cats, with dark blue markings and a pale blue ground color.
• **REMARK** These cats were granted recognition in the United States in 1962, but in the UK they have achieved only preliminary recognition.

good fur covering on tail •

• *blue nose*

FUR TYPE: long, thick, silky, and fine

• *tightly grouped dark lines*

clearly defined outline of an M •

cobby body; low on legs •

• *bushy tail*

Shorhair option Blue Tabby Exotic	Temperament Docile

| Country of origin Great Britain | Ancestry Angoras x Persians | Origins 1880s |

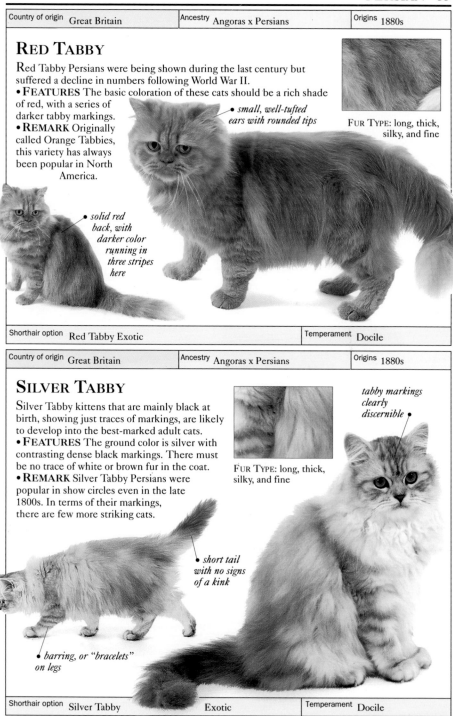

RED TABBY

Red Tabby Persians were being shown during the last century but suffered a decline in numbers following World War II.
• **FEATURES** The basic coloration of these cats should be a rich shade of red, with a series of darker tabby markings.
• **REMARK** Originally called Orange Tabbies, this variety has always been popular in North America.

• *small, well-tufted ears with rounded tips*

FUR TYPE: long, thick, silky, and fine

• *solid red back, with darker color running in three stripes here*

| Shorthair option Red Tabby Exotic | Temperament Docile |

| Country of origin Great Britain | Ancestry Angoras x Persians | Origins 1880s |

SILVER TABBY

Silver Tabby kittens that are mainly black at birth, showing just traces of markings, are likely to develop into the best-marked adult cats.
• **FEATURES** The ground color is silver with contrasting dense black markings. There must be no trace of white or brown fur in the coat.
• **REMARK** Silver Tabby Persians were popular in show circles even in the late 1800s. In terms of their markings, there are few more striking cats.

tabby markings clearly discernible •

FUR TYPE: long, thick, silky, and fine

• *short tail with no signs of a kink*

• *barring, or "bracelets" on legs*

| Shorthair option Silver Tabby | Exotic | Temperament Docile |

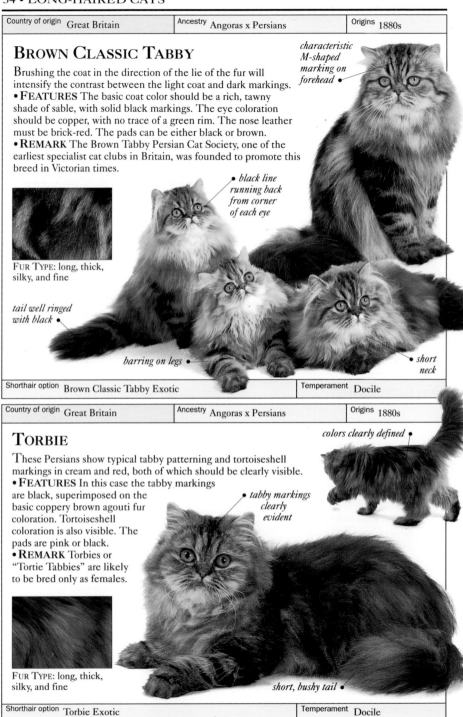

Country of origin	Ancestry	Origins
Great Britain	Angoras x Persians	1880s

BROWN CLASSIC TABBY

Brushing the coat in the direction of the lie of the fur will intensify the contrast between the light coat and dark markings.

characteristic M-shaped marking on forehead •

• **FEATURES** The basic coat color should be a rich, tawny shade of sable, with solid black markings. The eye coloration should be copper, with no trace of a green rim. The nose leather must be brick-red. The pads can be either black or brown.
• **REMARK** The Brown Tabby Persian Cat Society, one of the earliest specialist cat clubs in Britain, was founded to promote this breed in Victorian times.

• black line running back from corner of each eye

FUR TYPE: long, thick, silky, and fine

tail well ringed with black •

barring on legs •

• short neck

Shorthair option	Temperament
Brown Classic Tabby Exotic	Docile

Country of origin	Ancestry	Origins
Great Britain	Angoras x Persians	1880s

TORBIE

colors clearly defined •

These Persians show typical tabby patterning and tortoiseshell markings in cream and red, both of which should be clearly visible.
• **FEATURES** In this case the tabby markings are black, superimposed on the basic coppery brown agouti fur coloration. Tortoiseshell coloration is also visible. The pads are pink or black.

• tabby markings clearly evident

• **REMARK** Torbies or "Tortie Tabbies" are likely to be bred only as females.

FUR TYPE: long, thick, silky, and fine

short, bushy tail •

Shorthair option	Temperament
Torbie Exotic	Docile

| Country of origin Great Britain | Ancestry Angoras x Persians | Origins 1880s |

SHADED SILVER

There has been confusion in the past about the division between the Shaded Silver and the Chinchilla. Kittens of either form may occur in the same litter, and dark individuals may become paler, in effect becoming Chinchillas.
• **FEATURES** The black tipping, in the case of the Shaded Silver, should constitute about one third of the hair length.
• **REMARK** Breeders have concentrated on separating the two forms and on defining them clearly, by selective breeding.

tipping on face

FUR TYPE: long, thick, silky, and fine

pure white undercoat

black tipping shades from back to flanks

legs match face in coloration

| Shorthair option Shaded Silver Exotic | Temperament Docile |

| Country of origin Great Britain | Ancestry Angoras x Persians | Origins 1880s |

CHINCHILLA

The division between the Silver Shaded and the Chinchilla has now been reinstated, after being dropped at the beginning of the century.
• **FEATURES** The tipping in the Chinchilla is less pronounced than in the case of the Silver Shaded, resulting in a paler cat.
• **REMARK** Silver Tabbies may have led to the development of such cats in the 1800s.

tipping evenly distributed

FUR TYPE: long, thick, silky, and fine

kittens may be striped

pure white chest and chin

legs can be slightly tipped

| Shorthair option Chinchilla Exotic | Temperament Docile |

Country of origin Great Britain	Ancestry Angoras x Persians	Origins 1880s

CREAM SMOKE

The contrast in this case may not be quite as pronounced as in the darker colors, but it is nevertheless very attractive.

• **FEATURES** The basic body coloration is cream, shading to white on the sides and flanks. The undercoat becomes most evident as the cat walks.

• **REMARK** This variety needs very frequent grooming in order to show the Smoke effect to best advantage. As with all Smokes, kittens need to be at least six months old before they can be shown.

cream mask with no markings

cream feet

white frill extending from shoulders, and creating ruff on chest

short, bushy tail

FUR TYPE: long, thick, silky, and fine

Shorthair option Cream Smoke Exotic	Temperament Docile

Country of origin Great Britain	Ancestry Angoras x Persians	Origins 1880s

BLUE SMOKE

All Persians need extensive grooming; excessive grease in the coat can be overcome by rubbing corn starch into the coat and then brushing it out.

• **FEATURES** The blue coloration shades to silver on the sides of the body; the undercoat should be as white as possible to create an impressive contrast. The head and feet are also a deep shade of blue.

• **REMARK** The number of Blue Smokes has fluctuated as their popularity has risen and declined over the years.

blue coloration clearly evident along back

silver frill around neck

FUR TYPE: long, thick, silky, and fine

Shorthair option Blue Smoke Exotic	Temperament Docile

| Country of origin Great Britain | Ancestry Angoras x Persians | Origins 1880s |

BLACK SMOKE

There is some variation in the depth of black coloration in these cats. British breeders prefer the darker individuals. The contrast between the white undercoat and the black tipping on each hair is pronounced in the Black Smoke, frequent grooming being needed to emphasize the effect.

• **FEATURES** These cats resemble other Persians in type having a broad, round head, and cobby body. Their eye coloration should be deep copper.

• **REMARK** Black Smokes date back to the 1860s and are the traditional color form.

blackish back •

• *silver frill around neck*

black body coloration showing white undercoat when parted •

well-furnished tail •

FUR TYPE: long, thick, silky, and fine

| Shorthair option Black Smoke Exotic | Temperament Docile |

| Country of origin Great Britain | Ancestry Angoras x Persians | Origins 1880s |

BLUE-CREAM SMOKE

When assessing the potential of young Smoke kittens, choose those whose undercoats are lightest as they are likely to become the best adults in terms of their coloration. Regular grooming is especially important in maintaining the appearance of these cats.

• **FEATURES** In the case of the Blue-cream Smoke, the tipping should be a mixture of blue and cream, mingled together to create an attractive appearance. The contrasting undercoat should be as white as possible.

• **REMARK** Crossings involving Blue-cream Persians were used in the past to improve the type of other Smokes.

facial blaze •

• *coloration often most intense across head*

FUR TYPE: long, thick, silky, and fine

tufted paws •

short, powerful legs •

| Shorthair option Blue-cream Smoke Exotic | Temperament Docile |

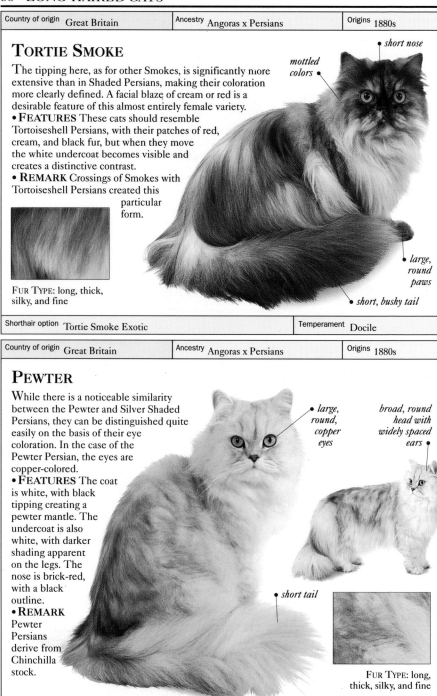

Country of origin Great Britain	Ancestry Angoras x Persians	Origins 1880s

TORTIE SMOKE

short nose

mottled colors

The tipping here, as for other Smokes, is significantly more extensive than in Shaded Persians, making their coloration more clearly defined. A facial blaze of cream or red is a desirable feature of this almost entirely female variety.

• FEATURES These cats should resemble Tortoiseshell Persians, with their patches of red, cream, and black fur, but when they move the white undercoat becomes visible and creates a distinctive contrast.

• REMARK Crossings of Smokes with Tortoiseshell Persians created this particular form.

large, round paws

FUR TYPE: long, thick, silky, and fine

short, bushy tail

Shorthair option Tortie Smoke Exotic	Temperament Docile

Country of origin Great Britain	Ancestry Angoras x Persians	Origins 1880s

PEWTER

While there is a noticeable similarity between the Pewter and Silver Shaded Persians, they can be distinguished quite easily on the basis of their eye coloration. In the case of the Pewter Persian, the eyes are copper-colored.

large, round, copper eyes

broad, round head with widely spaced ears

• FEATURES The coat is white, with black tipping creating a pewter mantle. The undercoat is also white, with darker shading apparent on the legs. The nose is brick-red, with a black outline.

• REMARK Pewter Persians derive from Chinchilla stock.

short tail

FUR TYPE: long, thick, silky, and fine

Shorthair option Pewter Exotic	Temperament Docile

Country of origin Great Britain	Ancestry Angoras x Persians	Origins 1880s

GOLDEN PERSIAN

The distinctive coloring of these cats results from the shading on the individual hairs.

• **FEATURES** The undercoat varies from apricot to gold, with seal-brown or black tipping on the head, back, flanks, and tail. The legs can be shaded, with a solid colored area that corresponds to the color of the tipping, extending from the paw up to the heel. Paw pads may be seal-brown or black.

• **REMARK** Only seal-brown tipping is allowed in North America, which results in a less pronounced effect.

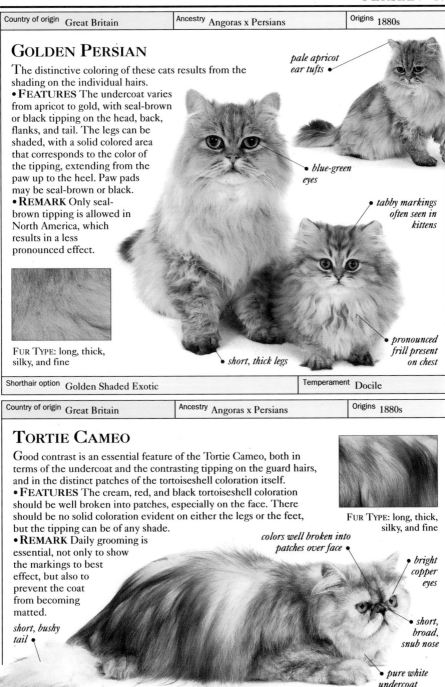

pale apricot ear tufts •

• *blue-green eyes*

• *tabby markings often seen in kittens*

• *pronounced frill present on chest*

FUR TYPE: long, thick, silky, and fine

• *short, thick legs*

Shorthair option Golden Shaded Exotic	Temperament Docile

Country of origin Great Britain	Ancestry Angoras x Persians	Origins 1880s

TORTIE CAMEO

Good contrast is an essential feature of the Tortie Cameo, both in terms of the undercoat and the contrasting tipping on the guard hairs, and in the distinct patches of the tortoiseshell coloration itself.

• **FEATURES** The cream, red, and black tortoiseshell coloration should be well broken into patches, especially on the face. There should be no solid coloration evident on either the legs or the feet, but the tipping can be of any shade.

• **REMARK** Daily grooming is essential, not only to show the markings to best effect, but also to prevent the coat from becoming matted.

FUR TYPE: long, thick, silky, and fine

colors well broken into patches over face •

• *bright copper eyes*

• *short, broad, snub nose*

short, bushy tail •

• *pure white undercoat*

Shorthair option Tortie Cameo Exotic	Temperament Docile

Country of origin Great Britain	Ancestry Angoras x Persians	Origins 1880s

CREAM SHADED CAMEO

The stunning appearance of these cats results from the contrast between the white undercoat and the cream shading.

• **FEATURES** The most pronounced cream areas occur on the mask and along the back to the tip of the tail. The legs and feet are well shaded; the ear tufts, flanks, frill, and underparts are pale.

• **REMARK** Cameos were developed in the United States, during the 1950s.

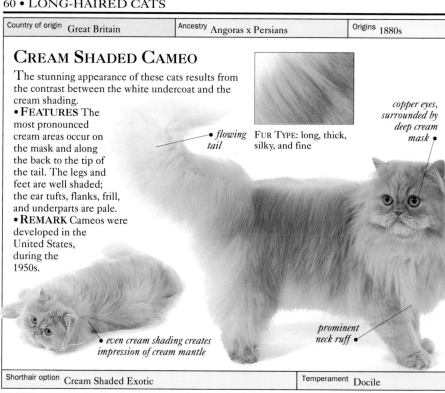

copper eyes, surrounded by deep cream mask •

• flowing tail FUR TYPE: long, thick, silky, and fine

prominent neck ruff •

• even cream shading creates impression of cream mantle

Shorthair option Cream Shaded Exotic	Temperament Docile

Country of origin Great Britain	Ancestry Angoras x Persians	Origins 1880s

CREAM SHELL CAMEO

Shell Cameos are lighter in the depth of their coloration than Shaded Cameos or darker Smokes; this difference is the result of shorter tipping on the individuals hairs.

• **FEATURES** The sparkling appearance of these cats results from the combination of predominantly white fur and slight cream tipping, giving a somewhat misty effect. The pads and the nose leather should be pink.

• **REMARK** Cameos were established in Australia, New Zealand, and North America in the 1960s. The first European Cameo was bred in Holland in 1962, two years after recognition in North America.

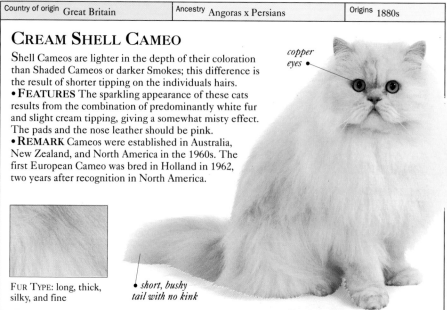

copper eyes •

FUR TYPE: long, thick, silky, and fine

• short, bushy tail with no kink

Shorthair option Cream Shell Cameo Exotic	Temperament Docile

Country of origin Great Britain	Ancestry Angoras x Persians	Origins 1880s

RED SHADED CAMEO

Although odd Cameos had been known for many years, it was not until the 1950s that a determined attempt was made by a breeder, Dr. Rachel Salisbury, to develop them. The American Cat Fanciers' Association accepted these cats in 1960, and they have since become widely known. The description "Cameo" is used for red equivalents of tipped colors such as the Chinchilla, Shaded, and Smoke. The difference between these three forms is in the extent of the tipping, which in turn influences the coloration. The tipping on the Red Shaded is of an intermediate shade.

deepest coloration apparent along cat's back

• **FEATURES** The white undercoat has red tips, creating contrast over the coat. The red coloration is most pronounced on the upper body, extending from the mask along the back to the tip of the tail. The underparts are pale, apart from the shaded legs and feet.
• **REMARK** There should be no tabby markings on the coat.

• small ears

bushy tail

• massive rump

tufted paws •

• broad, compact nose with clear stop

• relatively large body carried on short legs

short tail •

• large, round paws

• coppery eyes

• pink nose

muscular body •

• frill of longer hair begins over shoulders, extending between front legs

upper surface of tail redder than underside •

• paler coloration on flanks

FUR TYPE: long, thick, silky, and fine

Shorthair option Red Shaded Cameo Exotic	Temperament Docile

HIMALAYAN

K NOWN IN THE United Kingdom as Color Pointed Longhairs, long-haired cats with patterning such as this were originally developed in the 1920s by a Swedish geneticist, Dr. Tjebbes, for scientific study. Only when a later investigation into feline genetics attracted publicity was the potential for a new breed appreciated. The dark coloration on the points results from the "Himalayan" gene and is to be seen in other animals, including rabbits.

Country of origin USA	Ancestry Persians x Siamese	Origins 1920s

CREAM POINT

The quest to establish this breed began in 1935, using the results obtained from the original American breeding program. The crossing of a Black Persian with a Siamese had produced three black, short-haired kittens. Two of these were then mated, and a long-haired kitten resulted. When this cat, called *Debutante*, was paired with her father, a pointed Persian kitten was born. This showed that the normal self coloration and short-haired characteristics were dominant, but that the kittens carried both the pointed and the long-haired genes.

• **FEATURES** The body coloration is creamy white, with the points a darker shade of cream. In type, these cats resemble typical Persians, with large, round heads and cobby bodies.

• **REMARK** The mask tends to be more extensive in males of the breed.

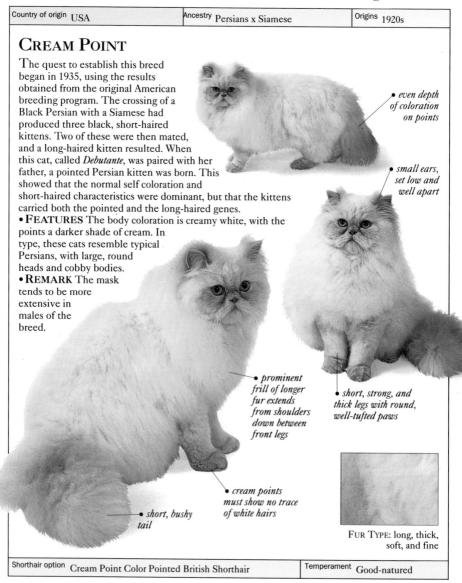

• *even depth of coloration on points*

• *small ears, set low and well apart*

• *prominent frill of longer fur extends from shoulders down between front legs*

• *short, strong, and thick legs with round, well-tufted paws*

• *short, bushy tail*

• *cream points must show no trace of white hairs*

FUR TYPE: long, thick, soft, and fine

Shorthair option Cream Point Color Pointed British Shorthair	Temperament Good-natured

Country of origin USA	Ancestry Persians x Siamese	Origins 1920s

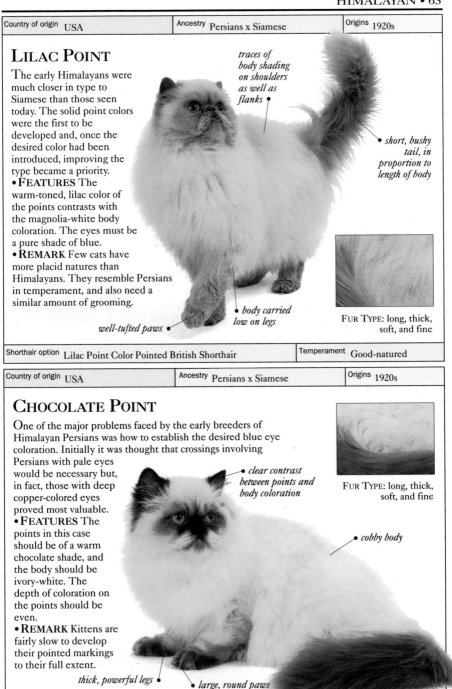

LILAC POINT

The early Himalayans were much closer in type to Siamese than those seen today. The solid point colors were the first to be developed and, once the desired color had been introduced, improving the type became a priority.

• **FEATURES** The warm-toned, lilac color of the points contrasts with the magnolia-white body coloration. The eyes must be a pure shade of blue.

• **REMARK** Few cats have more placid natures than Himalayans. They resemble Persians in temperament, and also need a similar amount of grooming.

traces of body shading on shoulders as well as flanks

• short, bushy tail, in proportion to length of body

• body carried low on legs

well-tufted paws •

FUR TYPE: long, thick, soft, and fine

Shorthair option Lilac Point Color Pointed British Shorthair	Temperament Good-natured

Country of origin USA	Ancestry Persians x Siamese	Origins 1920s

CHOCOLATE POINT

One of the major problems faced by the early breeders of Himalayan Persians was how to establish the desired blue eye coloration. Initially it was thought that crossings involving Persians with pale eyes would be necessary but, in fact, those with deep copper-colored eyes proved most valuable.

• **FEATURES** The points in this case should be of a warm chocolate shade, and the body should be ivory-white. The depth of coloration on the points should be even.

• **REMARK** Kittens are fairly slow to develop their pointed markings to their full extent.

• clear contrast between points and body coloration

FUR TYPE: long, thick, soft, and fine

• cobby body

thick, powerful legs •

• large, round paws

Shorthair option Chocolate Point Color Pointed British Shorthair	Temperament Good-natured

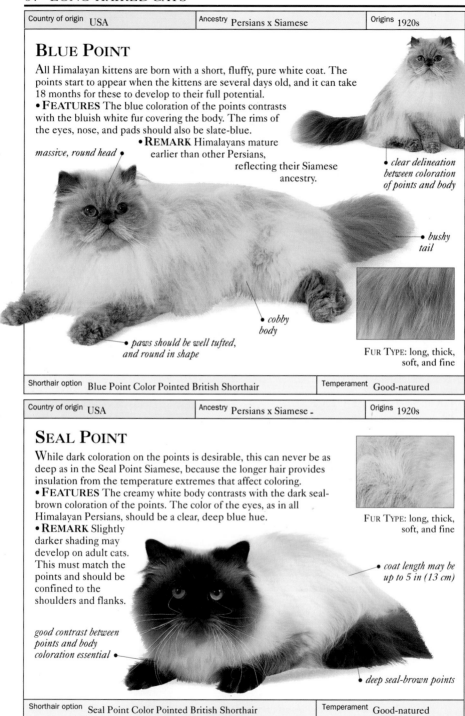

| Country of origin USA | Ancestry Persians x Siamese | Origins 1920s |

BLUE POINT

All Himalayan kittens are born with a short, fluffy, pure white coat. The points start to appear when the kittens are several days old, and it can take 18 months for these to develop to their full potential.

• **FEATURES** The blue coloration of the points contrasts with the bluish white fur covering the body. The rims of the eyes, nose, and pads should also be slate-blue.

• **REMARK** Himalayans mature earlier than other Persians, reflecting their Siamese ancestry.

massive, round head

clear delineation between coloration of points and body

bushy tail

cobby body

paws should be well tufted, and round in shape

FUR TYPE: long, thick, soft, and fine

| Shorthair option Blue Point Color Pointed British Shorthair | Temperament Good-natured |

| Country of origin USA | Ancestry Persians x Siamese | Origins 1920s |

SEAL POINT

While dark coloration on the points is desirable, this can never be as deep as in the Seal Point Siamese, because the longer hair provides insulation from the temperature extremes that affect coloring.

• **FEATURES** The creamy white body contrasts with the dark seal-brown coloration of the points. The color of the eyes, as in all Himalayan Persians, should be a clear, deep blue hue.

• **REMARK** Slightly darker shading may develop on adult cats. This must match the points and should be confined to the shoulders and flanks.

FUR TYPE: long, thick, soft, and fine

coat length may be up to 5 in (13 cm)

good contrast between points and body coloration essential

deep seal-brown points

| Shorthair option Seal Point Color Pointed British Shorthair | Temperament Good-natured |

Country of origin USA	Ancestry Persians x Siamese	Origins 1920s

LILAC TORTIE POINT

Whereas in some Himalayans, such as Seal Points, the body coloration may darken as the cat matures, this does not usually apply here.

FUR TYPE: long, thick, soft, and fine

- **FEATURES** The lilac points are broken by areas of cream, while the body coloration can vary from magnolia to glacial white. The darker mask should extend over the nose, reaching down to the whisker pads and chin, but it should not cover the whole of the cat's head.
- **REMARK** These cats first achieved recognition in the United States in 1957.

five toes on hind feet

powerful, muscular body

cream areas present on all points

lilac nose

magnolia-white body color

Shorthair option Lilac-cream Point Color Pointed British Shorthair	Temperament Good-natured

Country of origin USA	Ancestry Persians x Siamese	Origins 1920s

BLUE TORTIE POINT

Another tortie variant, this Blue-cream did not suffer any loss of type during its development, being created directly from crossings involving Persians. A difference has arisen between the Color Pointed Persian Longhairs in Europe and those in North America, where the type has become more exaggerated.

short, broad nose with distinctive stop

FUR TYPE: long, thick, soft and fine

- **FEATURES** The body coloration of these cats ranges from a glacial shade of white to a warm creamy white.
- **REMARK** Blue points are broken by areas of cream.

relatively large body

level back and massive rump

Shorthair option Blue-cream Point Color Pointed British Shorthair	Temperament Good-natured

Country of origin USA	Ancestry Persians x Siamese	Origins 1920s

RED LYNX POINT

Here both red coloration and tabby markings are combined with Himalayan patterning. This relatively recent development reflects the scope that exists for future breeding programs.

• **FEATURES** Tabby characteristics are apparent on the head, with an M-shaped scarab marking on the forehead and "spectacle" traces around the eyes.

• **REMARK** Whisker pads should be spotted.

small ears with round tips

FUR TYPE: long, thick, soft, and fine

lighter-colored hair within ears, creating pale rim

broken tabby rings on legs

apricot-white body color, with rich red markings on light apricot agouti points

tabby markings on tail

Shorthair option Red Lynx Point Color Pointed British Shorthair	Temperament Good-natured

Country of origin USA	Ancestry Persians x Siamese	Origins 1920s

LILAC LYNX POINT

The various lilac forms of the Himalayan evolved originally from chocolate stock, and they have since become popular. They must show the typically round, massive head, with no suggestion of a Pekinese face. The eyes are rounded in shape and relatively large in terms of size.

• **FEATURES** The magnolia-white body coloration is offset by the lilac tabby markings.

• **REMARK** Lynx Points are better known in Great Britain as "Tabby Points."

widely spaced ears emphasize rounded face shape

clear, brilliant blue eyes

short, thick neck leads to broad, deep chest

solid point color on back of hind legs

tabby markings on hind legs

FUR TYPE: long, thick, soft, and fine

Shorthair option Lilac Lynx Point Color Pointed British Shorthair	Temperament Good-natured

Country of origin USA	Ancestry Persians x Siamese	Origins 1920s

BLUE TORTIE LYNX POINT

The introduction of new features meant that the type of these cats initially showed a deterioration. Breeders then relied on matings with Persians to bring the type back to that of the Himalayan.

FUR TYPE: long, thick, soft, and fine

• **FEATURES** The body coloration can vary from a glacial to a creamy shade of white, with the points a combination of blue and cream; this is variable in depth of coloration, depending on the individual cat.
• **REMARK** The M-shaped marking on the forehead, characteristic of all tabbies, should be well defined.

spotted whisker pads

broken rings, confirming tabby patterning, extend up front legs from the toes

Shorthair option Blue-cream Lynx Pt Color Pointed British Shorthair	Temperament Good-natured

Country of origin USA	Ancestry Persians x Siamese	Origins 1920s

CHOCOLATE LYNX POINT

It is the darker forms of Lynx Point, such as the Chocolate, that show the clearest patterning. Kittens are much paler than adult cats.

FUR TYPE: long, thick, soft, and fine

• **FEATURES** The chocolate markings are displayed against a light bronze agouti background, offset by the ivory-white body coloration. It is acceptable for the fur above the nose to be bronze, with the nose itself corresponding in color to the points. The head markings include "spectacles."
• **REMARK** The "thumb-marks" on the ears are usually quite distinct in the darker forms.

lighter hair in ears

massive rump

adult cat showing darker points

five-and-a-half-month-old kitten with pale points

Shorthair option Chocolate Lynx Point Color Pointed British Shorthair	Temperament Good-natured

BIRMAN

L EGEND HAS IT that a white temple cat called *Sinh* came up to the head priest, Mun-Ha, as he lay dying. Whereas the cat's paws remained white where they had touched the priest, his yellow eyes were changed to blue. His head, tail, and legs took on an earthy brown hue, and the fur along his back became golden. The appearance of the other temple cats was then transformed to golden brown so that they resembled *Sinh*, the ancestor of the Birman breed.

Country of origin Burma (Myanmar)	Ancestry Nonpedigree cats	Origins Unknown

CREAM POINT

Although the traditional form of the Birman is the Seal Point, this is one of the newer, more recently developed forms. Contrast is not as marked in this case as in varieties with darker points but the characteristic white areas on the paws, extending partly up the hind legs, must be apparent.

• **FEATURES** The body coloration of the Cream Point is off-white with traces of a golden hue. The points are cream. In mature Birman cats, the color of the mask extends over the whole of the face, including the pads of the whiskers.

• **REMARK** There is no link between the Birman and the short-haired Burmese breed.

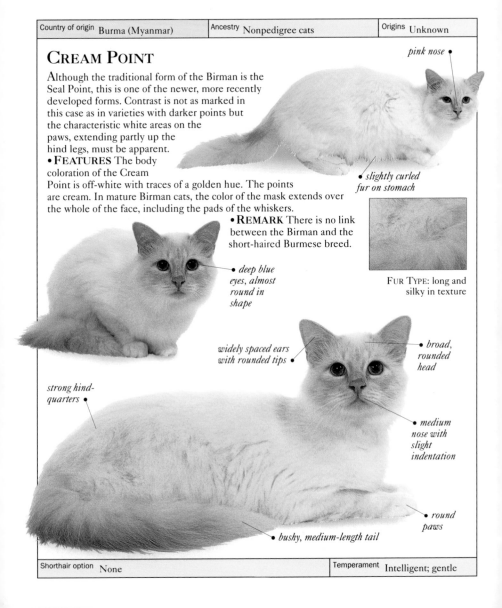

pink nose •

slightly curled fur on stomach •

FUR TYPE: long and silky in texture

• *deep blue eyes, almost round in shape*

widely spaced ears with rounded tips •

• *broad, rounded head*

strong hind-quarters •

• *medium nose with slight indentation*

• *round paws*

• *bushy, medium-length tail*

Shorthair option None	Temperament Intelligent; gentle

Country of origin Burma (Myanmar)	Ancestry Nonpedigree cats	Origins Unknown

RED POINT

Another recent addition to the Birman group, the Red Point shows an identical pattern of markings. On the front paws, the white gloves extend across the paw in a straight line and must be symmetrical; on the hind legs, the white "gauntlets" cover both paws completely.

• **FEATURES** Cream body hue, often with a hint of gold, is offset against a warm shade of orange-red on the nose, ears, and legs.

• **REMARK** Slight freckling, especially on nose and ears, is not judged to be a serious flaw.

• medium ears

FUR TYPE: long and silky in texture

• all points must be of even shade

• medium-length, thick-set legs

good contrast between points and body coloration •

Shorthair option None	Temperament Intelligent; gentle

Country of origin Burma (Myanmar)	Ancestry Nonpedigree cats	Origins Unknown

LILAC POINT

Although the Birman's coat is less susceptible to matting than that of Persians, daily grooming is essential, particularly during the shedding period. Regular grooming will prevent loose hair collecting in the cat's stomach and forming a furball, which can cause an obstruction.

• **FEATURES** The off-white magnolia body coloration contrasts with the soft, pink-gray color of the points.

• **REMARK** The Birman often proves to be a playful breed.

FUR TYPE: long and silky in texture

• distinctive ruff of longer hair around neck

pure white gloves •

• pinkish gray mask connected to ears by matching trace lines in mature cats

Shorthair option None	Temperament Intelligent; gentle

| Country of origin Burma (Myanmar) | Ancestry Nonpedigree cats | Origins Unknown |

BLUE POINT

tail shorter than body •

European development of the Birman has been carried out mainly in France, where the first Birman arrived in 1919. A pair had been given as a gift by temple priests to two Europeans who had helped defend their temple against attack, but only the pregnant female survived the journey.

• **FEATURES** Bluish white body coloration is offset against blue points.
• **REMARK** Eyes should be a deep shade of blue.

• *full cheeks, with rounded muzzle and heavy jaws*

white "gloves" should be symmetrical •

• *underparts are a lighter shade of bluish white than rest of body*

FUR TYPE: long and silky in texture

| Shorthair option None | Temperament Intelligent; gentle |

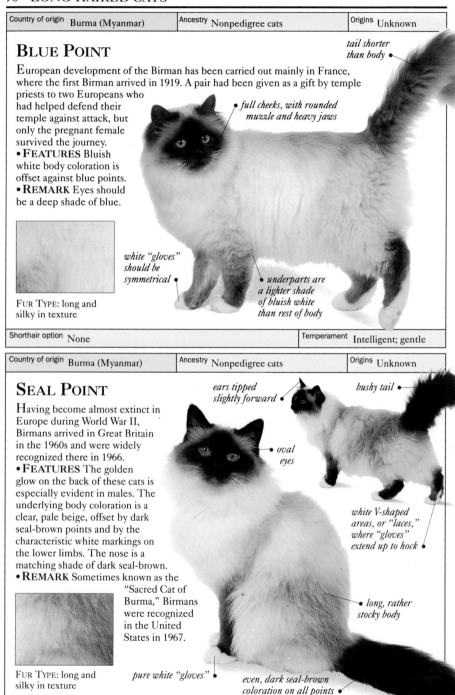

| Country of origin Burma (Myanmar) | Ancestry Nonpedigree cats | Origins Unknown |

SEAL POINT

ears tipped slightly forward •

bushy tail •

Having become almost extinct in Europe during World War II, Birmans arrived in Great Britain in the 1960s and were widely recognized there in 1966.

• **FEATURES** The golden glow on the back of these cats is especially evident in males. The underlying body coloration is a clear, pale beige, offset by dark seal-brown points and by the characteristic white markings on the lower limbs. The nose is a matching shade of dark seal-brown.
• **REMARK** Sometimes known as the "Sacred Cat of Burma," Birmans were recognized in the United States in 1967.

• *oval eyes*

white V-shaped areas, or "laces," where "gloves" extend up to hock •

• *long, rather stocky body*

FUR TYPE: long and silky in texture

pure white "gloves" •

even, dark seal-brown coloration on all points •

| Shorthair option None | Temperament Intelligent |

Country of origin Burma (Myanmar)	Ancestry Nonpedigree cats	Origins Unknown

CHOCOLATE POINT

As one of the darker-colored Birmans, the Chocolate may show some body shading, especially when adult, but this must match with the coloration of the points, and clear contrast must still be quite apparent.

• **FEATURES** The points in this case are of milk-chocolate coloration, offset against an ivory body coloration. In terms of type, these cats do not differ from other Birmans, having a relatively flat forehead and a dip in profile along the nose. The eyes should be as deep a shade of blue as possible; the nose leather should be chocolate-colored.

• **REMARK** Although the coat of these cats is semilong, it does not mat, and grooming is therefore straightforward.

well-spaced ears

full frill around neck; some curling of fur on stomach

bushy tail

FUR TYPE: long and silky in texture

white "gauntlets" cover hind paws

long fur on back

mask covers entire face, including whisker pads; dark tracings connect this area to matching ears

broad, rounded skull

round feet

medium-length tail, in proportion to body size

symmetrical white "gloves" on front paws

Shorthair option None	Temperament Intelligent; gentle

Country of origin Burma (Myanmar)	Ancestry Nonpedigree cats	Origins Unknown

SEAL TORTIE POINT

It is always difficult to produce quality Birmans that excel in type, coloration, and gloved patterning, but once tortie patterning is introduced the task becomes even harder.

• **FEATURES** The body coloration is a light fawn, shading to warm brown or red color on the back and sides.

• **REMARK** This is a female-only breed.

red and seal-brown fur evident on tail •

• facial blaze in mottled colors

intermingling of colors essential at each point •

• white paws and hocks

FUR TYPE: long and silky in texture

Shorthair option None	Temperament Intelligent; gentle

Country of origin Burma (Myanmar)	Ancestry Nonpedigree cats	Origins Unknown

SEAL TORTIE LYNX POINT

An additional element, in the form of tabby markings, is apparent in this cat. The typical tabby patterning should therefore be visible on the coat alongside the tortie coloration. The distribution of the markings is not significant.

• **FEATURES** The fawn body coloration is transformed unevenly into a more evident shade of brown, often merged with red, on the back and flanks. The points are seal-brown.

• **REMARK** The nose color in this case is a combination of mottled pink and darker markings.

• tabby markings on head

FUR TYPE: long and silky in texture

• actual coloration of Birmans can be variable in depth

• ruff of fur around neck

bushy, well-colored tail •

Shorthair option None	Temperament Intelligent

Country of origin Burma (Myanmar)	Ancestry Nonpedigree cats	Origins Unknown

BLUE LYNX POINT

Tabby markings are apparent on these cats although the "gloves" are unaffected. Good contrast, always an important feature in Birmans, tends to become more marked in the darker tabby forms, as seen here.

• **FEATURES** The blue points are offset against a light beige, agouti ground color with the body itself bluish white. A tail showing lighter and darker rings is preferred but such markings may occur only on the underside.

• **REMARK** It has not yet proved easy to develop good tail markings in Lynx Point Birmans.

• color on coat is more evident as cat grows older

"spectacle" marking at corner of eye

FUR TYPE: long and silky in texture

• colored legs

• darker tabby barring on legs

Shorthair option None	Temperament Intelligent; gentle

Country of origin Burma (Myanmar)	Ancestry Nonpedigree cats	Origins Unknown

SEAL LYNX POINT

Because Birmans shed much of their longer coat during the summer months, their appearance is apt to vary through the year.

• **FEATURES** Lynx Point Birmans must show solid markings above the "gauntlets" on the hind legs. The pale beige body with its golden hue is contrasted here against seal-brown markings over the points.

• **REMARK** All Birmans are born with a short, whitish coat.

• M-shaped tabby markings clearly defined on forehead

• seal-brown area above "gauntlet"

clear delineation of white "gloves" •

brown tail slightly barred •

FUR TYPE: long and silky in texture

Shorthair option None	Temperament Intelligent; gentle

TURKISH ANGORA

A S THE ANGORA became scarce, both in its native Turkey and elsewhere, the Turkish government set up a breeding program at Ankara Zoo during the 1960s with the aim of reviving the breed's fortunes. Surplus cats from the program were obtained by other breeders, particularly in the United States. The first overseas litter was born in 1963, but such cats did not reach Britain until the late 1970s. Turkish Angoras are one of the oldest surviving breeds and bloodlines must be kept pure for breeding purposes.

Country of origin Turkey	Ancestry Nonpedigree Persians	Origins 1400s

WHITE

White is the traditional color of this breed, which was originally known as the Angora. This name, however, was subsequently chosen for the recent recreation of the breed, using Oriental cats, which led to some confusion. The native form is now known as the Turkish Angora.

• **FEATURES** The Turkish Angora has a rounder and shorter head than the Angora, being less Oriental in its overall type. Its ears are less prominent too. Eye coloration in the white is variable, and deafness is likely to occur in blue-eyed forms.

• **REMARK** Traditionally, it is the odd-eyed variety, known as *Ankara kedi*, that is accepted as the original form, but the breed also occurs in other colors and patterned forms.

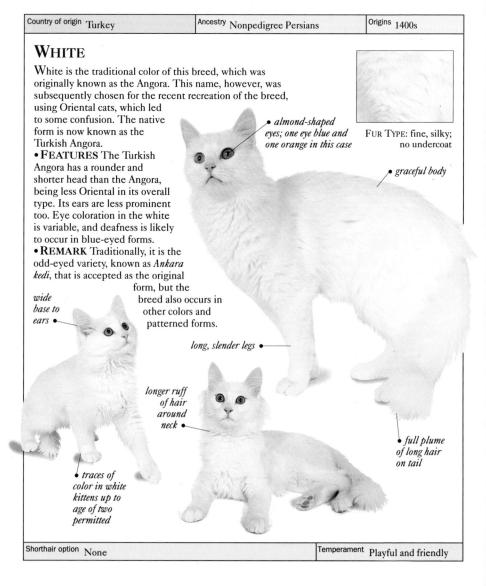

• *almond-shaped eyes; one eye blue and one orange in this case*

FUR TYPE: fine, silky; no undercoat

• *graceful body*

wide base to ears •

long, slender legs •

longer ruff of hair around neck •

• *full plume of long hair on tail*

• *traces of color in white kittens up to age of two permitted*

Shorthair option None	Temperament Playful and friendly

Country of origin Turkey	Ancestry Nonpedigree Persians	Origins 1400s

BLACK

This ancient breed has yet to achieve worldwide recognition, despite the fact that many of the breeds to which it has probably contributed, such as the Persians, are well established in the cat fancy.
• **FEATURES** The coloration of these cats should be a pure shade of dense black, with no hint of rusty brown in the coats. Scattered white hairs are considered to be a serious flaw.
• **REMARK** Crosses with other breeds are not permitted, and Turkish Angora bloodlines must be kept pure.

well-plumed tail

coat becomes shorter during summer months

widely spaced, pointed ears

rounded eyes

medium-length nose

slim, elegant neck

FUR TYPE: fine, silky; no undercoat

Shorthair option None	Temperament Playful and friendly

Country of origin Turkey	Ancestry Nonpedigree Persians	Origins 1400s

BLUE-CREAM

For many years, the white form was the only recognized color of Turkish Angora, but tabby, tortoiseshell, and Smoke forms are now being bred alongside the solid colors. The Blue-cream is essentially a female-only variety, as in other breeds.
• **FEATURES** The blue coloration may vary in shade from light to medium, as can the depth of the cream in the coat.
• **REMARK** The coats of these cats are softer and lighter than those of Persians. The distinctive tail is often carried lower than the body, although when the cat moves it is more likely to be curled forward, almost reaching to the head.

tufted ears

amber eyes

relatively small head, compared with body size

FUR TYPE: fine, silky; no undercoat

long, tapering tail

longish legs contribute to fine-boned appearance

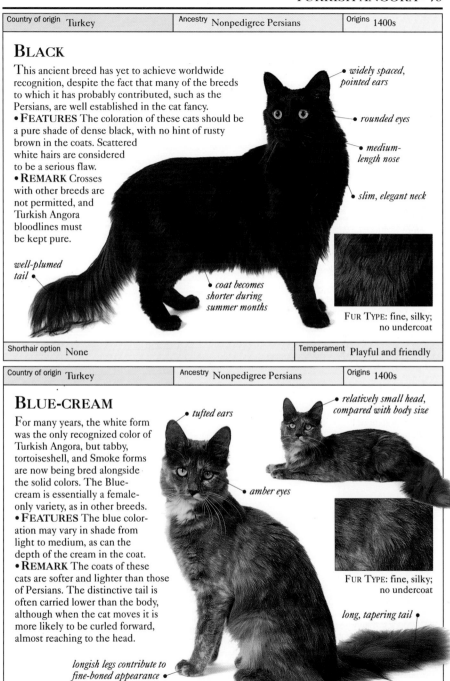

Shorthair option None	Temperament Playful and friendly

Country of origin Turkey	Ancestry Nonpedigree Persians	Origins 1400s

CREAM CLASSIC TABBY

The graceful shape of these cats is emphasized by their long, lithe body shape. Mature males are typically larger than females and may have jowls, but they should still appear lean and muscular in build.

• **FEATURES** The lighter shades of cream, and amber eyes, are preferred. The head is fairly small and wedge shaped. The fur on the underparts is slightly wavy.

• **REMARK** The overall appearance of these cats is fine boned, in contrast to the larger cobby type of the Persian to which they contributed.

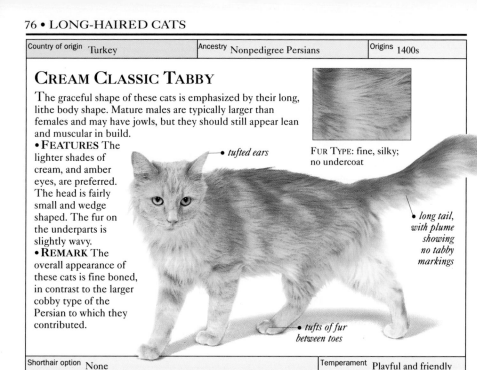

tufted ears

FUR TYPE: fine, silky; no undercoat

long tail, with plume showing no tabby markings

tufts of fur between toes

Shorthair option None		Temperament Playful and friendly

Country of origin Turkey	Ancestry Nonpedigree Persians	Origins 1400s

CREAM CLASSIC TABBY AND WHITE

darker blotch signifies Classic Tabby patterning

Like other Angoras, these cats tend to shed much of their longer fur in summer, so that they resemble shorthairs, although still retaining the distinctive plume of hair on the tail.

• **FEATURES** Both the cream and white areas in the coat should be prominent and clearly defined; the dark cream markings contrast with paler cream body coloration.

• **REMARK** The highly distinctive silky fur of the Angora shows little tendency to become matted, and the sleek appearance is emphasized by the complete absence of an undercoat. Regular daily grooming is still needed, however.

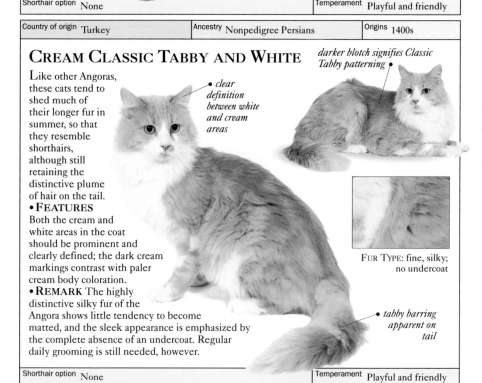

clear definition between white and cream areas

FUR TYPE: fine, silky; no undercoat

tabby barring apparent on tail

Shorthair option None		Temperament Playful and friendly

Country of origin Turkey	Ancestry Nonpedigree Persians	Origins 1400s

BLUE MACKEREL TABBY

Blue Turkish Angoras have the same delightful temperament as other Turkish Angoras, being lively, playful, and affectionate by nature. Part of their appeal stems from their characteristically large, expressive, almond-shaped eyes.

• FEATURES A light bluish shade which contrasts well with the darker blue tabby markings is preferred. The main characteristic is the narrow lines running down the sides of the body from the spine.

• REMARK Amber eye color predominates in the case of the Turkish Angora.

• typical tabby M-shaped marking

FUR TYPE: fine, silky; no undercoat

flat skull •

• unbroken darker "necklaces" on neck and upper chest

• evenly spaced rings on tail

None	Temperament Playful and friendly

Country of origin Turkey	Ancestry Nonpedigree Persians	Origins 1400s

BLACK TORTIE SMOKE

Another variety of the Turkish Angora, first documented in Britain in the late 1800s, the Smoke has been combined with Tortoiseshell in this case.

• FEATURES Only the typical tortoiseshell patterning of cream, red, and black is visible until the cat begins to move. The Smoke appearance is derived entirely from the silver-gray coloration at the base of the individual hairs.

• REMARK Several Victorian naturalists, including Charles Darwin, suggested that the Turkish Angora had evolved from Pallas's cat, not the African wild cat, but this is now thought unlikely.

• medium in overall size

• amber eyes

• tail curls forward to shoulders, tapering along its length

angular chest •

clearly defined areas of color, with paws correspondingly marked •

FUR TYPE: fine, silky; no undercoat

Shorthair option None	Temperament Playful and friendly

TURKISH VAN

THESE CATS all have a distinctively colored chalky white coat, which should display no hint of yellow. Their restricted markings should ideally be confined to the head and tail, although some cats may have localized "thumbprints" of color on their bodies. Auburn and Cream, the two most widely recognized colors, each exist in three different forms, distinguished on the basis of their eye coloration. The eyes can be either amber or blue, or an odd-eyed combination of both of these colors, with pink rims in all cases. Deafness is associated with blue-eyed Turkish Vans, and odd-eyed cats may well be afflicted with deafness on the side corresponding to the blue eye.

Country of origin Turkey	Ancestry Nonpedigree local cats	Origins 1600s

CREAM

Although their coats are relatively long, the grooming of Turkish Van cats is straightforward because they lack a thick woolly undercoat. A daily combing is still to be recommended, particularly in early summer, when these cats are shedding.
• FEATURES Cream markings contrast with the chalky white color of the coat. A vertical white blaze, extending over the nose, separates the colored areas of fur on the head. These are localized to the area above the eyes, not extending beyond the base of the rear of the ears. The ears themselves are white, with shell-pink interiors. The tail should be a solid shade of cream, which can extend slightly onto the back.
• REMARK Darker rings may be present on the tail; these are most likely to be apparent in kittens.

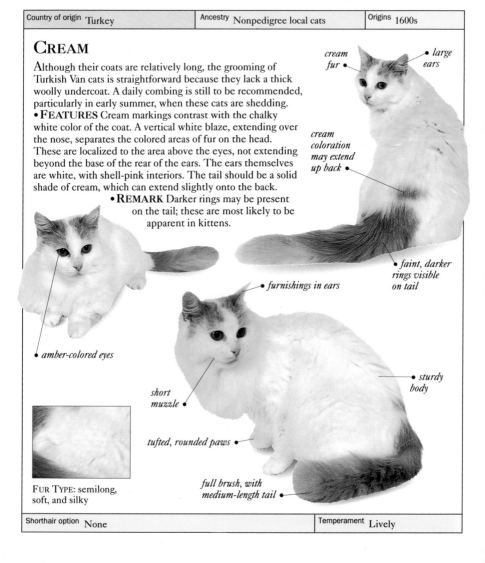

cream fur •

• large ears

cream coloration may extend up back •

• faint, darker rings visible on tail

• furnishings in ears

• amber-colored eyes

• sturdy body

short muzzle •

tufted, rounded paws •

FUR TYPE: semilong, soft, and silky

full brush, with medium-length tail •

Shorthair option None	Temperament Lively

Country of origin	Turkey	Ancestry	Nonpedigree local cats	Origins	1600s

AUBURN

These cats originated in the vicinity of Lake Van, in south-east Turkey. Their coat length varies throughout the year, being noticeably shorter in summer; in the winter it is much thicker providing protection against the freezing winters of their homeland. The development of this breed began in 1955, in Britain, when a pair of kittens was brought back by two photographers who were entranced with the cats.

• **FEATURES** The pattern of markings is significant in this case, with the auburn areas on the head confined to the area above the eyes and not extending behind the ears. The nose is white, and a clear white vertical blaze separates the auburn areas on the head. The tail is auburn.

• **REMARK** These cats are unusual in several respects, including their apparent affinity with water – they swim quite readily. Turkish Vans are also agile climbers and have a surprisingly melodious voice.

chalky white coloration with no hint of yellow

large ears, set high

long, sturdy body

amber-colored eyes with pink rims

short, wedge-shaped head

long, broad, muscular legs

fur long and silky to roots

medium-length tail with full brush

FUR TYPE: semilong, soft, and silky

Shorthair option	None	Temperament	Lively

ANGORA

A NGORAS ORIGINATED in Turkey, and were named after the capital city of Angora (or Ankara). They have been known in Europe since the 1600s and contributed to the development of the Persian Longhair. They then declined in numbers and eventually vanished. The breed known as Angora in the UK today is, in fact, the result of a program to recreate the original Turkish Angora, the longhair gene being provided by Oriental Shorthairs.

Country of origin Great Britain	Ancestry Oriental Shorthair crosses	Origins 1960s

BLUE-EYED WHITE

The prolific nature of the Oriental bloodlines helped to ensure that these cats increased quite rapidly in numbers. Although they have evolved to resemble the original Turkish Angora, they have retained the more vocal natures of their Oriental ancestors. Breeders have placed particular emphasis on coat quality, and have developed these cats in a much wider range of colors than formerly. In appearance, however, they can still be distinguished from the traditional Turkish form by their longer, more angular heads and larger ears.
• FEATURES White has traditionally been the most significant fur color in cats originating in Turkey. Although there is a clear link between blue-eyed white cats and deafness, such individuals have remained popular. In the case of Odd-eyed Whites, deafness may affect the ear on the side of the blue eye.
• REMARK Turkish legends suggest that the famous ruler Atatürk would be reincarnated as a deaf, white cat.

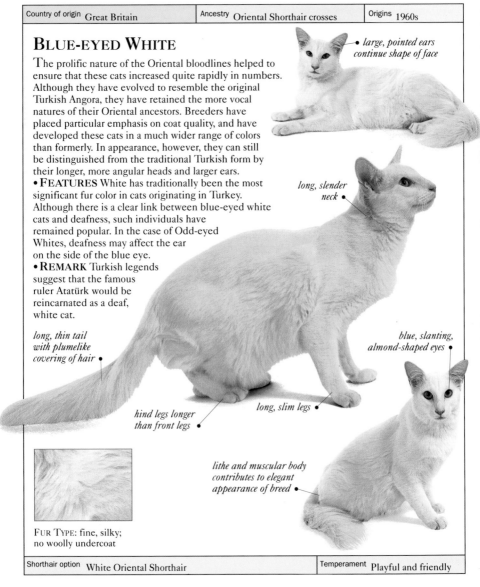

large, pointed ears continue shape of face

long, slender neck •

blue, slanting, almond-shaped eyes •

long, thin tail with plumelike covering of hair •

hind legs longer than front legs •

long, slim legs •

lithe and muscular body contributes to elegant appearance of breed •

FUR TYPE: fine, silky; no woolly undercoat

Shorthair option White Oriental Shorthair	Temperament Playful and friendly

Country of origin Great Britain	Ancestry Oriental Shorthair crosses	Origins 1960s

GREEN-EYED WHITE

The combination of bright green eyes and pure white coat stems from the use of Oriental blood when the Angora breed was recreated in Great Britain. In fact, green eyes are not a typical feature of the traditional Turkish Angora, but they do create an attractive contrast.
• FEATURES The graceful shape of these cats is emphasized by their wedge-shaped heads, slender necks, lithe bodies, and gently tapering tails.
• REMARK These cats are not affected by deafness.

eyes slant in direction of nose, with no squint •

• pure green eyes

• small, dainty paws with tufts of hair developing on toes

• all kittens are born with blue eyes

FUR TYPE: fine, silky; no woolly undercoat

Shorthair option White Oriental Shorthair	Temperament Playful and friendly

Country of origin Great Britain	Ancestry Oriental Shorthair crosses	Origins 1960s

LAVENDER

This is one of the newer colors. The coat lies relatively flat against the body and is a little shorter than that of most long-hairs, especially during the summer when Angoras tend to shed heavily. They can then be confused with shorthairs, although the plume of longer hair on the tail is a consistent feature.
• FEATURES The body coloration should be frosty gray, with an overall pinkish hue. The eyes are green.
• REMARK These slender cats have an almost tubular body outline.

tapering tail •

fine muzzle •

• wide bases to ears; typically large and tufted

• tubular body

dainty, tufted paws •

FUR TYPE: fine, silky; no woolly undercoat

Shorthair option Lavender Oriental Shorthair	Temperament Playful and friendly

Country of origin Great Britain	Ancestry Oriental Shorthair crosses	Origins 1960s

CINNAMON

The long wedge of the head is an important feature of this breed, forming straight lines that extend from the base of the nose up to the tips of the ears, and creating a triangle within this area. The only acceptable variance is in the case of mature males, whose jowl development distorts their facial contours, creating a more rounded appearance.

• **FEATURES** Coloration should be a warm shade of cinnamon-brown throughout the coat, with no white hairs apparent. The pads can vary in color from pink to cinnamon-brown.

• **REMARK** Litters comprising fewer than three kittens are rare.

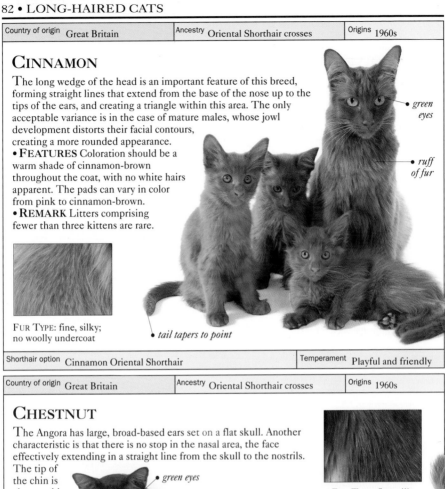

green eyes

ruff of fur

FUR TYPE: fine, silky; no woolly undercoat

tail tapers to point

Shorthair option Cinnamon Oriental Shorthair	Temperament Playful and friendly

Country of origin Great Britain	Ancestry Oriental Shorthair crosses	Origins 1960s

CHESTNUT

The Angora has large, broad-based ears set on a flat skull. Another characteristic is that there is no stop in the nasal area, the face effectively extending in a straight line from the skull to the nostrils. The tip of the chin is also roughly in line with the end of the nose in this variety.

• **FEATURES** It can take up to two years for this rich shade of chestnut-brown color to develop; the nose and paws must be similarly colored. These cats are sometimes described as Chocolate, notably in Great Britain.

• **REMARK** This chocolate colour has not yet been recognized in the Turkish Angora.

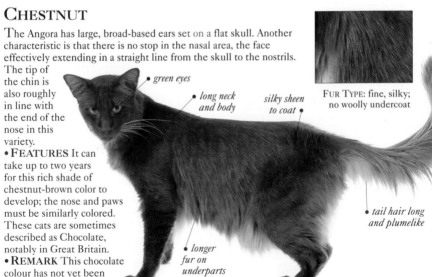

green eyes

long neck and body

silky sheen to coat

FUR TYPE: fine, silky; no woolly undercoat

tail hair long and plumelike

longer fur on underparts

Shorthair option Havana Brown Oriental Shorthair	Temperament Playful and friendly

JAVANESE (UK)

CONFUSION STILL ARISES over cats known by this name. In North America, the name is often applied to forms of the Balinese that do not correspond to the four traditional Siamese point colors, while in New Zealand it is the self and spotted forms of the Balinese that are so called. In Great Britain, however, the name Javanese is given to the cats that emerged from a breeding program aimed at recreating the Angora.

Country of origin Great Britain	Ancestry Abyssinian / Siamese hybrids	Origins 1973

CINNAMON

Cuckoo, one of the kittens from the original breeding program, was noted to be very similar in appearance to the old Turkish Angora. He was distinguished by a whitish undercoat, which contrasted with his longer chocolate-brown hair. All of these Javanese cats resulted from a breeding program that attempted to recreate the traditional Angora. The breed was granted championship status in 1984. In October 1989 the breed's name was changed from Angora to Javanese, to accord more with its Oriental appearance.
• **FEATURES** The Javanese shows the typical features of an Oriental cat, being graceful and lithe, with a wedge-shaped head. It has now been developed in a range of colors and patterns.
• **REMARK** The Javanese has more recently been introduced in the United States, where there is already one Supreme Grand Champion.

long tail reaches shoulder when cat is lying down

Oriental-shaped eyes, slanting downward in direction of nose

large, wide ears with rounded tips

long, svelte body

angular, wedge-shaped face with straight nose

fur shortest on sides of body and head

longer fur on tail

FUR TYPE: semilong, fine, soft, and silky

Shorthair option Cinnamon Oriental Shorthair	Temperament Affectionate

MAINE COON

T HIS IS THE FIRST long-haired breed to have emerged naturally in North America. As the name suggests, the breed originated on the east coast, in the vicinity of Maine. These are large cats, and the males can weigh up to 18 lb (8 kg); the females are only slightly lighter. They are tough, hardy cats with a dense, rugged coat, which is longer on the back and legs. The undercoat is soft and fine, and the tail fur is long and profuse.

Country of origin USA	Ancestry Nonpedigree Persians	Origins 1770s

GOLDEN-EYED WHITE

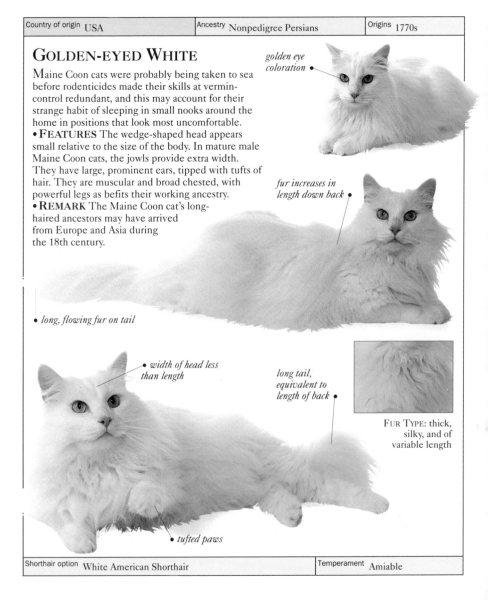

golden eye coloration •

Maine Coon cats were probably being taken to sea before rodenticides made their skills at vermin-control redundant, and this may account for their strange habit of sleeping in small nooks around the home in positions that look most uncomfortable.
• FEATURES The wedge-shaped head appears small relative to the size of the body. In mature male Maine Coon cats, the jowls provide extra width. They have large, prominent ears, tipped with tufts of hair. They are muscular and broad chested, with powerful legs as befits their working ancestry.
• REMARK The Maine Coon cat's long-haired ancestors may have arrived from Europe and Asia during the 18th century.

fur increases in length down back •

• long, flowing fur on tail

• width of head less than length

long tail, equivalent to length of back •

FUR TYPE: thick, silky, and of variable length

• tufted paws

Shorthair option White American Shorthair	Temperament Amiable

Country of origin	USA	Ancestry	Nonpedigree Persians	Origins	1770s

BLACK

Maine Coon cats are very affectionate, but
they do like the freedom to explore out-of-
doors, making them most suitable for rural
living. The Black is a very imposing cat.
• **FEATURES** The coat is pure black, as
are the paw pads, nose, and eye rims.
• **REMARK** At the first cat show in New
York in 1860 this breed was prevalent, but
its numbers had declined by 1900.

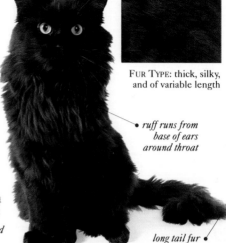

FUR TYPE: thick, silky,
and of variable length

• *ruff runs from
base of ears
around throat*

*firm
chin* •

• *longer fur toward
hindquarters*

long tail fur •

Shorthair option	Black American Shorthair	Temperament	Amiable

Country of origin	USA	Ancestry	Nonpedigree Persians	Origins	1770s

BLUE AND WHITE

One remarkable feature of the
Maine Coon cat is the way it
grooms its long tail by wrapping
it around a front leg and then
spiraling around. During hot
weather, these cats frequently
shed their longer hair and the
ruff becomes less distinctive.
• **FEATURES** While having
typical Maine Coon proportions,
the bicolor forms should display
white fur covering one third of the
body, as well as on the face and
underparts. Clear delineation of white
and colored areas is also desirable.
• **REMARK** One of the earliest Maine
Coons to be
exhibited, in 1861,
was a Black and
White male.

• *large, tall ears,
tapering to point*

• *large,
wide-set
eyes*

• *longish neck and
back emphasize
body length*

white paws •

FUR TYPE: thick, silky,
and of variable length

• *long tail, with wide base
tapering toward tip*

Shorthair option	Blue and White American Shorthair	Temperament	Amiable

| Country of origin | USA | Ancestry | Nonpedigree Persians | Origins | 1770s |

SILVER TABBY

These intelligent cats sometimes use their front paws to pick up food and twigs. They are not averse to water: their dense coat provides protection against the elements, and in the home they often delight in playing with water dripping from a tap.
•FEATURES The basic ground color in this case should be silver, with black tabby markings that are dense and well defined.
•REMARK Both Classic and Mackerel tabby patterning have been long associated with Maine Coon cats, but this particular color is relatively scarce.

M-shaped marking

tabby patterning

large, round paws

FUR TYPE: thick, silky, and of variable length

| Shorthair option | Silver Tabby American Shorthair | Temperament | Amiable |

| Country of origin | USA | Ancestry | Nonpedigree Persians | Origins | 1770s |

CREAM SILVER TABBY

Maine Coons can be bred in a vast array of color forms, this being one of the more unusual combinations currently available. These cats do not differ significantly in temperament, and all members of the breed have an unusual, chirping call.
•FEATURES The ground color in this case is silver, offset by rich cream tabby markings. The pads and nose are pink.
•REMARK Maine Coons were first seen outside North America, in West Germany, in 1978.

wide-based, pointed ears

FUR TYPE: thick, silky, and of variable length

some white markings permitted on chin

flowing tail

tabby markings on leg

| Shorthair option | Cream Silver Tabby American Shorthair | Temperament | Amiable |

Country of origin USA	Ancestry Nonpedigree Persians	Origins 1770s

BROWN CLASSIC TABBY

The striped tail of this breed may have given rise to the name "Coon," as the tail is similar to that of the raccoon, or "coon" as such animals are popularly known in North America.

• **FEATURES** The ground coloration in this case should be a warm shade of copper, with contrasting black tabby markings. In the Classic Tabby form, the markings should be blotched on the body and solid in color. The nose leather should be brick-red.

• **REMARK** Brown Classic Tabbies are a common form of the Maine Coon.

ruff around neck •

broad chest •

ears well spaced and high on head •

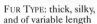

FUR TYPE: thick, silky, and of variable length

black tip to tail •

Shorthair option Brown Classic Tabby American Shorthair	Temperament Amiable

Country of origin USA	Ancestry Nonpedigree Persians	Origins 1770s

BROWN TABBY AND WHITE

This form of Maine Coon has been developed from the more common Brown Tabby ancestry.

• **FEATURES** Brown coloration should predominate in this case, with the tabby markings clearly evident. White fur should be confined essentially to the underparts and the feet.

• **REMARK** Originally known in Europe as American Forest Cats, the Maine Coon first arrived in Britain in 1984.

M-shaped tabby marking on head •

FUR TYPE: thick, silky, and of variable length

moderately long neck •

characteristic Mackerel markings •

wide base to tail •

bushy, flowing tail •

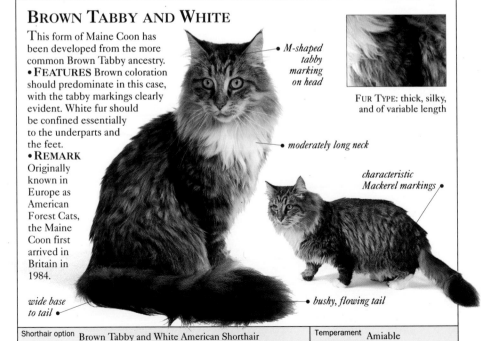

Shorthair option Brown Tabby and White American Shorthair	Temperament Amiable

Country of origin USA	Ancestry Nonpedigree Persians	Origins 1770s

TORBIE AND WHITE

Maine Coons are very easy to
train and can be taught to walk
with a harness and leash. Although
they are not prolific breeders, and
often produce just one litter a
year, they are good mothers.
• **FEATURES** The ground
color is a warm shade of copper
agouti, with cream and red areas,
and black tabby markings. The
white fur is somewhat variable in
distribution but should ideally be
restricted to the face, chest, and
belly, and down the legs to the feet.
• **REMARK** More than 60 color and
patterning
combinations
have been
recorded to
date for the
Maine
Coon cat.

wide-set eyes

firm chin

clear division between white and colored areas

solid, muscular body

FUR TYPE: thick, silky,
and of variable length

tail at least as long as body

Shorthair option Torbie and White American Shorthair	Temperament Amiable

Country of origin USA	Ancestry Nonpedigree Persians	Origins 1770s

SILVER PATCHED TABBY

When viewed from the front, the head of this cat is similar to that of a
shorthair, the longer fur being most apparent on the sides of the body.
• **FEATURES** These cats are distinguished from the Silver Tabby by
their red and cream patching. The ground color is silver, offset by clearly
defined, darker black tabby
markings.
• **REMARK** This
variety is better
known in Great
Britain as the
"Silver
Tortoiseshell
Tabby."

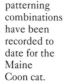

FUR TYPE: thick, silky,
and of variable length

M-shaped head marking

black tabby patterning clearly apparent

barring on legs

powerful legs with large, round paws

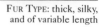

Silver Patched Tabby American Shorthair	Temperament Amiable

Country of origin USA	Ancestry Nonped. Persians	Origins 1770s

BLUE SILVER PATCHED TABBY

• profuse tail fur

Because of the wide range of colors within this breed, there is usually great diversity in the coloration of the kittens in any litter.
• **FEATURES** The ground color is a pale, clear shade of bluish silver. Tortoiseshell markings, in the form of patches of cream, are apparent in the coat, as well as the denser, dark blue tabby markings.
• **REMARK** The diversity in coloration and markings in this breed has resulted partly from its widespread natural evolution; this may change as the breed is now restricted to pedigrees only.

full, round eyes •

• tortie coloration

• tabby markings

FUR TYPE: thick, silky, and of variable length

Shorthair option Blue Silver Patched Tabby American Shorthair	Temperament Amiable

Country of origin USA	Ancestry Nonpedigree Persians	Origins 1770s

BLACK SMOKE AND WHITE

Although there can be considerable variation in the size of these cats, this factor alone is not sufficient to determine the quality of a cat.
• **FEATURES** The coat markings of this variety are equivalent to other Smokes; the white undercoat is most clearly visible when the cat walks, showing through the black tipping on individual outer hairs. The ear tufts and flanks are lightest in color; the head, back, and legs are darkest.
• **REMARK** Smoke forms of all the self colors, and of the Calico combinations, are now being bred.

ears wide at base •

rectangular body shape desirable •

• prominent ruff around neck

FUR TYPE: thick, silky, and of variable length

• well-tufted white paws

plumelike end to long tail •

Shorthair option Black Smoke and White American Shorthair	Temperament Amiable

NORWEGIAN FOREST

T HIS BREED is not dissimilar to the Maine Coon cat and may even have contributed to the development of that breed. Known in their Norwegian homeland as *Norsk Skaukatt*, these cats are very well adapted to survival there during the freezing winter months. The long, double-layered coat is water-repellent and is not affected even by heavy rain. Although, in the past, Norwegian Forest Cats have not been well known outside their homeland, they are now being more widely kept. Despite their origins in the forests and mountains of Scandinavia, Norwegian Forest Cats will thrive in the home as long as they have sufficient space to indulge their love of exploration.

Country of origin Norway	Ancestry Angoras x Shorthairs	Origins 1520s

BLACK AND WHITE

The origin of these cats is something of a mystery, although it has been suggested that they were developed from Angoras that had been brought by ship to Norway, where they mated with the local shorthairs. Yet despite the fact that the breed has been kept in Norway for centuries, it was only during the 1930s that it attracted any serious interest from breeders.
• FEATURES Large and muscular, these cats are solidly built. The head has the shape of an equilateral triangle, with a long, straight profile.
• REMARK A breeding program for these cats was begun in earnest in 1973 and, since then, a number have been sent overseas.

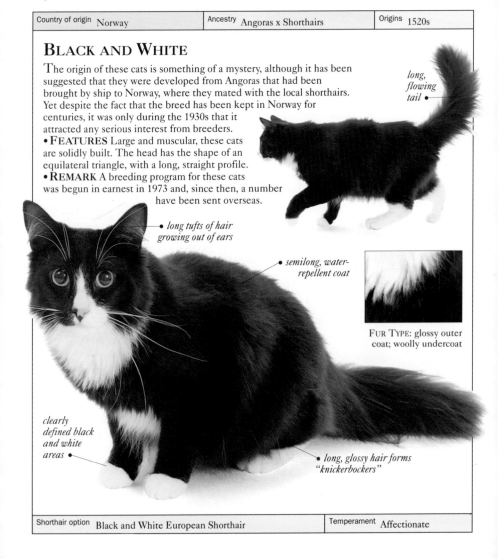

long, flowing tail

long tufts of hair growing out of ears

semilong, water-repellent coat

FUR TYPE: glossy outer coat; woolly undercoat

clearly defined black and white areas

long, glossy hair forms "knickerbockers"

Shorthair option Black and White European Shorthair	Temperament Affectionate

Country of origin Norway	Ancestry Angoras x Shorthairs	Origins 1520s

BLUE TABBY AND WHITE

In spite of its similarity to the Maine Coon, the Norwegian Forest Cat is distinctive in type, having hind legs longer than its forelegs. The eyes of adult cats should be almond shaped and slightly angled, with the inner corner lower than the outer. In young cats, the eyes may be more rounded.

• FEATURES White fur, when present, is confined to the chest and paws. There may be a slight difference in coat type between the different colors, with tabbies tending to have the thickest coats.

• REMARK Color has never been as important a feature of this breed as its type and coat.

FUR TYPE: glossy outer coat; woolly undercoat

• large, open, obliquely set eyes

• glossy topcoat

• long, flowing tail

large, round, tufted paws •

Shorthair option Blue Tabby and White European Shorthair	Temperament Affectionate

Country of origin Norway	Ancestry Angoras x Shorthairs	Origins 1520s

BLUE-CREAM SMOKE AND WHITE

This form of the Norwegian Forest Cat reflects the extensive range of colors associated with the breed. As a tortie, it is essentially a female-only variety and is therefore smaller than other forms, in which males are invariably larger.

• FEATURES Straight noses are preferred, but they may sometimes display a slight curve along the length.

• REMARK Traditionally, torties of this breed have softer, smoother coats than those of tabbies.

tufted ears •

FUR TYPE: glossy outer coat; woolly undercoat

• long tail should reach to neck

Shorthair option Blue Tortie Smoke and White European Shorthair	Temperament Affectionate

Country of origin	Norway	Ancestry	Angoras x Shorthairs	Origins	1520s

BLACK SMOKE AND WHITE

The distinctive double coat is a feature of this breed; pressing on it ought to leave an indentation in the fur. During the summer months much of the coat is shed but the tufts of hair on the toes, as well as the long, flowing tail, will remain evident, indicating the true, semilonghaired nature of the breed.

• **FEATURES** The Smoke coloration results from the contrast between the white undercoat and the dark shading on the outer fur.

• **REMARK** All colors, except chocolate, lavender, and Siamese-style points, are permitted for showing.

FUR TYPE: glossy outer coat; woolly undercoat

long, flowing tail with bushy appearance •

white normally present on the chest •

	Black Smoke and White European Shorthair	Temperament	Affectionate

Country of origin	Norway	Ancestry	Angoras x Shorthairs	Origins	1520s

BROWN TABBY AND WHITE

triangular head with strong chin •

An important feature of this breed is the neck ruff, consisting of a full bib, a short back, and, in winter, a final section sometimes called "side muttonchops."

• **FEATURES** The fur of these cats is affected by their living conditions: those kept indoors, in the warmth, have shorter and softer coats than do those living outdoors in Scandinavia.

• **REMARK** The ears of the Norwegian Forest Cat are high and open, and wide at the base, with lynxlike tufts.

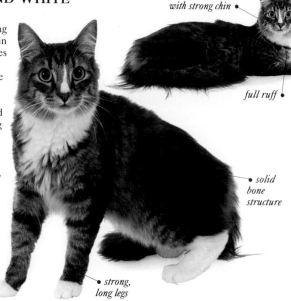

full ruff •

• solid bone structure

FUR TYPE: glossy outer coat; woolly undercoat

• strong, long legs

Shorthair option	Brown Tabby and White European Shorthair	Temperament	Affectionate

SIBERIAN CAT

I T IS NOW THOUGHT that these cats could be the ancestral form of all long-haired breeds, including the original Persians and Angoras. It is not clear when this coat mutation first appeared, but there is some evidence to suggest that these cats have been in existence for a thousand years or more, and have altered little during that time.

Studies in the former USSR have shown that the greatest incidence of the long-haired gene is in the vicinity of St. Petersburg (formerly Leningrad), and it seems likely that these cats first emerged in the northern part of the country. The extra thickness of the coat would have been very beneficial in the harsh weather conditions of that area.

Country of origin Russian	Ancestry Nonpedigree long-haired cats	Origins 1000s

BROWN SPOTTED AND WHITE

There is a fairly high incidence of tabby markings in this breed, possibly the result of matings with wild cats. The Siberian has been fostered and selectively bred in St. Petersburg, and, more recently, in the US and Germany, but they are still quite scarce. The traditional color of the breed is the golden tabby.
• FEATURES In the individual illustrated here, the spotted tabby markings are clearly off-set against the white areas of the coat.
  • REMARK One of the first mentions of this breed outside of Russia was made by Harrison Weir, founder of the cat fancy, who described and illustrated a long-haired Russian cat in his book *Our Cats and All About Them* (1889).

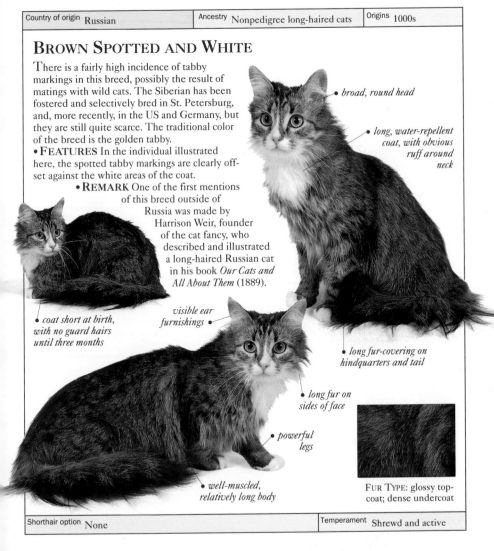

broad, round head

long, water-repellent coat, with obvious ruff around neck

coat short at birth, with no guard hairs until three months

visible ear furnishings

long fur-covering on hindquarters and tail

long fur on sides of face

powerful legs

well-muscled, relatively long body

FUR TYPE: glossy top-coat; dense undercoat

Shorthair option None	Temperament Shrewd and active

RAGDOLL

I N THEIR EARLY DAYS, Ragdolls were reputed to be insensitive to pain, but this is entirely fallacious; the belief arose when the original white Persian gave birth to her kittens after having been injured in a road accident.

These cats do, however, have a knack of becoming extraordinarily relaxed, like limp ragdolls, when being stroked by their owners, and they make ideal family pets, as they are usually very docile and tolerant toward children.

Country of origin USA	Ancestry Nonpedigree cats	Origins 1960s

SEAL POINT

There are currently three coat patterns, the Seal Point being an example of the Color Pointed variety. Blue, Chocolate, and Lilac Points are identical in markings, differing simply in their coloration. Ragdolls are large cats and take three years or so to reach full adult size and coloration.

• **FEATURES** The head is large and wedge shaped, with a flat-topped skull and rounded muzzle. There is a slight stop on the short nose. Coat length is long on the neck, giving the impression of a bib. The coat grows longer in cold weather and is then shed during the summer months. Females are smaller and lighter in color than males.

• **REMARK** The early development of this breed was controlled by the original breeder, by franchise.

• broad hind-quarters

• even, dense shade of seal-brown on tail

beige coloration shading to cream on belly and chest •

• large, heavy body

• heavy-boned legs

• large, rounded, seal-brown paws

FUR TYPE: medium-length, silky, and dense

Shorthair option None	Temperament Docile and quiet

Country of origin	USA	Ancestry	Nonpedigree cats	Origins	1960s

BLUE MITTED

The Ragdoll was granted recognition in the United States in 1965 and in Great Britain in 1983, two years after its arrival there.
• **FEATURES** Similar to the equivalent Color Pointed form, the Mitted Ragdoll is distinguished by the white "mittens" on its front paws, which must be evenly matched in size and which should not extend beyond the angle of the paw and the leg. The white "boots" on the hind legs continue up to the hocks; the entire underbody, from chin to tail, is also white.

• **REMARK** Ragdoll kittens begin to develop their characteristic points at about one week of age.

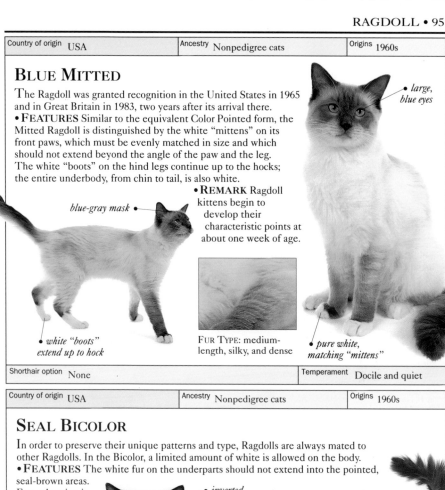

large, blue eyes

blue-gray mask

white "boots" extend up to hock

FUR TYPE: medium-length, silky, and dense

pure white, matching "mittens"

Shorthair option	None	Temperament	Docile and quiet

Country of origin	USA	Ancestry	Nonpedigree cats	Origins	1960s

SEAL BICOLOR

In order to preserve their unique patterns and type, Ragdolls are always mated to other Ragdolls. In the Bicolor, a limited amount of white is allowed on the body.
• **FEATURES** The white fur on the underparts should not extend into the pointed, seal-brown areas. Eye coloration is deep blue. The body is long and muscular, with a broad chest and strong, short, heavy-set neck.
• **REMARK** The V-shape on the face is an important feature.

inverted white V

odd white spots on body areas

long, tapering tail

white on back legs extends up to hocks

fatty pad on lower abdomen

FUR TYPE: medium-length, silky, and dense

Shorthair option	None	Temperament	Docile and quiet

SOMALI

THESE CATS are named after the country of Somalia, which borders Ethiopia (formerly Abyssinia), in Africa, and the name was chosen to reflect the breed's close relationship with the Abyssinian. Long-haired kittens had occurred in Abyssinian litters for a number of years, but it was only in 1967 that the first steps were taken to develop these cats into a new breed. Somalis display ticking along each hair similar to that of the Abyssinian.

Country of origin USA	Ancestry Long-haired Abyssinians	Origins 1967

SORREL SILVER

The Somali is a medium-size cat of muscular build and harmonious proportions. The head is wedge shaped, with soft contours and a slightly curved profile. A slight nose break is essential. The pricked ears are widely spaced and tufted at the tips.

• **FEATURES** All silver forms of the Somali should have white hair with appropriate ticking; in this case, the chocolate ticking gives rise to a sparkling, silvery peach impression. The ears and tail should each be tipped with chocolate coloration.

• **REMARK** Although breeders in many countries welcomed the development of the Somali, it was not until 1983 that the breed was recognized by the CA of Britain, and the breed only received championship status there from the GCCF in 1991.

lithe, muscular body

chocolate-brown tufting between toes

dark skin on eyelids, with lighter "spectacles" encircling eyes

almond-shaped hazel-colored eyes

medium-length coat, shorter over shoulders

long, tapering tail

five toes on front foot

chocolate tip to tail

FUR TYPE: soft, fine, and double-coated

Shorthair option Sorrel Silver Abyssinian	Temperament Extrovert

| Country of origin | USA | Ancestry | Long-haired Abyssinians | Origins | 1967 |

SORREL

This breed has a double-layered coat, with at least three bands of ticking along each hair.
• **FEATURES** The warm, red fur is ticked with chocolate-brown, and the ears and tail are similarly tipped. The undercoat is deep apricot.
• **REMARK** Two Sorrel Somali kittens, born in a litter with four Sorrel Abyssinians in 1971, caused controversy when they were exhibited in Britain.

FUR TYPE: soft, fine, and double-coated

• *rich copper coloration preferred*

short hair on head •

• *soft, curved wedge*

fine, long legs •

tail with full brush •

| Shorthair option | Sorrel Abyssinian | Temperament | Extrovert |

| Country of origin | USA | Ancestry | Long-haired Abyssinians | Origins | 1967 |

RUDDY

bands of ticking with dark tips •

This form of the Somali, which is better known in some countries as the "Usual," was one of the first colors, along with the Sorrel Somali, to be recognized for show purposes in Britain.
• **FEATURES** The coloration should be a rich, golden brown with black ticking most evident on the spine and tail. The underparts are apricot, with no trace of darker markings.
• **REMARK** A ruff around the neck and "breeches" of longer fur on the legs are desirable.

• *ruff gives full-coated appearance*

black tip to tail with no trace of rings •

• *fur longer on underparts*

FUR TYPE: soft, fine, and double-coated

• *"breeches" of longer fur*

| Shorthair option | Usual Abyssinian | Temperament | Extrovert |

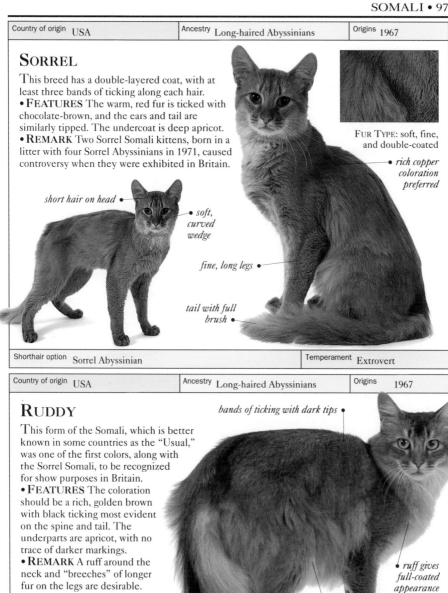

| Country of origin USA | Ancestry Long-haired Abyssinians | Origins 1967 |

BLUE

The popularity of the Somali is increasing rapidly, and these cats are being produced in an ever-expanding array of colors.
• **FEATURES** The depth of blue coloration varies between individuals, but the ticking should be darker in all cases. The undercoat can be cream or a slightly deeper shade, often known as blush beige.
• **REMARK** Because the coat of the Somali is not woolly, it shows no tendency to mat.

FUR TYPE: soft, fine, and double-coated

• *broad-based ears set wide apart on head*

• *oatmeal-colored underparts*

mauvish blue pads •

• *tufted toes*

| Shorthair option Blue Abyssinian | Temperament Extrovert |

| Country of origin USA | Ancestry Long-haired Abyssinians | Origins 1967 |

CREAM SILVER

pricked ears •

Somali kittens can take up to 18 months to develop their pattern of adult ticking. Although Somalis mated together will produce only Somali kittens, either coat length may result from Somali x Abyssinian pairings.
• **FEATURES** The base hair in this typical Somali is white with cream ticking, so that the resulting impression is of a cat with a sparkling, silvery cream appearance. The ears and tail are cream, and the underparts are whitish.
• **REMARK** In a mixed litter, Somalis tend to be slightly larger than Abyssinians.

• *medium, wedge-shaped head with rounded chin*

• *silvery underparts*

full, plumed tail •

FUR TYPE: soft, fine, and double-coated

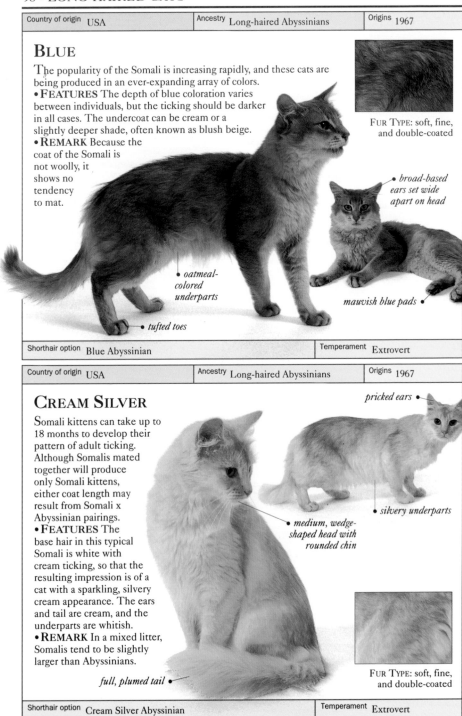

| Shorthair option Cream Silver Abyssinian | Temperament Extrovert |

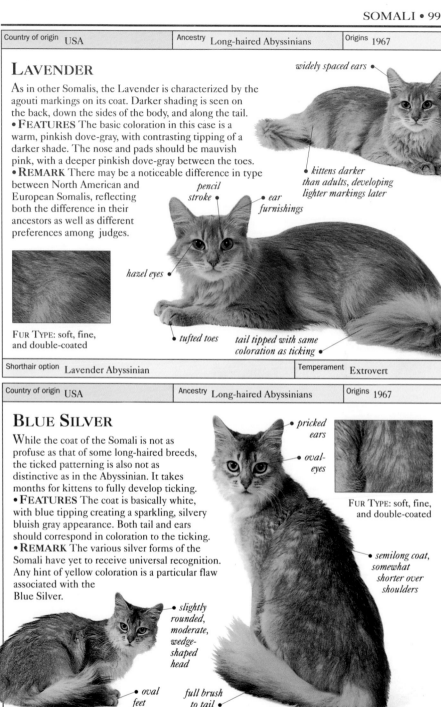

Country of origin USA	Ancestry Long-haired Abyssinians	Origins 1967

LAVENDER

As in other Somalis, the Lavender is characterized by the agouti markings on its coat. Darker shading is seen on the back, down the sides of the body, and along the tail.
• **FEATURES** The basic coloration in this case is a warm, pinkish dove-gray, with contrasting tipping of a darker shade. The nose and pads should be mauvish pink, with a deeper pinkish dove-gray between the toes.
• **REMARK** There may be a noticeable difference in type between North American and European Somalis, reflecting both the difference in their ancestors as well as different preferences among judges.

widely spaced ears

kittens darker than adults, developing lighter markings later

pencil stroke

ear furnishings

hazel eyes

FUR TYPE: soft, fine, and double-coated

tufted toes

tail tipped with same coloration as ticking

Shorthair option Lavender Abyssinian	Temperament Extrovert

Country of origin USA	Ancestry Long-haired Abyssinians	Origins 1967

BLUE SILVER

While the coat of the Somali is not as profuse as that of some long-haired breeds, the ticked patterning is also not as distinctive as in the Abyssinian. It takes months for kittens to fully develop ticking.
• **FEATURES** The coat is basically white, with blue tipping creating a sparkling, silvery bluish gray appearance. Both tail and ears should correspond in coloration to the ticking.
• **REMARK** The various silver forms of the Somali have yet to receive universal recognition. Any hint of yellow coloration is a particular flaw associated with the Blue Silver.

pricked ears

oval eyes

FUR TYPE: soft, fine, and double-coated

semilong coat, somewhat shorter over shoulders

slightly rounded, moderate, wedge-shaped head

oval feet

full brush to tail

Shorthair option Blue Silver Abyssinian	Temperament Extrovert

Country of origin USA	Ancestry Long-haired Abyssinians	Origins 1967

RUDDY SILVER

The Somali is actually a ticked tabby, and the presence of the silver gene in this case results in a glacial white ground color. There is no hint of gold or reddish hues in the ground color.

• **FEATURES** The combination of a white undercoat and black ticking creates an impression of silver in the coat. There should be no ticking or any other dark markings on the underparts. The pads can be either brown or black in color, with the black coloration extending up along the hind legs. This cat has five toes on each of the front feet, and only four on the back.

• **REMARK** The quality of the coat is an important feature, and there should be at least three bands of ticking on each of the hairs. The dark coloration of the eyelids emphasizes the color of the eyes, which can range from amber, through hazel, to green.

pricked ears •

• brick-red nose with black outline

• long legs

• black tip

• black ticking

• thick base to tail

• coloration most evident on upper surface of tail

• black tipping on large, well-spaced ears

FUR TYPE: soft, fine, and double-coated

well-spaced, expressive eyes, encircled by lighter-colored "spectacles" •

shorter fur on shoulders •

• muscular legs

• longer fur ruff forms here

oval feet •

• black tufts between toes

• moderate, wedge-shaped head

• lithe body

white under-parts contrast with dense ticking on spine •

• medium-length coat

Shorthair option Ruddy Silver Abyssinian	Temperament Extrovert

| Country of origin USA | Ancestry Long-haired Abyssinians | Origins 1967 |

CHOCOLATE SILVER

The alternate light and dark bands of ticking on the individual hairs create the distinctive patterning of Somalis. There can be up to four distinct light and dark bands along the length of any one hair.
• FEATURES Dark ticking on the white base hair gives these cats a sparkling, silvery chocolate appearance.
• REMARK Kittens are darker in coloration.

• *short, dark "pencil" stroke extends vertically above each eye*

• *ruff of fur clearly apparent around neck*

• *"breeches" of longer fur on hind legs*

dark chocolate toetufts •

• *chocolate-brown pads, with color extending up hocks*

FUR TYPE: soft, fine, and double-coated

| Shorthair option Chocolate Silver Abyssinian | Temperament Extrovert |

| Country of origin USA | Ancestry Long-haired Abyssinians | Origins 1967 |

BLUE-CREAM

Somali kittens are born with short hair, which very quickly turns fluffy, but they only gradually acquire their smooth, sleek coat as they mature.
• FEATURES The blue-gray coloration is here mixed with a rich shade of cream, the coloration of the belly reflecting that of the underlying base hair. Coloring on the back, hind legs, and the tip of the tail should be darker. The areas of tortie patterning may be even on both sides of the cat's body, or entirely random, with a blaze present in some cases.

• *hazel-green, almond-shaped eyes with dark rims and lighter colored "spectacles"*

• *medium-length nose*

• *legs quite long in relation to body size*

tail thickest at base •

FUR TYPE: soft, fine, and double-coated

| Shorthair option Blue Tortie Abyssinian | Temperament Extrovert |

BALINESE / JAVANESE

T HESE CATS ARE the long-haired counterparts of Siamese and Colorpoint Shorthairs; some registries in the US classify only the four traditional colors as Siamese, others being known as Javanese, but in the UK they are all known as Balinese, and the name Javanese is reserved for cats that emerged from a breeding program aimed at recreating the Angora. The long-haired gene was probably introduced to Siamese from Angoras.

Country of origin USA	Ancestry Siamese x Angoras	Origins 1940s

LILAC POINT BALINESE

When they first appeared in what were believed to be pure Siamese bloodlines, breeders had little interest in these cats, but gradually the appeal of the Balinese spread, and the breed began to evolve. Since long hair is a recessive characteristic, any two Balinese mated together will inevitably produce Balinese kittens, but outcrossings to preserve Siamese type were also used.
• FEATURES Balinese have a long, wedge-shaped head, and a slim, elegant body. Fur may grow to 2 in (5 cm) in length.
• REMARK The name of this group of cats stems from the graceful dancers on the island of Bali in Indonesia. The first known breeder was Marion Dorsey, of California, who collaborated on a breeding program with another cat fancier in New York, during the 1960s.

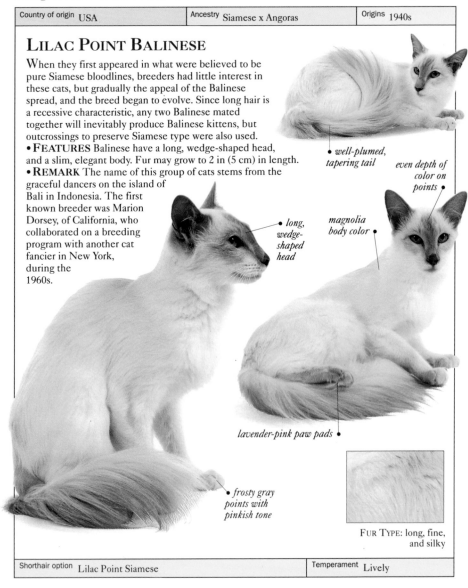

well-plumed, tapering tail

even depth of color on points

long, wedge-shaped head

magnolia body color

lavender-pink paw pads

frosty gray points with pinkish tone

FUR TYPE: long, fine, and silky

Shorthair option Lilac Point Siamese	Temperament Lively

Country of origin USA	Ancestry Siamese x Angoras	Origins 1940s

BLUE POINT BALINESE

Kittens are born with white coats and only later does the characteristic coloration begin to develop. Adult cats, on the other hand, become somewhat darker as they start to age.

• **FEATURES** The color of the body is a glacial shade of bluish white, which is darker on the back. The points should be slate-blue, with matching pads and nose coloration.

• **REMARK** The first Balinese to reach Europe arrived from the United States during the 1970s.

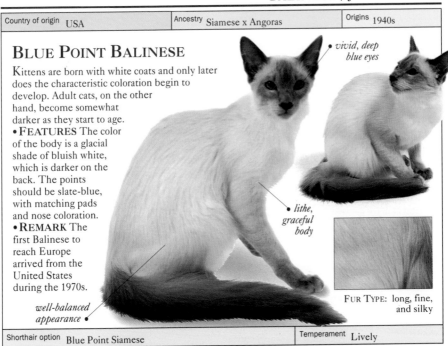

vivid, deep blue eyes

lithe, graceful body

well-balanced appearance •

FUR TYPE: long, fine, and silky

Shorthair option Blue Point Siamese	Temperament Lively

Country of origin USA	Ancestry Siamese x Angoras	Origins 1940s

CHOCOLATE POINT BALINESE

Balinese were recognized as a breed for the first time in the United States in 1963, and a specialist breed club was formed for them five years later.

• **FEATURES** The ivory body color contrasts with warm, milk-chocolate points. The nose and paw pads are a cinnamon-pink shade.

• **REMARK** Grooming is easy, as the silky hair texture helps prevent matting.

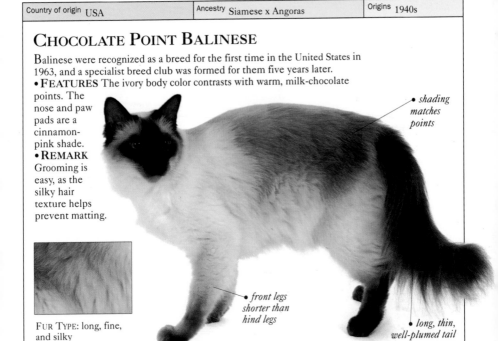

shading matches points

FUR TYPE: long, fine, and silky

front legs shorter than hind legs

long, thin, well-plumed tail

Shorthair option Chocolate Point Siamese	Temperament Lively

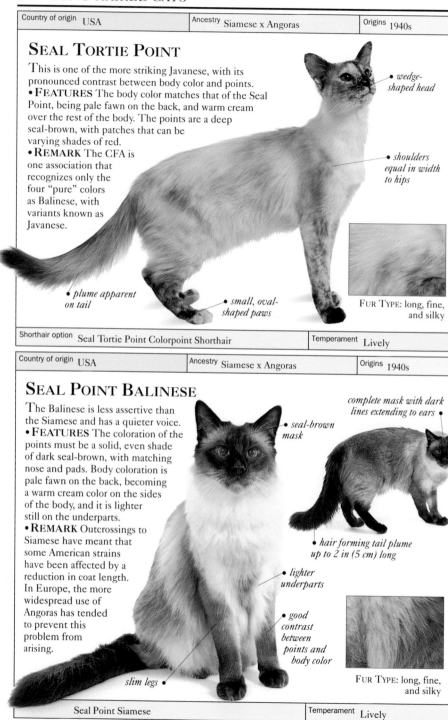

| Country of origin USA | Ancestry Siamese x Angoras | Origins 1940s |

SEAL TORTIE POINT

This is one of the more striking Javanese, with its pronounced contrast between body color and points.
• **FEATURES** The body color matches that of the Seal Point, being pale fawn on the back, and warm cream over the rest of the body. The points are a deep seal-brown, with patches that can be varying shades of red.
• **REMARK** The CFA is one association that recognizes only the four "pure" colors as Balinese, with variants known as Javanese.

• *wedge-shaped head*

• *shoulders equal in width to hips*

• *plume apparent on tail*

• *small, oval-shaped paws*

FUR TYPE: long, fine, and silky

| Shorthair option Seal Tortie Point Colorpoint Shorthair | Temperament Lively |

| Country of origin USA | Ancestry Siamese x Angoras | Origins 1940s |

SEAL POINT BALINESE

The Balinese is less assertive than the Siamese and has a quieter voice.
• **FEATURES** The coloration of the points must be a solid, even shade of dark seal-brown, with matching nose and pads. Body coloration is pale fawn on the back, becoming a warm cream color on the sides of the body, and it is lighter still on the underparts.
• **REMARK** Outcrossings to Siamese have meant that some American strains have been affected by a reduction in coat length. In Europe, the more widespread use of Angoras has tended to prevent this problem from arising.

complete mask with dark lines extending to ears •

• *seal-brown mask*

• *hair forming tail plume up to 2 in (5 cm) long*

• *lighter underparts*

• *good contrast between points and body color*

slim legs •

FUR TYPE: long, fine, and silky

| Seal Point Siamese | Temperament Lively |

Country of origin USA	Ancestry Siamese x Angoras	Origins 1940s

SEAL TORTIE LYNX POINT

The coat obscures the markings in Tortie and Tabby Points, especially on the tail. During judging the tail is held at its tip, shaken, and assessed from behind for a clear view of the patterning.
• **FEATURES** The combination of tortie and tabby markings is reflected by the presence of shades of red superimposed on the basic tabby patterning.
• **REMARK** In the United Kingdom these cats are known as "tortie tabby points."

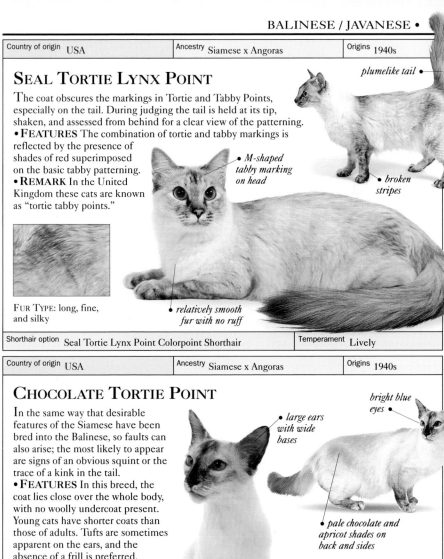

plumelike tail •

• *M-shaped tabby marking on head*

• *broken stripes*

FUR TYPE: long, fine, and silky

• *relatively smooth fur with no ruff*

Shorthair option Seal Tortie Lynx Point Colorpoint Shorthair	Temperament Lively

Country of origin USA	Ancestry Siamese x Angoras	Origins 1940s

CHOCOLATE TORTIE POINT

In the same way that desirable features of the Siamese have been bred into the Balinese, so faults can also arise; the most likely to appear are signs of an obvious squint or the trace of a kink in the tail.
• **FEATURES** In this breed, the coat lies close over the whole body, with no woolly undercoat present. Young cats have shorter coats than those of adults. Tufts are sometimes apparent on the ears, and the absence of a frill is preferred.
• **REMARK** As in the case of other tortie varieties, these cats are usually exclusively female.

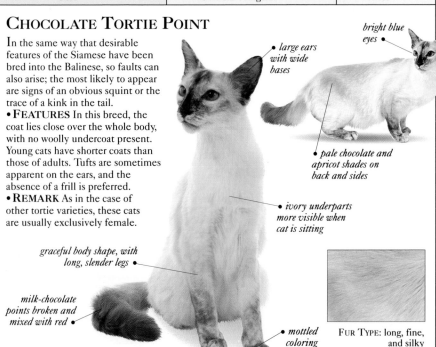

bright blue eyes •

• *large ears with wide bases*

• *pale chocolate and apricot shades on back and sides*

• *ivory underparts more visible when cat is sitting*

graceful body shape, with long, slender legs •

milk-chocolate points broken and mixed with red •

• *mottled coloring*

FUR TYPE: long, fine, and silky

Shorthair option Chocolate Tortie Point Colorpoint Shorthair	Temperament Lively

Country of origin USA	Ancestry Siamese x Angoras	Origins 1940s

RED LYNX POINT

Better known in Great Britain as the "Red Tabby Point Balinese," these cats are Siamese in type and have a desirable erminelike coat. They are a playful, intelligent, and naturally friendly breed.

• FEATURES Here, the basic body color is creamy white, with points varying from orange through to red, contrasting with blue eyes. Tabby markings must be clearly evident on the head and on the legs and tail.

• tabby rings apparent on legs

• REMARK The Javanese category was introduced in the United States in 1980.

• large, pointed ears

• M-shaped tabby marking on head

FUR TYPE: long, fine, and silky

• tapering tail showing tabby markings

contrast between points and body color •

Shorthair option Red Lynx Point Colorpoint Shorthair	Temperament Lively

Country of origin USA	Ancestry Siamese x Angoras	Origins 1940s

BLUE LYNX POINT

Elegance and balance are vital features of the Balinese, with all parts of the cat's body in proportion to each other. The body is lithe with slender legs, and the long, tapering tail emphasizes the body length.

• FEATURES The body is pale, glacial white, becoming more blue on the back. Points are light blue, set against darker blue tabby. Definite stripes surround the eyes and nose; tail markings are not as clear.

FUR TYPE: long, fine, and silky

• REMARK This breed is known as "Blue Tabby Point Balinese" in the United Kingdom.

• almond-shaped blue eyes slant toward nose

• triangular head

well-plumed, long tail •

Shorthair option Blue Lynx Point Colorpoint Shorthair	Temperament Lively

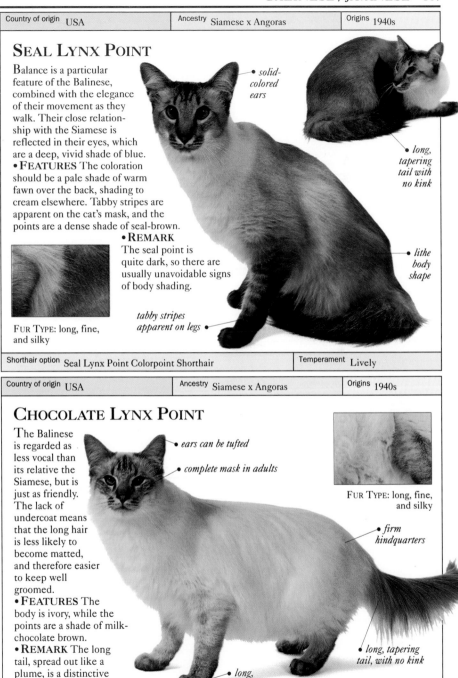

Country of origin USA	Ancestry Siamese x Angoras	Origins 1940s

SEAL LYNX POINT

Balance is a particular feature of the Balinese, combined with the elegance of their movement as they walk. Their close relationship with the Siamese is reflected in their eyes, which are a deep, vivid shade of blue.

• **FEATURES** The coloration should be a pale shade of warm fawn over the back, shading to cream elsewhere. Tabby stripes are apparent on the cat's mask, and the points are a dense shade of seal-brown.

• **REMARK** The seal point is quite dark, so there are usually unavoidable signs of body shading.

solid-colored ears

long, tapering tail with no kink

lithe body shape

FUR TYPE: long, fine, and silky

tabby stripes apparent on legs

Shorthair option Seal Lynx Point Colorpoint Shorthair	Temperament Lively

Country of origin USA	Ancestry Siamese x Angoras	Origins 1940s

CHOCOLATE LYNX POINT

The Balinese is regarded as less vocal than its relative the Siamese, but is just as friendly. The lack of undercoat means that the long hair is less likely to become matted, and therefore easier to keep well groomed.

• **FEATURES** The body is ivory, while the points are a shade of milk-chocolate brown.

• **REMARK** The long tail, spread out like a plume, is a distinctive feature of this breed.

ears can be tufted

complete mask in adults

FUR TYPE: long, fine, and silky

firm hindquarters

long, tapering tail, with no kink

long, slim legs

Shorthair option Chocolate Lynx Point Colorpoint Shorthair	Temperament Lively

TIFFANY

T HE TIFFANY, sometimes spelled "Tiffanie," is essentially a long-haired form of the Burmese. Similar in type to the Burmese, with a medium, wedge-shaped head and a short nose, they have well-spaced ears that are slightly rounded at the tips. The widely spaced eyes are set slightly obliquely, and the Burmese ancestry is reflected in the eye coloration, which can vary in shade from yellow to amber, although a rich golden yellow color is preferred.

Country of origin USA	Ancestry Burmese crosses	Origins 1970s

RED

Originally Tiffanies were known in the United States simply as long-haired Burmese and did not attract much attention in Britain. However, it is there that they have recently been developed, as a by-product of the breeding of Asian Shorthairs like the Burmilla.
• **FEATURES** The coloration matches that of the Red Burmese, but the fur itself is noticeably longer, forming a ruff around the neck, as well as being much longer on the tail.
• **REMARK** Tiffanies are still relatively scarce but, as they become available in a wider range of colors, their popularity is likely to increase.

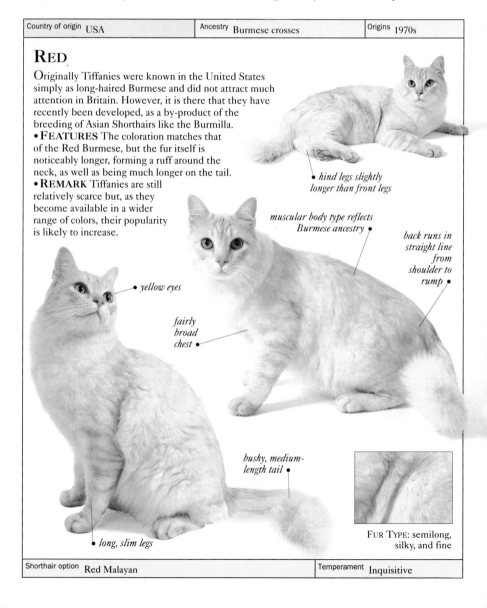

• *hind legs slightly longer than front legs*

muscular body type reflects Burmese ancestry •

back runs in straight line from shoulder to rump •

• *yellow eyes*

fairly broad chest •

bushy, medium-length tail •

• *long, slim legs*

FUR TYPE: semilong, silky, and fine

Shorthair option Red Malayan	Temperament Inquisitive

Country of origin USA	Ancestry Burmese crosses	Origins 1970s

BROWN

Although Tiffanies are now being developed in a wide range of colors in Great Britain, the traditional brown form shown here tends to be most popular in North America.
• **FEATURES** Kittens' coats are shorter than those of adults, and take several months to grow; they also tend to be paler.
• **REMARK** Tiffanies in North America differ from those in Europe because of the variations in their Burmese ancestry; in general, European cats are more elegant in conformation.

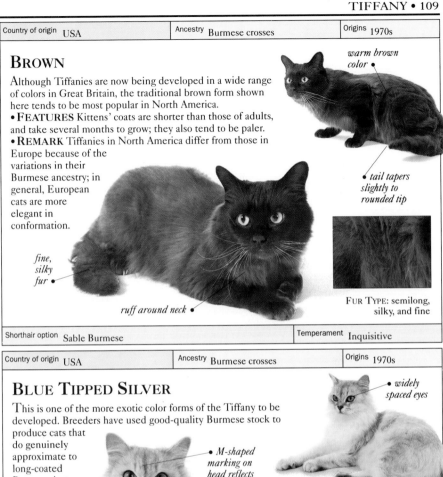

warm brown color

tail tapers slightly to rounded tip

fine, silky fur

ruff around neck

FUR TYPE: semilong, silky, and fine

Shorthair option Sable Burmese	Temperament Inquisitive

Country of origin USA	Ancestry Burmese crosses	Origins 1970s

BLUE TIPPED SILVER

This is one of the more exotic color forms of the Tiffany to be developed. Breeders have used good-quality Burmese stock to produce cats that do genuinely approximate to long-coated Burmese in type.
• **FEATURES** Blue tipping of the silver coat creates an attractive color contrast, just as distinctive as in the Blue Tipped Silver Burmilla.
• **REMARK** The long-haired gene that enabled this breed to develop was introduced by pairing Chinchilla Persians with Burmese during the development of the Burmilla.

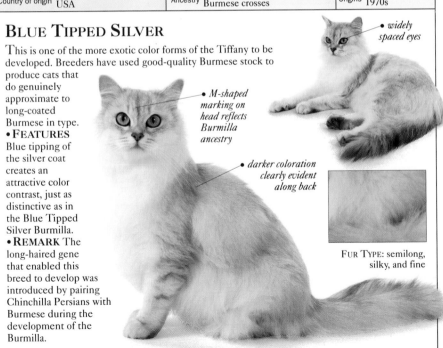

widely spaced eyes

M-shaped marking on head reflects Burmilla ancestry

darker coloration clearly evident along back

FUR TYPE: semilong, silky, and fine

Shorthair option Blue Tipped Silver Malayan	Temperament Inquisitive

CYMRIC

T HE CYMRIC is the long-haired form of the Manx and, as such, it is distinguished by a similar absence of tail. There are three different forms: Rumpy Cymrics have no trace of a tail, but just a hollow at the base; Stumpies have some vertebrae present in this area; the Longie has a tail that is only slightly shorter than that of other breeds. Most forms of coloration and markings are accepted by those associations that recognize the breed.

Country of origin Canada	Ancestry Long-haired Manx x Persians	Origins 1960s

ORANGE-EYED WHITE

Although the Cymric (pronounced KUMRIC, after the traditional name for Wales) is a long-haired breed, its dense coat does not mat easily, and it is quite easy to groom. Because of the lethal gene associated with taillessness, Cymrics are never mated together, and the longer-tailed forms play an important part in breeding programs.

• **FEATURES** All colors, except for Chocolate, Lilac, and Himalayan forms, are accepted with eye coloration matching the coat. The Cymric is similar to the Manx in terms of its type.

• **REMARK** Evolved directly from Manx, these cats are best known, currently, in North America and the United Kingdom.

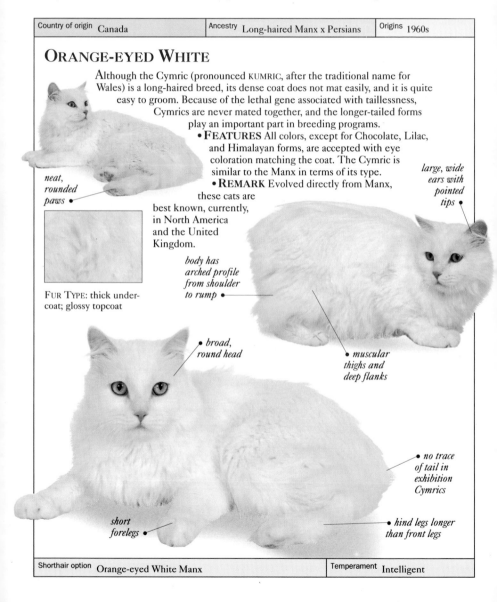

neat, rounded paws •

FUR TYPE: thick undercoat; glossy topcoat

large, wide ears with pointed tips •

body has arched profile from shoulder to rump •

• broad, round head

• muscular thighs and deep flanks

• no trace of tail in exhibition Cymrics

short forelegs •

• hind legs longer than front legs

Shorthair option Orange-eyed White Manx	Temperament Intelligent

SCOTTISH FOLD

T HE LONG-HAIRED gene appears to have been present in the original bloodline of these cats. Although the first recorded Scottish Fold was actually short-haired (*see p.144*), both she and her daughter *Snooks* went on to produce long-haired cats with the characteristic folded ears. Later, the use of British Shorthair breeds probably contributed further long-haired genes, via previous Persian crosses, and long-haired kittens frequently crop up in today's Scottish Fold litters. The short-haired form was the first to be recognized, and it was not until May 1987 that the long-haired Scottish Fold was given championship status for the first time by The International Cat Association (TICA). These cats are now beginning to make a big impact on the show scene.

Country of origin Scotland	Ancestry Nonpedigree Shorthairs	Origins 1950s

BLUE-CREAM AND WHITE

Scottish Folds make ideal companions, being very amenable and generally tolerant of other pets, dogs included. They should display the same rounded face as their short-haired counterparts, with the medium-size ears lying rather like a cap on the side of the head. There is a slight stop on the nose, and the large, round eyes emphasize the friendly nature of these cats.
• **FEATURES** The colored areas of fur should be discrete, and not merge with the white hair. The distinctive semilong coat stands away from the body.
• **REMARK** It takes two to three weeks for the ears of a Scottish Fold kitten to start folding over.

FUR TYPE: medium-length; dense; resilient

bushy tail

medium-sized ears

semi-cobby body

muscular thighs

sturdy legs

tightly folded ears

large, round eyes

clearly defined patches of colored and white fur

strong, muscular neck

short legs

rounded face

flexible tail

Shorthair option Blue-cream and White Short-haired Scottish Fold	Temperament Placid

AMERICAN CURL

T HE HIGHLY UNUSUAL appearance of these cats results from a mutation affecting the ears. Originally seen in long-haired cats, the mutation has now been transferred to short-haired cats; both forms are now popular.

The breed first appeared in 1981, when two kittens were adopted by John and Grace Ruga, of Lakewood, California. The Rugas noticed that the ear cartilage of the kittens curled backwards, and when one of the kittens, *Shulamith*, had her first litter, two of these kittens also had curled ears. This confirmed that the curled-ear trait could be passed on from one generation to the next, and provided the potential for developing the breed.

Country of origin USA	Ancestry Nonpedigree Curl	Origins 1981

BLACK

Mercedes, one of the original curly-eared kittens, and her offspring were spotted in California by Nancy Kiester, who obtained both a long- and a short-haired specimen. She and the Rugas then decided to exhibit *Shulamith* and the two kittens at a show in Palm Springs in October 1983. The cats attracted considerable attention and, as a result, the Rugas and another breeder set out to establish a breed standard and to provide a sound base for the development of these cats.

• FEATURES All kittens in a litter of American Curls are born with apparently normal ears; about half then develop curled ears. The changes may become evident from four to seven days of age.

• REMARK All colors and coat patterns are accepted in this breed.

• *cartilage at base of ears feels firm to touch*

legs moderately thick, with rounded paws •

• *plumed tail quite wide at base, tapering along length*

curled tip •

silky coat, with little undercoat •

FUR TYPE: semilong and silky

• *hind legs slightly longer than front legs*

Shorthair option Black Short-haired American Curl	Temperament Gentle

Country of origin USA	Ancestry Nonpedigree Curl	Origins 1981

BLACK AND WHITE

It can take up to six months for the adult shape of the ears to become apparent, although they may continue unfurling for a time after this stage. The American Curl is relatively slow to mature, taking two or three years; it is of medium size, with a weight of 5–10 lb (2–4.5 kg).
• **FEATURES** The ears curl through at least 90 degrees, and usually through a greater angle. The cat actually swivels its ears so the tips point toward each other.
• **REMARK** Judges assess both the size and shape of the ears and their positioning, as well as the degree of curl and the ear furnishings.

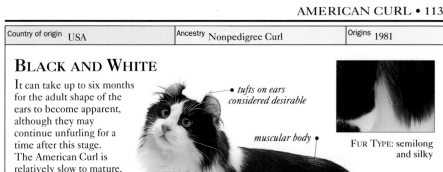

tufts on ears considered desirable

muscular body

FUR TYPE: semilong and silky

medium-length coat lies flat

short, straight legs

Shorthair option Black and White Short-haired American Curl	Temperament Gentle

Country of origin USA	Ancestry Nonpedigree Curl	Origins 1981

BROWN MACKEREL TABBY AND WHITE

The American Curl is a muscular, medium-sized cat with a softly rounded face and a straight nose. The silky, medium-length coat lies flat on the body.
• **FEATURES** The ears of the American Curl should be angled toward the middle of the back of the skull. The hair in the ears, known as furnishings, needs to be clearly visible. The eyes are quite large and slanted towards the nose and contribute to the friendly and alert appearance of this popular breed.
• **REMARK** American Curls make intelligent and playful companions and appear to suffer no ill effects from their unusual ear formation.

tips of ears may be soft to touch

furnishings clearly apparent within ears

typical Mackerel stripes

FUR TYPE: semilong and silky

plumed tail

long tail, reaching to shoulders when folded forward

tight, round paws

Shorthair option Brown Tabby Short-haired American Curl	Temperament Gentle

NONPEDIGREE

A S WITH WILD CATS, it is likely that the coats of domestic cats evolved in response to their environment. Cats that originated in colder northern areas have longer, thicker fur, while those from southeastern Asia are often short-haired. The first long-haired cats in Great Britain came from France.

Country of origin Turkey	Ancestry Crossbred cats	Origins 1500s

BLUE

Since they have not been bred to specific standards, the appearance of nonpedigree Persians can be quite variable. Their coats can be less profuse than those of purebred Persians, and the depth of coloration may vary between individuals.
• **FEATURES** There are often traces of tabby markings and small white areas that would be penalized in purebred Blue Persians. The head shape is less rounded than in pedigree Blue Persians.
• **REMARK** There was very little interest in establishing strains of pure colors until the advent of cat shows at the end of the last century. The earliest Blue Persians of that period were probably rather like the nonpedigree cats of today.

• *narrow head shape*

• *longish fur on tail*

• *largish, upright ears*

• *straight legs*

• *fur tufts between toes unlikely in nonpedigrees*

• *relatively little frill extending around shoulders and between legs compared to pedigree Persians*

FUR TYPE: thick and soft

Shorthair option Blue Nonpedigree Shorthair	Temperament Friendly

Country of origin Turkey	Ancestry Crossbred cats	Origins 1500s

BLACK

Black coloration may have been one of the first domestic color mutations, and Persian Longhairs, although scarce, were much in demand in Victorian Britain. Today, these cats are most commonly to be found in urban areas.
• **FEATURES** Nonpedigree cats can be quite diverse in appearance, resulting from random matings. Coloration may include grayish or brownish hues.
• **REMARK** Black cats may have originated in the eastern Mediterranean region, about 2,000 years ago.

stocky body shape with variable fur length

FUR TYPE: thick and soft

• shorter hair on large paws

fluffy tail •

Shorthair option Black Nonpedigree Shorthair	Temperament Friendly

Country of origin Turkey	Ancestry Crossbred cats	Origins 1500s

CREAM AND WHITE

Bicolor nonpedigree cats are very appealing, although they do not show the precise pattern of markings of their pedigree counterparts. Such cats can be found in any of the usual color combinations.
• **FEATURES** The fur of nonpedigrees is usually quite short compared with that of exhibition Persians.
• **REMARK** Most nonpedigree Persians are the result of entirely random matings.

FUR TYPE: thick and soft

cream coloration may show traces of tabby markings •

• clear delineation between colored and white areas is common

• stocky legs

medium-long tail •

Shorthair option Cream and White Nonpedigree Shorthair	Temperament Friendly

Country of origin	Turkey	Ancestry	Crossbred cats	Origins	1500s

RED SPOTTED

Cats of this color are better known as "ginger" rather than red. It is believed that the color may be of Asiatic origin.
• **FEATURES** The spotted markings are random and the coloration and coat length vary, so some individuals will be more attractive than others.

tabby markings

• **REMARK** There is often a class for non-pedigrees at cat shows, judging being based on beauty, condition, and temperament.

longish tail, less bushy than in pedigree Persians •

narrow head •

• *rounded cheeks with relatively short fur*

FUR TYPE: thick and soft

• *tabby markings on legs*

Shorthair option	Red Spotted Nonpedigree Shorthair	Temperament	Friendly

Country of origin	Turkey	Ancestry	Crossbred cats	Origins	1500s

BROWN TABBY

Tabby patterning in cats dates back to the earliest days of their domestication, about 5,000 years ago. However, longer coat length may tend to obscure these markings.
• **FEATURES** Tabby cats have darker patterning, offset against their basic color, which in this case is light brown. In nonpedigree tabbies, the tabby markings are less precise. For example, the tip of this cat's tail does not terminate in black fur, as specified by the show standard for a pedigree Brown Tabby Persian.
• **REMARK** Cats showing this patterning have been common for centuries.

agouti coat with dense black markings •

• *upright, rounded ears*

FUR TYPE: thick and soft

slight ruff evident here •

• *strong body*

Shorthair option	Brown Tabby Nonpedigree Shorthair	Temperament	Friendly

Country of origin	Ancestry	Origins
Turkey	Crossbred cats	1500s

SILVER AND WHITE

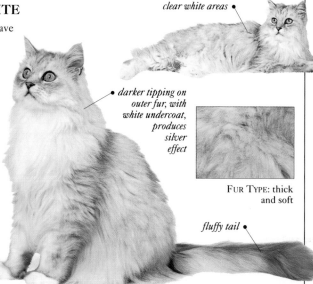

clear white areas

Today's purebred Persians have been selectively developed from nonpedigree stock over the past 120 years. However, nonpedigree cats are no less attractive than their pure-bred counterparts – they are simply of a different type. Although they are bred in the usual combinations, rarer variants, such as this silver and white, also arise.

darker tipping on outer fur, with white undercoat, produces silver effect

FUR TYPE: thick and soft

• **FEATURES** Cats that are the result of shorthair x longhair pairings often have shorter coats than those bred from long-haired parents.
• **REMARK** In pedigree circles, the Tipped Silver Persian is better known as the Chinchilla.

fluffy tail

Shorthair option	Temperament
Silver and White Nonpedigree Shorthair	Friendly

Country of origin	Ancestry	Origins
Turkey	Crossbred cats	1500s

CALICO

These cats have a reputation for being excellent mothers and mousers; these skills, however, are passed on by example as well as by inheritance. Being torties, they are predominantly female.
• **FEATURES** Variable blotches of black, red, cream and white fur distinguish these cats, with the patterning largely depending on the individual. No two cats will have identical markings.
• **REMARK** Traditionally associated with farms, Calico Persians have evolved into a pure breed since 1956, with a rigorous standardization of type and patterning imposed.

colors clearly defined

round head

cobby body shape

FUR TYPE: thick and soft

bushy, mottled tail

Shorthair option	Temperament
Calico Nonpedigree Shorthair	Friendly

SHORT-HAIRED CATS

BRITISH SHORTHAIR

BRED ORIGINALLY from ordinary domestic cats, and then refined in terms of size, British Shorthairs are now distinguished by their massive, cobby shape and rounded faces. Adult males are considerably larger than females.

Following a period of decline at the turn of the century, interest in these cats revived during the 1930s. The self colors have always been in great demand and new colors, such as the Lilac, are still being developed.

Country of origin Great Britain	Ancestry Nonpedigree Shorthairs	Origins 1880s

GOLDEN-EYED WHITE

There are three forms of the White British Shorthair, distinguished by eye coloration. Congenital deafness is not associated with the golden-eyed variety as it is with Blue-eyed Whites. Like other white cats, however, they can be at risk of sunburn.

• **FEATURES** Some individuals suffer from a condition known as polydactylism, which literally means "many digits." Although this is considered a serious fault in show-judging terms, the condition does not cause any real handicap and will not prevent the cat from proving a healthy and delightful companion.

• **REMARK** White cats have always been very popular, in contrast to their black counterparts, which have been regarded as symbols of darkness and evil.

eyes may vary from deep gold, through orange, to copper

round, massive head

deep chest and broad shoulders

cobby body shape

pure white coat with no hint of yellow

FUR TYPE: short, dense, resilient, and firm

Longhair option Orange-eyed White Persian	Temperament Placid and friendly

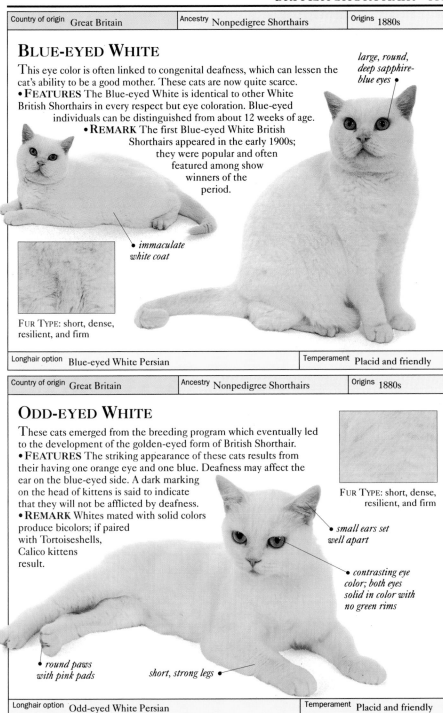

Country of origin	Great Britain	Ancestry	Nonpedigree Shorthairs	Origins	1880s

BLUE-EYED WHITE

This eye color is often linked to congenital deafness, which can lessen the cat's ability to be a good mother. These cats are now quite scarce.
• **FEATURES** The Blue-eyed White is identical to other White British Shorthairs in every respect but eye coloration. Blue-eyed individuals can be distinguished from about 12 weeks of age.
• **REMARK** The first Blue-eyed White British Shorthairs appeared in the early 1900s; they were popular and often featured among show winners of the period.

large, round, deep sapphire-blue eyes

immaculate white coat

FUR TYPE: short, dense, resilient, and firm

Longhair option	Blue-eyed White Persian	Temperament	Placid and friendly

Country of origin	Great Britain	Ancestry	Nonpedigree Shorthairs	Origins	1880s

ODD-EYED WHITE

These cats emerged from the breeding program which eventually led to the development of the golden-eyed form of British Shorthair.
• **FEATURES** The striking appearance of these cats results from their having one orange eye and one blue. Deafness may affect the ear on the blue-eyed side. A dark marking on the head of kittens is said to indicate that they will not be afflicted by deafness.
• **REMARK** Whites mated with solid colors produce bicolors; if paired with Tortoiseshells, Calico kittens result.

FUR TYPE: short, dense, resilient, and firm

small ears set well apart

contrasting eye color; both eyes solid in color with no green rims

round paws with pink pads

short, strong legs

Longhair option	Odd-eyed White Persian	Temperament	Placid and friendly

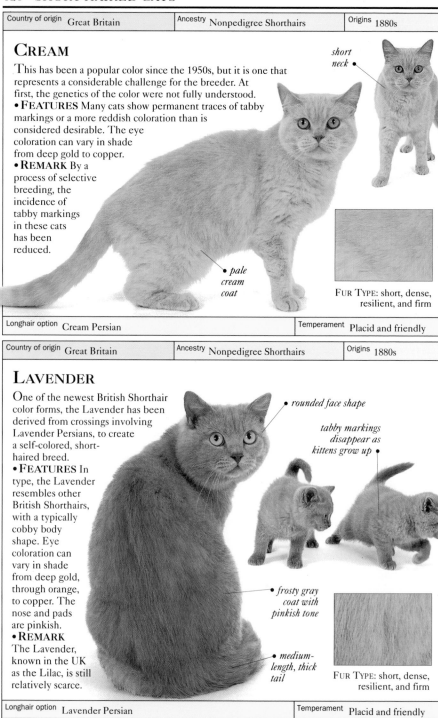

| Country of origin | Great Britain | Ancestry | Nonpedigree Shorthairs | Origins | 1880s |

CREAM

This has been a popular color since the 1950s, but it is one that represents a considerable challenge for the breeder. At first, the genetics of the color were not fully understood.
• FEATURES Many cats show permanent traces of tabby markings or a more reddish coloration than is considered desirable. The eye coloration can vary in shade from deep gold to copper.
• REMARK By a process of selective breeding, the incidence of tabby markings in these cats has been reduced.

short neck

pale cream coat

FUR TYPE: short, dense, resilient, and firm

| Longhair option | Cream Persian | Temperament | Placid and friendly |

| Country of origin | Great Britain | Ancestry | Nonpedigree Shorthairs | Origins | 1880s |

LAVENDER

One of the newest British Shorthair color forms, the Lavender has been derived from crossings involving Lavender Persians, to create a self-colored, short-haired breed.
• FEATURES In type, the Lavender resembles other British Shorthairs, with a typically cobby body shape. Eye coloration can vary in shade from deep gold, through orange, to copper. The nose and pads are pinkish.
• REMARK The Lavender, known in the UK as the Lilac, is still relatively scarce.

rounded face shape

tabby markings disappear as kittens grow up

frosty gray coat with pinkish tone

medium-length, thick tail

FUR TYPE: short, dense, resilient, and firm

| Longhair option | Lavender Persian | Temperament | Placid and friendly |

Country of origin Great Britain	Ancestry Nonpedigree Shorthairs	Origins 1880s

BLUE

This is probably the most popular of all the self colors.

• **FEATURES** British Blues have a typically rounded face and stocky body shape. Males of the breed may develop prominent jowls as they mature, especially if they have not been neutered early in life.

• **REMARK** This breed nearly became extinct during World War II, due to a shortage of male cats, and did not begin to recover until the 1950s. The quality of the coat had to be maintained by a process of selective breeding.

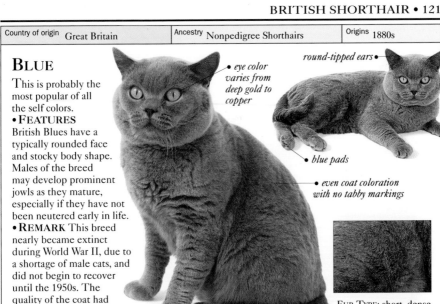

eye color varies from deep gold to copper

round-tipped ears

blue pads

even coat coloration with no tabby markings

FUR TYPE: short, dense, resilient, and firm

Longhair option Blue Persian	Temperament Placid and friendly

Country of origin Great Britain	Ancestry Nonpedigree Shorthairs	Origins 1880s

CHOCOLATE

The Chocolate is not yet very common, but the attractive coloration should ensure their popularity as they become more readily available.
• **FEATURES** The short, glossy coat is a rich, dark brown color with no tabby markings, shading, or white marks. Paw pads are pinkish.
• **REMARK** This breed originated from the use of Chocolate Persians followed by careful breeding to maintain the coat type of the British Shorthair. These cats are not currently recognized by all associations.

FUR TYPE: short, dense, resilient, and firm

short, straight nose

rich dark brown coloration

tabby markings may be present in kittens

large jowls

tail slightly rounded at tip

Longhair option Chocolate Persian	Temperament Placid and friendly

Country of origin Great Britain	Ancestry Nonpedigree Shorthairs	Origins 1880s

BLACK

Black British Shorthairs were often seen at the early cat shows but had lost their popularity by the outbreak of World War I, and only started to become a common sight at cat shows again in the 1950s.

broad chest •

• **FEATURES** Cobby in shape, with a short, glossy coat, this is a very striking cat. A potential fault is any hint of green in the eye coloration, thought to be a legacy of outcrosses with Blues early in their development. Eyes should be copper, orange, or deep gold.
• **REMARK** These cats should be discouraged from sunbathing because this can bleach the coat slightly, and give it a rusty brown hue.

• short, level back

• pure black coat

• powerful, muscular body

• thick tail

FUR TYPE: short, dense, resilient, and firm

Longhair option Black Persian	Temperament Placid and friendly

Country of origin Great Britain	Ancestry Nonpedigree Shorthairs	Origins 1880s

CREAM AND WHITE

Bicolored cats have never been as popular in show circles as their self-colored counterparts, possibly because of the difficulty in breeding well-marked individuals.
• **FEATURES** The white areas should be restricted to no more than one half of the body area and preferably only one third. The markings should be symmetrical, but this is impossible to predict with certainty, even in the case of well-marked parents.
• **REMARK** The Cream and White is the rarest of the four traditional bi-colored forms, the other variants being black, blue, and red, all combined with white.

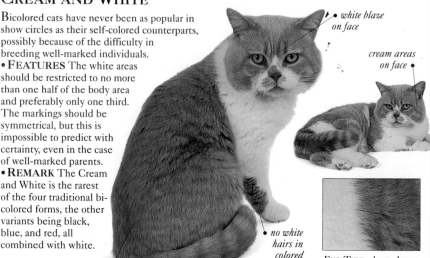

• white blaze on face

cream areas on face •

cobby body shape •

• no white hairs in colored areas

FUR TYPE: short, dense, resilient, and firm

Longhair option Cream and White Persian	Temperament Placid and friendly

| Country of origin | Great Britain | Ancestry | Nonpedigree Shorthair | Origins | 1880s |

DILUTE CALICO

All forms of the tortoiseshell are highly valued as pets, being gentle and affectionate by nature. This more unusual breed is no exception to the rule.

• **FEATURES** As the "dilute" version of the Calico British Shorthair, blue replaces the black coloration, and cream replaces the red. The white areas should predominate on the lower parts of the body. A blaze is considered desirable in this breed.

• **REMARK** The name "tortie" is simply an abbreviation of "tortoiseshell," and applies to any cat in the group.

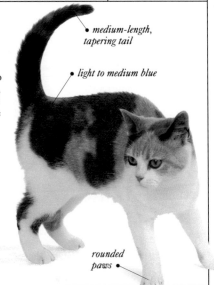

• *medium-length, tapering tail*

• *light to medium blue*

clear coloration

FUR TYPE: short, dense, resilient, and firm

rounded paws

| Longhair option | Dilute Calico Persian | Temperament | Placid and friendly |

| Country of origin | Great Britain | Ancestry | Nonpedigree Shorthairs | Origins | 1880s |

CALICO

This ancient variety was originally known in Great Britain as the "Chintz and White." It is now called the Tortoiseshell and White.

• **FEATURES** Unlike the Tortoiseshell, this is a patched variant, with each of the three colors being distinctly visible against a white ground. Kittens are invariably duller than adults, and take about nine months to acquire their full color.

• **REMARK** Although males are rare in this variety, one named *Ballochmyle Batchelor* won at a show in London in 1912. His winning career continued, but he obviously sired no kittens, tortoiseshell males being invariably sterile.

white facial blaze

• *deep orange eyes*

• *pale red fur*

white fur covers one third to one half of body

• *dense black*

FUR TYPE: short, dense, resilient, and firm

| Longhair option | Calico Persian | Temperament | Placid and friendly |

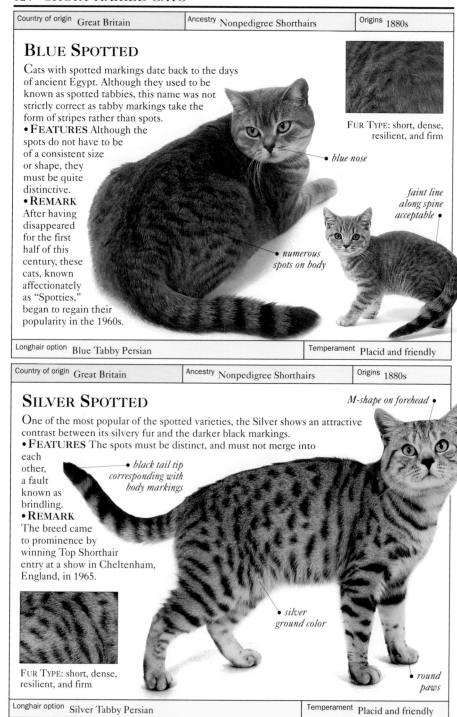

| Country of origin Great Britain | Ancestry Nonpedigree Shorthairs | Origins 1880s |

BLUE SPOTTED

Cats with spotted markings date back to the days of ancient Egypt. Although they used to be known as spotted tabbies, this name was not strictly correct as tabby markings take the form of stripes rather than spots.

• FEATURES Although the spots do not have to be of a consistent size or shape, they must be quite distinctive.

• REMARK After having disappeared for the first half of this century, these cats, known affectionately as "Spotties," began to regain their popularity in the 1960s.

FUR TYPE: short, dense, resilient, and firm

• blue nose

faint line along spine acceptable •

• numerous spots on body

| Longhair option Blue Tabby Persian | Temperament Placid and friendly |

| Country of origin Great Britain | Ancestry Nonpedigree Shorthairs | Origins 1880s |

SILVER SPOTTED

M-shape on forehead •

One of the most popular of the spotted varieties, the Silver shows an attractive contrast between its silvery fur and the darker black markings.

• FEATURES The spots must be distinct, and must not merge into each other, a fault known as brindling.

• REMARK The breed came to prominence by winning Top Shorthair entry at a show in Cheltenham, England, in 1965.

• black tail tip corresponding with body markings

• silver ground color

FUR TYPE: short, dense, resilient, and firm

• round paws

| Longhair option Silver Tabby Persian | Temperament Placid and friendly |

Country of origin	Great Britain	Ancestry	Nonpedigree Shorthairs	Origins	1880s

BROWN CLASSIC TABBY

It appears that all the early Brown Tabbies exhibited in Victorian times originated from nonpedigree stock, and little is known about their origins. They now tend to be less common than other forms of the tabby.
• FEATURES The basic coloration should be a rich, coppery brown, often difficult to achieve; the tabby markings must be black.
• REMARK The Tabby Cat Club, which helps develop the breed, was set up in 1968.

points of M extend from above eyes to between ears

ground color rich and even in all areas

FUR TYPE: short, dense, resilient, and firm

Longhair option	Brown Classic Tabby Persian	Temperament	Placid and friendly

Country of origin	Great Britain	Ancestry	Nonpedigree Shorthairs	Origins	1880s

RED SPOTTED

Although the spots on the back of a Spotted British Shorthair will not be confused with the broken bars of a Mackerel tabby, this breed retains the M-shaped tabby head markings.
• FEATURES Good contrast between the two distinctive shades of red in the coat is important. The type of these cats is distinctly British, with their massive round heads and cobby bodies.
• REMARK In Egyptian mythology, the god *Ra* is portrayed in the form of a spotted cat killing *Apep*, the serpent of darkness.

M-shape on head

deep orange eyes

spots follow the typical distribution of tabby patternings

narrow tail rings

dark red spots clearly visible

FUR TYPE: short, dense, resilient, and firm

Longhair option	Red Tabby Persian	Temperament	Placid and friendly

| Country of origin | Great Britain | Ancestry | Nonpedigree Shorthairs | Origins | 1880s |

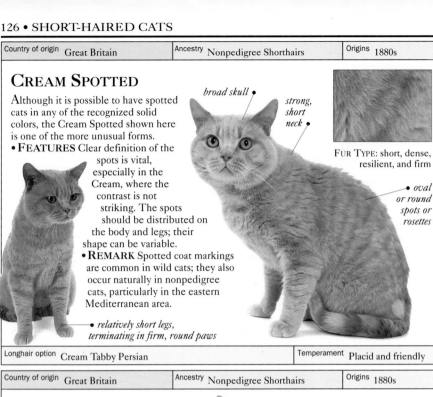

CREAM SPOTTED

broad skull •

strong, short neck •

Although it is possible to have spotted cats in any of the recognized solid colors, the Cream Spotted shown here is one of the more unusual forms.
• **FEATURES** Clear definition of the spots is vital, especially in the Cream, where the contrast is not striking. The spots should be distributed on the body and legs; their shape can be variable.
• **REMARK** Spotted coat markings are common in wild cats; they also occur naturally in nonpedigree cats, particularly in the eastern Mediterranean area.

FUR TYPE: short, dense, resilient, and firm

• oval or round spots or rosettes

• relatively short legs, terminating in firm, round paws

| Longhair option | Cream Tabby Persian | Temperament | Placid and friendly |

| Country of origin | Great Britain | Ancestry | Nonpedigree Shorthairs | Origins | 1880s |

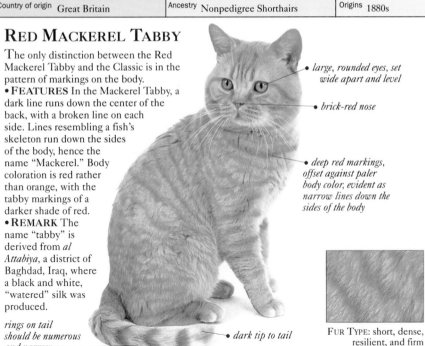

RED MACKEREL TABBY

The only distinction between the Red Mackerel Tabby and the Classic is in the pattern of markings on the body.
• **FEATURES** In the Mackerel Tabby, a dark line runs down the center of the back, with a broken line on each side. Lines resembling a fish's skeleton run down the sides of the body, hence the name "Mackerel." Body coloration is red rather than orange, with the tabby markings of a darker shade of red.
• **REMARK** The name "tabby" is derived from *al Attabiya*, a district of Baghdad, Iraq, where a black and white, "watered" silk was produced.

• large, rounded eyes, set wide apart and level

• brick-red nose

• deep red markings, offset against paler body color, evident as narrow lines down the sides of the body

rings on tail should be numerous and narrow •

• dark tip to tail

FUR TYPE: short, dense, resilient, and firm

| Longhair option | Red Mackerel Tabby Persian | Temperament | Placid and friendly |

Country of origin Great Britain	Ancestry Nonpedigree Shorthairs	Origins 1880s

BLUE-CREAM

This breed came to prominence after World War II, but it is still relatively scarce. The earliest Blue-cream individuals appeared in Tortoiseshell litters and from matings between Blues and Creams.
• FEATURES In the UK, there should be no pronounced patches of color in the coat, the aim being to produce cats with evenly mixed cream and blue coloration.
• REMARK In contrast, in the United States, the colors should be clearly apparent.

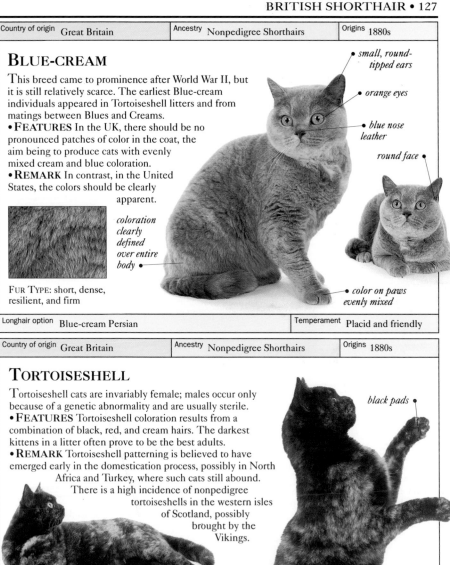

small, round-tipped ears

orange eyes

blue nose leather

round face

coloration clearly defined over entire body

FUR TYPE: short, dense, resilient, and firm

color on paws evenly mixed

Longhair option Blue-cream Persian	Temperament Placid and friendly

Country of origin Great Britain	Ancestry Nonpedigree Shorthairs	Origins 1880s

TORTOISESHELL

Tortoiseshell cats are invariably female; males occur only because of a genetic abnormality and are usually sterile.
• FEATURES Tortoiseshell coloration results from a combination of black, red, and cream hairs. The darkest kittens in a litter often prove to be the best adults.
• REMARK Tortoiseshell patterning is believed to have emerged early in the domestication process, possibly in North Africa and Turkey, where such cats still abound. There is a high incidence of nonpedigree tortoiseshells in the western isles of Scotland, possibly brought by the Vikings.

black pads

short, strong legs

cobby body shape

coat colors evenly intermingled

FUR TYPE: short, dense, resilient, and firm

thick tail with rounded tip

Longhair option Tortoiseshell Persian	Temperament Placid and friendly

Country of origin Great Britain	Ancestry Nonpedigree Shorthairs	Origins 1880s

BLUE AND WHITE

The bicolored appearance is common in non-pedigree cats, but producing exhibition British Shorthairs with the right pattern of markings invariably proves difficult.
• **FEATURES** British breeders aim to produce cats showing just one third white fur, with the remainder being a solid, even shade of blue. Ideally, coloration should be distributed along the top of the head and ears, back, and down the sides, with the underparts white; in practice, however, this is difficult to achieve.
• **REMARK** Originally, only combinations of white with red, black, blue, or cream were permitted but now any of the solid colors, combined with white, is generally acceptable.

• any tabby markings should soon disappear

FUR TYPE: short, dense, resilient, and firm

• thick base to tail

• no white hairs marring blue coloration

Longhair option Blue and White Persian	Temperament Placid and friendly

Country of origin Great Britain	Ancestry Nonpedigree Shorthairs	Origins 1880s

BLACK AND WHITE

Black and White British Shorthairs were the most highly prized bi-colors in Victorian times, although never numerous. They have proved valuable in the development of Calicos.
• **FEATURES** As well as having the typical stocky British Shorthair shape, these cats must show a very clear contrast between black and white areas of fur.
• **REMARK** In the early cat shows, the markings on the Black and White had to be even, with white chest and feet, and a white blaze on the face.

• white blaze between eyes

FUR TYPE: short, dense, resilient, and firm

• jet black

Longhair option Black and White Persian	Temperament Placid and friendly

Country of origin Great Britain	Ancestry Nonpedigree Shorthairs	Origins 1880s

RED CLASSIC TABBY

Like other British Shorthairs, these cats are
affectionate, hardy, and usually very healthy.
• **FEATURES** In the Classic tabby, the markings
must be clearly defined and perfectly symmetrical.
Any trace of white is a serious fault in these tabbies.
The Classic Tabby form is distinguished from its
Mackerel counterpart by the pattern of the
markings; these extend in swirls in the
Classic Tabby, but form vertical stripes
running down the body in the Mackerel.
• **REMARK** Only since the advent of
cat shows have attempts been made to
breed tabbies
with a
particular
patterning.

*line runs from corner
of each eye •*

*butterfly markings
on shoulder •*

*• legs
ringed
with
darker
fur*

FUR TYPE: short, dense,
resilient, and firm

*typical oyster-
shaped markings
surrounded by rings •*

Longhair option Red Classic Tabby Persian	Temperament Placid and friendly

Country of origin Great Britain	Ancestry Nonpedigree Shorthairs	Origins 1880s

BLUE CLASSIC TABBY

These tabbies are becoming increasingly popular, their markings
making an attractive contrast against the paler ground color.
• **FEATURES** In Classic tabby patterning, an M shape is
visible on the forehead. Darker lines extend to the shoulders,
forming butterfly shapes.
An unbroken line
continues down the back
to the tail, with oyster-
shaped patches on each
flank. Small narrow rings
of darker fur encircle the
tail, which has a dark tip.
• **REMARK** Producing
tabbies with the ideal
pattern of markings is a
difficult task for the breeder.

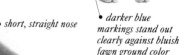

• short, straight nose

*• darker blue
markings stand out
clearly against bluish
fawn ground color*

FUR TYPE: short, dense,
resilient, and firm

pink pads •

Longhair option Blue Classic Tabby Persian	Temperament Placid and friendly

| Country of origin Great Britain | Ancestry Nonpedigree Shorthairs | Origins 1880s |

BLACK SMOKE

The silver undercoat and contrasting topcoat of these cats produce an unusual shimmering effect.
• **FEATURES** When sitting still, Black Smokes are indistinguishable from solid Black Shorthairs but, when moving, the silver undercoat becomes apparent, to wonderful effect. Any odd white hairs in the coat are considered a fault.
• **REMARK** Smokes derive from matings of Silver Tabbies and self British Shorthairs.

typical rounded face •

FUR TYPE: short, dense, resilient, and firm

• eye color varies from deep gold to orange or copper

• black topcoat conceals silver undercoat

black pads •

• relatively short legs

| Longhair option Black Smoke Persian | Temperament Placid and friendly |

| Country of origin Great Britain | Ancestry Nonpedigree Shorthairs | Origins 1880s |

TORTIE SMOKE

The distinctive qualities of the Smoke result from a gene that inhibits coloration of the undercoat. Another gene emphasizes coloration along the full length of the guard hairs, creating a rippling effect.
• **FEATURES** Characteristic tortoiseshell patterning should be distributed evenly throughout the coat. The silver undercoat contributes to the breed's soft, hazy appearance.
• **REMARK** Any British breed can be produced in a Smoke equivalent, but the darker color forms have proved most popular.

• well-spaced eyes

• short, strong neck

• cobby body

FUR TYPE: short, dense, resilient, and firm

• round paws

• good mix of colors visible

| Longhair option Tortie Smoke Persian | Temperament Placid and friendly |

Country of origin	Great Britain	Ancestry	Nonpedigree Shorthairs	Origins	1880s

BLACK TIPPED

Originally known as Chinchilla Shorthairs, these cats have been officially recognized under their present name only since 1978.
• **FEATURES** Only the tips of the outer coat should show dark markings; this coloration is evident on the upper part of the body, and extends down the flanks, legs, and tail. The underparts, from the chin to the tail, should be pure white, and free from any sign of tipping.
• **REMARK** The Chinchilla Persian legacy may still be apparent in kittens before they acquire their adult coats.

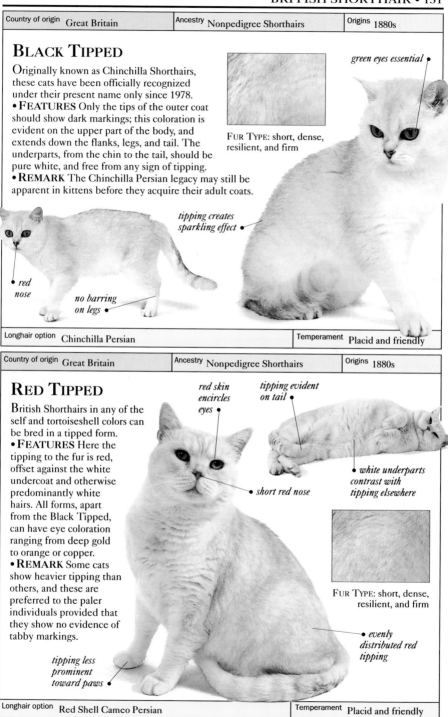

green eyes essential

FUR TYPE: short, dense, resilient, and firm

tipping creates sparkling effect

red nose

no barring on legs

Longhair option	Chinchilla Persian	Temperament	Placid and friendly

Country of origin	Great Britain	Ancestry	Nonpedigree Shorthairs	Origins	1880s

RED TIPPED

British Shorthairs in any of the self and tortoiseshell colors can be bred in a tipped form.
• **FEATURES** Here the tipping to the fur is red, offset against the white undercoat and otherwise predominantly white hairs. All forms, apart from the Black Tipped, can have eye coloration ranging from deep gold to orange or copper.
• **REMARK** Some cats show heavier tipping than others, and these are preferred to the paler individuals provided that they show no evidence of tabby markings.

red skin encircles eyes

tipping evident on tail

white underparts contrast with tipping elsewhere

short red nose

FUR TYPE: short, dense, resilient, and firm

evenly distributed red tipping

tipping less prominent toward paws

Longhair option	Red Shell Cameo Persian	Temperament	Placid and friendly

COLOR POINTED BRITISH SHORTHAIR

T HESE CATS, which have been recognized as a breed in Britain only since 1991, have been developed to conform in type to British Shorthairs while displaying Siamese-type colored points. Unfortunately, the name given to this breed is similar to that of the Colorpoint Shorthair grouping in the United States: the latter is quite separate from Color Pointed British Shorthairs, however, being comprised only of cats of distinctly Siamese type.

Country of origin	Ancestry	Origins
Great Britain	British Shorthairs x Siamese	1980s

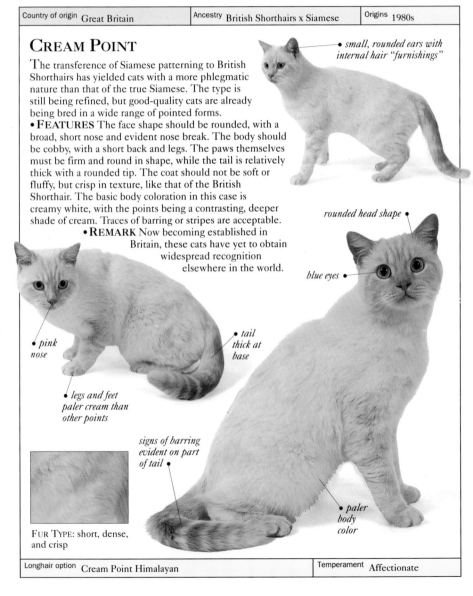

CREAM POINT

The transference of Siamese patterning to British Shorthairs has yielded cats with a more phlegmatic nature than that of the true Siamese. The type is still being refined, but good-quality cats are already being bred in a wide range of pointed forms.
• FEATURES The face shape should be rounded, with a broad, short nose and evident nose break. The body should be cobby, with a short back and legs. The paws themselves must be firm and round in shape, while the tail is relatively thick with a rounded tip. The coat should not be soft or fluffy, but crisp in texture, like that of the British Shorthair. The basic body coloration in this case is creamy white, with the points being a contrasting, deeper shade of cream. Traces of barring or stripes are acceptable.
• REMARK Now becoming established in Britain, these cats have yet to obtain widespread recognition elsewhere in the world.

• small, rounded ears with internal hair "furnishings"

rounded head shape •

blue eyes

• pink nose

• tail thick at base

• legs and feet paler cream than other points

signs of barring evident on part of tail •

• paler body color

FUR TYPE: short, dense, and crisp

Longhair option	Temperament
Cream Point Himalayan	Affectionate

| Country of origin | Great Britain | Ancestry | British Shorthairs x Siamese | Origins | 1980s |

BLUE POINT

The popularity of these cats is likely to increase rapidly as the potential within the group is explored further by breeders.
• **FEATURES** The body coloration of the Blue Point should be a glacial shade of white, contrasting with the medium blue coloration of the points themselves.
• **REMARK** Coat quality is a vital feature of these cats; it must be short, and any tendency toward a soft or woolly coat is a fault.

thick neck

FUR TYPE: short, dense, and crisp

good contrast between points and coat color

medium blue

firm, round paws

| Longhair option | Blue Point Himalayan | Temperament | Affectionate |

| Country of origin | Great Britain | Ancestry | British Shorthairs x Siamese | Origins | 1980s |

SEAL POINT

The blue eyes that are characteristic of Color Pointed British Shorthairs must be round in shape and set wide apart on the head, revealing no trace of the Siamese ancestry of these cats. In the case of the Seal Point, though, heavier dark shading on the flanks is quite common, especially as the young cat starts to mature.
• **FEATURES** The coloration of the body should create an overall impression of light, warm fawn. The points are a contrasting and significantly darker shade of seal-brown.
• **REMARK** The shape of the head may alter somewhat in mature males, which develop noticeable jowls.

clearly defined mask

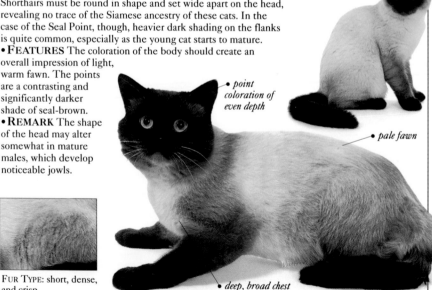

point coloration of even depth

pale fawn

FUR TYPE: short, dense, and crisp

deep, broad chest

| Longhair option | Seal Point Himalayan | Temperament | Affectionate |

Country of origin	Great Britain	Ancestry	British Shorthairs x Siamese	Origins	1980s

RED POINT

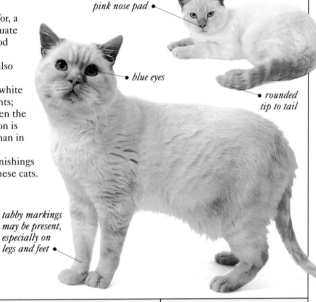

pink nose pad

blue eyes

rounded tip to tail

These cats are easy to care for, a weekly combing being adequate to maintain their coats in good condition when they are not shedding. Regular stroking also helps to remove dead hairs.
• **FEATURES** The apricot-white body is offset by the red points; however, the contrast between the points and the body coloration is less distinctive in this case than in the darker colored varieties.
• **REMARK** Internal ear furnishings should not be excessive in these cats.

tabby markings may be present, especially on legs and feet

FUR TYPE: short, dense, resilient, and firm

Longhair option	Red Point Himalayan	Temperament	Affectionate

Country of origin	Great Britain	Ancestry	British Shorthairs x Siamese	Origins	1980s

CHOCOLATE POINT

The large eyes of British Shorthairs are always expressive, but the contrasting color of the mask emphasizes this feature. The eyes should be quite widely spaced, so that there is at least the width of an eye between them.
• **FEATURES** Another of the more darkly pointed forms, the Chocolate has an ivory body color and contrasting milk-chocolate points. These should be of an even color, and clearly defined against the body.
• **REMARK** A level bite is essential in these cats, as in other British Shorthairs.

FUR TYPE: short, dense, resilient, and firm

mask clearly marked against body coloration

small ears with rounded tips

tail thick at base

solid colored tail

Longhair option	Chocolate Point Himalayan	Temperament	Affectionate

Country of origin Great Britain	Ancestry British Shorthairs x Siamese	Origins 1980s

BLUE-CREAM POINT

The dilute form of the Tortie, the Blue-cream Point is essentially a female-only variety, as in the case of other tortoiseshell breeds.

• **FEATURES** There may be signs of pale blue or cream coloration on the back and down the sides of an otherwise whitish body. Paw pads may be blue, pink or a combination.

• **REMARK** Blue points are broken by cream markings.

blue and cream coloration most apparent on back

round face with full cheeks

blue and cream areas

FUR TYPE: short, dense, resilient, and firm

blue points should be broken with cream markings

round, firm paws

Longhair option Blue-cream Point Himalayan	Temperament Affectionate

Country of origin Great Britain	Ancestry British Shorthairs x Siamese	Origins 1980s

SEAL TORTIE POINT

Another tortoiseshell variant, again showing the characteristic blue eyes of this group. These friendly cats invariably prove good mothers.

• **FEATURES** The basic body coloration is fawn, with shadings of warm brown and red on the sides and over the back. All the points should be seal-brown in color, and broken with various areas of differing shades of red.

• **REMARK** The highly individual markings of these cats also extend to the nose and pads.

short, level back, contributing to breed's cobby appearance

short, broad nose

points broken with varying shades of red

FUR TYPE: short, dense, resilient, and firm

mottled seal color

Longhair option Seal Tortie Point Himalayan	Temperament Affectionate

EXOTIC

T HE ORIGINS of these cats date back to the attempts of American Shorthair breeders to introduce the coat texture qualities of the Persian into their cats. Some fanciers liked the resulting hybrids and decided to use them as the basis for a new breed. The Exotic Shorthair was first recognized in 1967. Although Burmese were used in the early days, outcrosses with only Persian or American Shorthairs are permitted in American pedigrees today.

Country of origin USA	Ancestry American Shorthair x Persian	Origins 1960s

BLUE

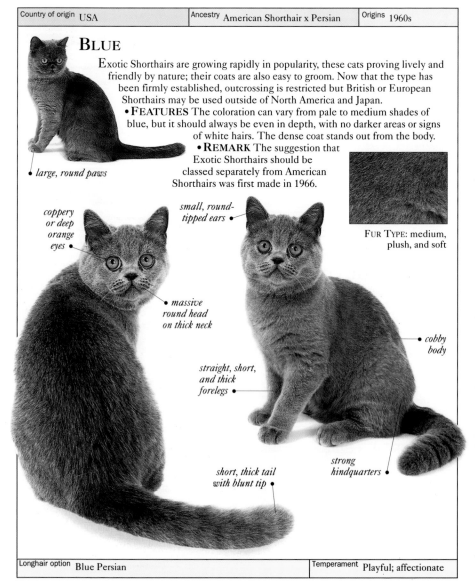

Exotic Shorthairs are growing rapidly in popularity, these cats proving lively and friendly by nature; their coats are also easy to groom. Now that the type has been firmly established, outcrossing is restricted but British or European Shorthairs may be used outside of North America and Japan.

• **FEATURES** The coloration can vary from pale to medium shades of blue, but it should always be even in depth, with no darker areas or signs of white hairs. The dense coat stands out from the body.

• **REMARK** The suggestion that Exotic Shorthairs should be classed separately from American Shorthairs was first made in 1966.

FUR TYPE: medium, plush, and soft

large, round paws

coppery or deep orange eyes

small, round-tipped ears

massive round head on thick neck

cobby body

straight, short, and thick forelegs

short, thick tail with blunt tip

strong hindquarters

Longhair option Blue Persian	Temperament Playful; affectionate

| Country of origin | USA | Ancestry | American Shorthair x Persian | Origins | 1960s |

BLACK

These cats resemble
Persians in all but coat
length; their well-spaced
ears are small with
rounded tips and set so
they tilt slightly forward.
• **FEATURES** The black
coloration should be of a deep,
lustrous shade, with no hint of a
rusty hue in adult cats. There must
be no signs of barring or white hairs.

• **REMARK**
The coloration
of kittens may
be slightly gray
or rusty, but
this improves
with age.

• *broad, short, snub nose, with noticeable break in profile*

thick tail •

• *deep-chested body, set low on legs*

• *tight, round paws*

strong legs •

FUR TYPE: medium,
plush, and soft

| Longhair option | Black Persian | Temperament | Playful; affectionate |

| Country of origin | USA | Ancestry | American Shorthair x Persian | Origins | 1960s |

BLUE POINT COLORPOINT

These attractive colorpoints, sometimes dubbed
"panda bears" because of their large, round eyes
and cuddly appearance, have yet to receive wide
recognition, but they are growing in numbers.
They should have a good undercoat, combined
with guard hairs of medium length.
• **FEATURES** The Blue Point is characterized
by the color of its points, contrasting with an off-
white body color and lighter underparts.
• **REMARK** The massive head and short, stubby nose
distinguish these cats from other short-haired colorpoints.

• *well-spaced, large, round, appealing eyes*

• *no kink in tail*

FUR TYPE: medium,
plush, and soft

• *blue tail*

• *blue nose complements point color*

• *dense fur stands out*

| Longhair option | Blue Point Himalayan | Temperament | Playful; affectionate |

Country of origin USA	Ancestry American Shorthair x Persian	Origins 1960s

SHADED GOLDEN

Selective breeding has helped ensure that the type of these cats matches that of their long-haired ancestors. They are also similarly good-natured. Their dense fur must be freestanding and never so long that it hangs down like that of the Persian.

• **FEATURES** The shading results from either seal-brown or black tipping on the golden yellow fur. The undercoat varies from apricot to light gold.

• **REMARK** It is quite usual for Exotic kittens to appear rather indolent, compared with those of other breeds.

broad and powerful jaws, with full cheeks

FUR TYPE: medium, plush, and soft

short, thick legs

Longhair option Shaded Golden Persian	Temperament Playful; affectionate

Country of origin USA	Ancestry American Shorthair x Persian	Origins 1960s

SILVER TORBIE

Both tabby and tortie patterning should be clearly apparent in these cats. The Silver Tabby combination is one of the most striking, offset in this case with shades of red.

• **FEATURES** The dense black tabby markings should stand out well against the clear silver ground color. The underparts tend to be paler than other areas of the body, while unbroken black lines, or "necklaces," extend across the neck and top of the chest.

• **REMARK** The description "Exotic" was chosen for these cats to distinguish them from the American Shorthair and to emphasize their link with the imported Persian.

ears set low on head

deep chest and massive shoulders

oyster-shaped tabby patterning

black tip to tail

FUR TYPE: medium, plush, and soft

Longhair option Silver Torbie Persian	Temperament Playful; affectionate

Country of origin USA	Ancestry American Shorthair x Persian	Origins 1960s

LILAC LYNX POINT COLORPOINT

This particular variety has not become widely recognized yet, although it is a very attractive combination. The coat in this case, as in other Exotics, should be dense and stand out from the body. The nose is broader and shorter than in other shorthairs, reflecting the breed's Persian ancestry.

• **FEATURES** The warm, lilac tabby markings, contrasting with a magnolia-white body color, are offset in this case by the frosty gray of the points. Darker shading on the back and sides of the body may be present.

• **REMARK** The tail of the Exotic Shorthair is normally kept straight and beneath the level of the back when the cat is moving.

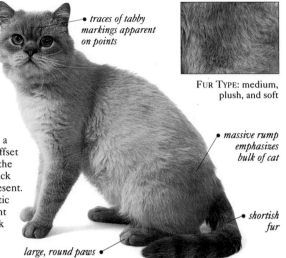

traces of tabby markings apparent on points

FUR TYPE: medium, plush, and soft

massive rump emphasizes bulk of cat

shortish fur

large, round paws

Longhair option Lilac Lynx Point Himalayan	Temperament Playful; affectionate

Country of origin USA	Ancestry American Shorthair x Persian	Origins 1960s

BROWN SPOTTED

A typical M-shaped tabby marking is clearly apparent on the head, with lines running backward down to the shoulders. The ears, edged with black, have a central, coppery brown "thumbprint."

• **FEATURES** The dense, black, spotted pattern contrasts with a coppery brown agouti ground color. The round, oval, or rosette-shaped spots should be well defined, extending over the body and legs. Spots can be present on the tail, though this usually shows a ringed pattern.

• **REMARK** The Exotic Shorthair is sometimes described as a "Persian in its petticoat," and certainly, these cats shed quite heavily compared with other shorthairs.

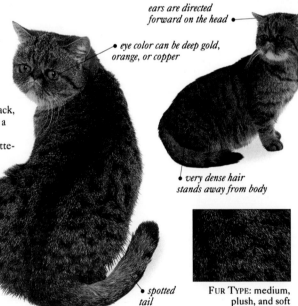

ears are directed forward on the head

eye color can be deep gold, orange, or copper

very dense hair stands away from body

spotted tail

FUR TYPE: medium, plush, and soft

Longhair option Brown Spotted Persian	Temperament Playful; affectionate

MANX

I T HAS BEEN SUGGESTED that the Manx breed may be descended from cats that swam ashore to the Isle of Man, off England's west coast, from a shipwrecked Spanish galleon in 1588. It is more likely, however, that the breed arose from cats native to the island. Although absolute absence of tail is essential in a true Manx (the Rumpy), cats with varying degrees of tail (Risers, Stumpies, and Longies) are useful in Manx breeding programs.

Country of origin Great Britain	Ancestry Nonpedigree Shorthairs	Origins 1600s

WHITE

There is no trace of a tail in the Rumpy Manx, just a hollow where the tail would normally start. In the Rumpy Riser, however, some vertebrae can be discerned in this region. The vertebral column of the Manx tends to differ from that of other cats, the shortened vertebrae giving the breed a curved profile.
• FEATURES Manx are powerfully built cats that do not appear to suffer greatly from the lack of a tail. They have been bred in a vast range of colors, although those showing Siamese-type markings are not recognized by all associations. The coat in this case should be pure white. The "double coat" consists of a dense, short undercoat, with a coarser, slightly longer topcoat. During the summer months, the undercoat is shed, resulting in a sleeker appearance.
• REMARK Manx are traditionally longlived cats and show few signs of aging.

ears wide at base, tapering to tip •

"double coat" •

hollow where tail normally begins •

• rounded, broad rump

• front legs shorter than hind legs

• straight front legs

• muscular thighs contribute to distinctive gait

FUR TYPE: thick undercoat; longer topcoat

Longhair option White Cymric		Temperament Intelligent

Country of origin Great Britain	Ancestry Nonpedigree Shorthairs	Origins 1600s

BLACK AND WHITE

Manx have always been popular, and have
become something of a symbol of their
native Isle of Man, featuring on
the coinage of the island.
• **FEATURES** The quality of
the double coat is considered
to be more important in Manx
than their color or markings.
• **REMARK** Because of their
longer hind legs, Manx tend to
have an
unusual
hopping
walk; this
is deemed
a fault in all
but kittens.

*curved back with rump
higher than shoulder*

*• clearly
defined
colored
areas*

FUR TYPE: thick under-
coat; longer topcoat

Longhair option Black and White Cymric	Temperament Intelligent

Country of origin Great Britain	Ancestry Nonpedigree Shorthairs	Origins 1600s

RED CLASSIC TABBY

Tabby markings are not uncommon
in the Manx; in fact, the first
Manx champion was actually a
Silver Tabby called *Bonhaki*.
• **FEATURES** The basic
coloration of these cats is
red rather than orange, with
the tabby patterning clearly
discernible against the ground
color. The markings on each of the
different forms of tabby should be
dense and clearly defined.
• **REMARK** Breeding Manx cats is
a slow and frustrating process. The
litter sizes are small and some of the
kittens are likely to show traces of tail
of variable length. It is important to
check that the anal
opening is properly
formed in newborn
Manx kittens.

rounded rump •

*compact body
shape •*

*• darker
tabby
markings*

tabby rings •

*• rabbit-
like posture*

FUR TYPE: thick under-
coat; longer topcoat

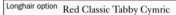

Longhair option Red Classic Tabby Cymric	Temperament Intelligent

Country of origin Great Britain	Ancestry Nonpedigree Shorthairs	Origins 1600s

RED CLASSIC TABBY AND WHITE

Rumpy Manx are paired to cats showing at least a trace of a tail because the gene responsible for taillessness is also linked to defects in kittens bred from like-to-like pairings; these tend to result in the death of the kittens, either before or just after birth.

• **FEATURES** In this case, there is a combination of red and white coloration, with the darker red, Classic pattern, tabby markings superimposed on the red areas.

• **REMARK** The hair beneath the hocks on the hind legs of Manx may be rather thin, as they often rest on their legs rather than on their paws.

widely spaced, medium ears

large, round, expressive eyes

great depth to flanks

clear delineation between red and white areas

no trace of tail

FUR TYPE: thick under-coat; longer topcoat

Longhair option Red Classic Tabby and White Cymric	Temperament Intelligent

Country of origin Great Britain	Ancestry Nonpedigree Shorthairs	Origins 1600s

TORTOISESHELL

Manx kittens are at risk of *spina bifida*, and possibly of constipation in later life, because of their particular spinal structure.

• **FEATURES** This cat shows the typical tortoiseshell coloration of black, and light and dark red. This Stumpy's tail is long enough to be moved, but is not as long as that of a Longie. These cats are useful in breeding programs, although not always accepted for exhibiting.

• **REMARK** A cattery has been set up on the Isle of Man, to preserve the Manx on their native island.

furnishings of hair within ears

clear evidence of short tail visible here

solid body profile

FUR TYPE: thick under-coat; longer topcoat

Longhair option Tortoiseshell Cymric	Temperament Intelligent

JAPANESE BOBTAIL

C ATS WITH DEFORMED TAILS are well documented in various parts of Asia. The genes responsible for this mutation were probably introduced with the early cats taken to Japan from China about 1,000 years ago. Asian cats with stubby and kinked tails may share a common ancestry with the Japanese Bobtail, but there is no connection between the Bobtail and the Manx: these are now known to be entirely separate mutations. This breed has a long history in its native Japan but is still scarce in other parts of the world. The tail of the Japanese Bobtail is about 4 in (10 cm) long and is relatively inflexible; the joints are virtually fused. It is usually kept curled close to the body when the cat is resting, but when walking, the tail may be held upright.

Country of origin Japan	Ancestry Nonpedigree Shorthairs	Origins 1000s

RED AND WHITE

Because the tail fur of this breed is longer than on the rest of the body, the tail resembles a pom-pom, most of all when held above the body.
• **FEATURES** Coloration is a significant feature of the Japanese Bobtail, the tortoiseshell form of black, red, and white (known as the *Mi-ke*) being the favored variety. The red and white form shown here is also popular. In fact there are virtually no restrictions on their coloration, but patterned varieties are more common than selfs. Other distinctive features include the high cheekbones and slanting, oval eyes.
• **REMARK** The breed was first seen outside of Japan, in the United States, in 1968.

recessed eyes, not protruding beyond forehead or cheekbones

pom-pom tail flexible at its base

forelegs and shoulders form straight line when standing upright

medium-size, muscular, slender body

head shaped like equilateral triangle

long nose

hind legs noticeably longer than forelegs

FUR TYPE: soft and silky; little undercoat

Longhair option Red and White Long-haired Japanese Bobtail	Temperament Affectionate

SCOTTISH FOLD

I N 1951, A KITTEN with folded ears appeared in a litter born to a farm cat. Originating close to Coupar Angus in Scotland, these cats have since become known as Scottish Folds. The original cat, christened *Susie*, gave birth to another white kitten with folded ears. It was then that a local shepherd, named William Ross, decided to try and establish a whole new breed with the folded ear characteristic. He started with this kitten, who was called *Snooks*.

Country of origin Scotland	Ancestry Nonpedigree Shorthairs	Origins 1951

BLACK AND WHITE

During the early days of the breed's development, in the 1950s, crossings were undertaken with other nonpedigree shorthairs, and only later were British Shorthair cats introduced to help develop the Scottish Fold bloodline.
• **FEATURES** The folded ears are directed forward but, because the flaps are also folded down, the tips of the ears point in the direction of the nose. A less obvious feature of the breed today is its thickened, short legs, which have been actively discouraged by out-crossings to other cat breeds.
• **REMARK** Fears that the ear shape would encourage ear infections have proved to be false.

copper eyes

cobby body

small ears folded forward and downward

clear definition between white and black areas

FUR TYPE: short, dense, and resilient

round head with full cheeks

black areas in coat may develop brownish hue in sunshine

tail must be flexible, and at least two thirds of body length

Longhair option Black and White Long-haired Scottish Fold	Temperament Placid

Country of origin Scotland	Ancestry Nonpedigree Shorthairs	Origins 1951

BLUE AND WHITE

The appearance of these distinctive cats attracts great interest although, ironically, they are now far more common outside of Great Britain than in their Scottish homeland. This has arisen largely because the breed was not recognized by the GCCF, with the result that it attracted little interest from breeders within the United Kingdom.

• **FEATURES** In this case, the blue coloration may vary from a pale to a medium shade, depending on the individual cat, and contrasts with the white areas in the coat. The blue fur may become slightly rusty in color before shedding. Bicolored forms of the Scottish Fold tend to be the most popular, especially where there is good contrast in coloration, as seen in this case.

• **REMARK** This breed was accepted for registration in the United States in 1973, and by the CA of Britain in 1984.

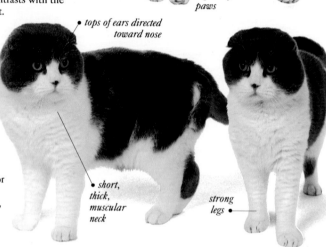

copper or deep orange eyes

powerful paws

tops of ears directed toward nose

short, thick, muscular neck

strong legs

white blaze extending over face

well-padded body

well-rounded face, with short, straight nose

medium-long, flexible tail

FUR TYPE: short, dense, and resilient

Longhair option Blue and White Long-haired Scottish Fold	Temperament Placid

Country of origin Scotland	Ancestry Nonpedigree Shorthairs	Origins 1951

CALICO

Scottish Folds have been bred in a wide range of colors and patterns. It has been relatively easy to produce so many forms because this characteristic is a dominant mutation: only one Scottish Fold parent is needed in order to produce a proportion of similar offspring.
• **FEATURES** The typical tortoiseshell patterning is clearly evident here, being broken by white areas of fur.
• **REMARK** All the kittens in a litter have normal ears at first, but the Folds become recognizable by their ears when they are about two to three weeks old.

folded ears emphasize overall round shape of face

FUR TYPE: short, dense, and resilient

clearly defined markings

medium-size body

long, flexible tail tapering along length

medium-boned, short, sturdy legs

Longhair option Calico Long-haired Scottish Fold	Temperament Placid

Country of origin Scotland	Ancestry Nonpedigree Shorthairs	Origins 1951

BLACK SMOKE AND WHITE

In its homeland, the careful registration policy adopted by the Cat Association of Britain insists that only one parent may be a Fold. The standard also penalizes short, inflexible tails or excessively thick limbs, to ensure the health of these cats.
• **FEATURES** The mainly white under-coat and black guard hairs contrast with the variable pure white areas, depending on the individual cat.
• **REMARK** In the United States, the only outcrosses allowable in Scottish Fold breeding programs are British and American Shorthairs.

full, rounded cheeks and muzzle

FUR TYPE: short, dense, and resilient

Longhair option Black Smoke and White Long-haired Scottish Fold	Temperament Placid

SNOWSHOE

T HIS BREED WAS developed during the 1960s by Dorothy Hinds-Daugherty, a breeder of Siamese cats from Philadelphia. She faced some opposition at first because of fears that the characteristic white markings of the Snowshoe could become widespread in Siamese bloodlines as a result of ill-judged crossings. Progress was rather slow until the 1980s, but now these cats are bred in various countries around the world. In spite of the white paws, which give the breed its name, their ancestry does not include Birmans.

Country of origin USA	Ancestry American Shorthairs x Siamese	Origins 1960s

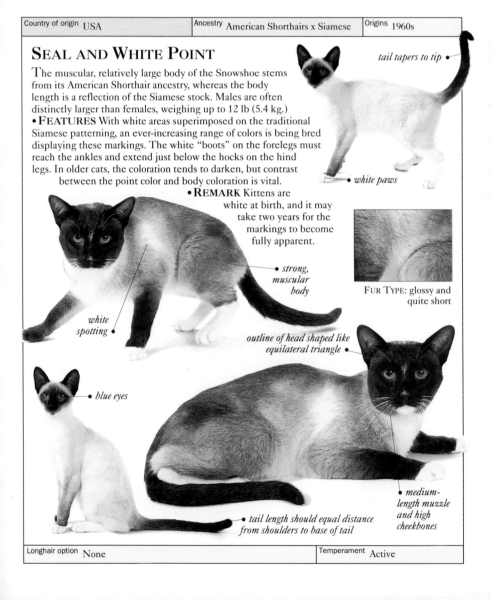

SEAL AND WHITE POINT

The muscular, relatively large body of the Snowshoe stems from its American Shorthair ancestry, whereas the body length is a reflection of the Siamese stock. Males are often distinctly larger than females, weighing up to 12 lb (5.4 kg.)

• FEATURES With white areas superimposed on the traditional Siamese patterning, an ever-increasing range of colors is being bred displaying these markings. The white "boots" on the forelegs must reach the ankles and extend just below the hocks on the hind legs. In older cats, the coloration tends to darken, but contrast between the point color and body coloration is vital.

• REMARK Kittens are white at birth, and it may take two years for the markings to become fully apparent.

tail tapers to tip •

• white paws

FUR TYPE: glossy and quite short

• strong, muscular body

white spotting •

outline of head shaped like equilateral triangle •

• blue eyes

• medium-length muzzle and high cheekbones

• tail length should equal distance from shoulders to base of tail

Longhair option None	Temperament Active

AMERICAN SHORTHAIR

T HE AMERICAN SHORTHAIR has evolved from European cats taken to North America during the early years of exploration and settlement. Ships' cats, highly valued as a means of controlling the rodent population on board, traveled the world and, not surprisingly, some were occasionally left at ports-of-call. Also, the early settlers would almost certainly have taken cats with them, not just as pets, but also for their hunting skills.

Prior to the establishment of the first European colonies in the late 1500s, there was no indigenous domestic cat population in North America, but the number of cats soon increased, especially after the founding of permanent colonies in New England and Virginia. The American Shorthair has developed through a process of evolution and selective breeding.

Country of origin USA	Ancestry Nonpedigree Shorthairs	Origins 1600s

BLACK

American Shorthairs were allowed to evolve without undue human interference, particularly in the early days, and they have developed into a versatile, hardy breed with a friendly and intelligent disposition. Their dense coats provide them with good protection especially if they are hunting in undergrowth.

• FEATURES The most significant distinction between American and European Shorthairs is the shape of the face, which is less rounded, and with a slightly longer nose. Overall, the American Shorthairs are also slightly larger than their European counterparts.

• REMARK Although early North American cats evolved in relative isolation, the American Shorthairs seen in show halls today have been selectively bred for specific characteristics.

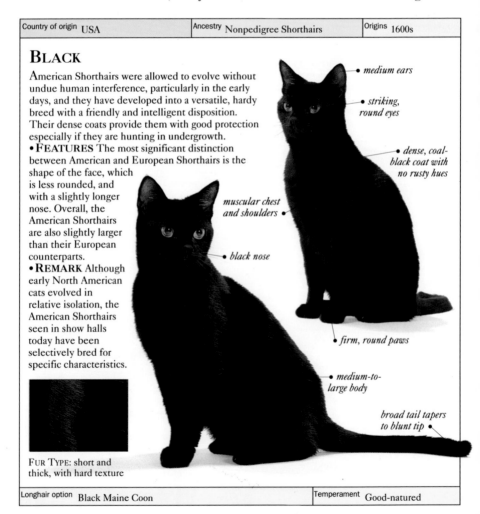

• medium ears

• striking, round eyes

• dense, coal-black coat with no rusty hues

muscular chest and shoulders •

• black nose

• firm, round paws

• medium-to-large body

broad tail tapers to blunt tip •

FUR TYPE: short and thick, with hard texture

Longhair option Black Maine Coon	Temperament Good-natured

Country of origin USA	Ancestry Nonpedigree Shorthairs	Origins 1600s

ODD-EYED WHITE

The White American Shorthair can be bred in three varieties, differing only in eye coloration. However, deafness is associated with the blue-eyed form and, in this case, the ear on the side of the blue eye may be afflicted.
• **FEATURES** Overall, these cats should give the impression of being feline athletes, with their muscular bodies clearly outlined beneath the short fur.
• **REMARK** Despite existing for centuries in an unrefined state, the first American Shorthair was registered about 1900; even this, however, was actually a cat born in Great Britain.

one eye deep blue

pink nose matches coloration of pads

powerfully built body

medium-length tail

FUR TYPE: short and thick, with hard texture

Longhair option White Maine Coon	Temperament Good-natured

Country of origin USA	Ancestry Nonpedigree Shorthairs	Origins 1600s

BLACK SMOKE

This is a cat of striking contrasts, with the pure white undercoat becoming clearly visible as the cat moves.
• **FEATURES** The American Shorthair's coat is not as plush as that of its British relative. Having adapted over centuries to a harsh outdoor existence, it is perhaps not surprising that the coat is inevitably thicker during the colder winter months. They have less rounded faces than those of their British and European counterparts as well as slightly larger bodies.
• **REMARK** *Buster Brown*, the first all-American cat to be registered, was a Smoke of un-known street cat origins.

brilliant gold eyes

broad, round head with full cheeks

powerful, muscular legs emphasize cat's jumping abilities

tail tapers along length

heavy paws

FUR TYPE: short and thick, with hard texture

Longhair option Black Smoke Maine Coon	Temperament Good-natured

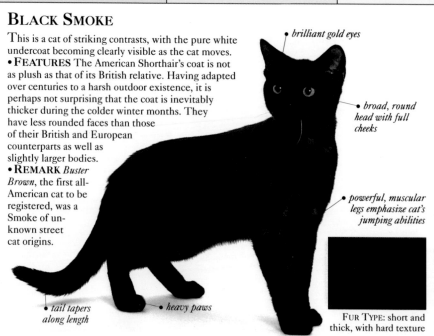

Country of origin USA	Ancestry Nonpedigree Shorthairs	Origins 1600s

RED CLASSIC TABBY

• *unbroken line extends from corner of each eye*

This form of the American Shorthair tends to be slightly larger than its British counterpart. The Red is always popular, with the deep, rich red markings displayed against a paler, red ground color.
• **FEATURES** When viewed from above, the shoulder markings should appear rather like a butterfly, with the outline of the wings clearly visible. A dark line runs through the center of the "butterfly" down to the tail, with two darker stripes on either side, separated by areas of the paler ground color.

brilliant gold eyes •

• **REMARK** Grooming is simple, and helps to emphasize contrasts in the coat.

• *blotched patterning*

FUR TYPE: short and thick, with hard texture

Longhair option Red Classic Tabby Maine Coon	Temperament Good-natured

Country of origin USA	Ancestry Nonpedigree Shorthairs	Origins 1600s

BROWN CLASSIC TABBY

Classic patterning with "bullseye" visible •

The Brown Classic Tabby tends to be less popular than other, more striking tabby forms of American Shorthair, although some top examples of this form have come to prominence within the American cat fancy.
• **FEATURES** This variety is characterized by a coppery brown ground color, broken by a dense black pattern of markings, the latter surrounded by a lighter ring of of coppery brown.
• **REMARK** The development of this breed was placed in jeopardy in the 1960s by matings with Persians and Burmese. Such pairings have now been outlawed, and American Shorthairs conform once more to their traditional type.

• *shortish, muscular neck*

• *muscular legs emphasize cat's athletic nature*

leg length should correspond to depth of body •

FUR TYPE: short and thick, with hard texture

Longhair option Brown Classic Tabby Maine Coon	Temperament Good-natured

Country of origin	USA	Ancestry	Nonpedigree Shorthairs	Origins	1600s

BROWN PATCHED TABBY

The American Shorthair is a breed well equipped for survival: its muzzle length is ideally suited to catching prey, and its moderately short and square shape means that there is considerable strength in the cat's jaws.

• FEATURES The unusual patterning of these tabbies results from the presence of tortoiseshell markings superimposed both on their basic coloration and on the tabby markings. "Patching" describes the appearance of red or cream areas of color, or sometimes both, in the coat.

• REMARK These cats are sometimes known as "torbies," which is simply an abbreviated form of "tortie tabby."

cheeks less well developed in kittens

random patterning, varying from one individual to another

tabby markings apparent

FUR TYPE: short and thick with hard texture

Longhair option	Brown Patched Tabby Maine Coon	Temperament	Good-natured

Country of origin	USA	Ancestry	Nonpedigree Shorthairs	Origins	1600s

RED AND WHITE VAN TABBY

muscular shoulders

The excellent temperament of the American Shorthair, coupled with its healthy disposition and wide range of colors, gives plenty of choice to the intending exhibitor or pet owner. Years of fending for themselves in the wild have endowed this breed with a natural intelligence.

• FEATURES While these tabbies do not differ in type from other American Shorthairs, their pattern of markings is distinctive. Mainly white, their darker coloring and tabby markings are restricted to the head, legs, and tail.

predominantly white body

brilliant blue eyes

• REMARK The description "Van" originated from the Turkish Van breed (*see pp.78–79*), which shows this patterning.

FUR TYPE: short and thick with hard texture

tabby barring on legs

pink pads

even tabby rings apparent on tail

Longhair option	Red and White Van Tabby Maine Coon	Temperament	Goodnatured

Country of origin	USA	Ancestry	Nonpedigree Shorthairs	Origins	1600s

CREAM MACKEREL TABBY

Tabby forms of the American Shorthair are among the most popular; their coat texture emphasizes the pattern of markings with excellent contrast. The Mackerel Tabby is sometimes described as the "natural" or "wild" type, because it occurs in wild cats.

dark buff-cream markings on light cream ground color •

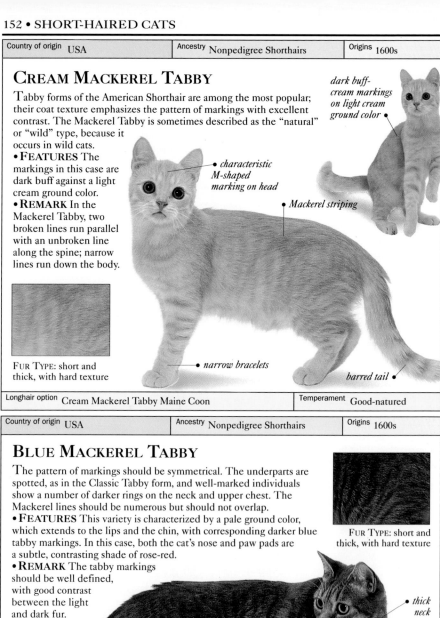

• **FEATURES** The markings in this case are dark buff against a light cream ground color.
• **REMARK** In the Mackerel Tabby, two broken lines run parallel with an unbroken line along the spine; narrow lines run down the body.

• characteristic M-shaped marking on head

Mackerel striping

FUR TYPE: short and thick, with hard texture

• narrow bracelets

barred tail •

Longhair option	Cream Mackerel Tabby Maine Coon	Temperament	Good-natured

Country of origin	USA	Ancestry	Nonpedigree Shorthairs	Origins	1600s

BLUE MACKEREL TABBY

The pattern of markings should be symmetrical. The underparts are spotted, as in the Classic Tabby form, and well-marked individuals show a number of darker rings on the neck and upper chest. The Mackerel lines should be numerous but should not overlap.
• **FEATURES** This variety is characterized by a pale ground color, which extends to the lips and the chin, with corresponding darker blue tabby markings. In this case, both the cat's nose and paw pads are a subtle, contrasting shade of rose-red.

FUR TYPE: short and thick, with hard texture

• **REMARK** The tabby markings should be well defined, with good contrast between the light and dark fur.

• thick neck

deep blue markings encircle tail •

barred legs •

• "necklaces"

Longhair option	Blue Mackerel Tabby Maine Coon	Temperament	Good-natured

Country of origin USA	Ancestry Nonpedigree Shorthairs	Origins 1600s

BLUE-CREAM

This is the dilute form of the tortoiseshell, sometimes described as the Blue Tortie. In type, these shorthairs should not differ from other colors although, being an essentially female-only form like other torties, they will not show as much development of the cheeks as can be seen in some male American Shorthairs.
• **FEATURES** No tabby markings should be apparent in this case. The muzzle must be square, and a dip in the nose profile is essential. Nose coloration can be blue, pink, or a combination of both colors.
• **REMARK** The leg length of the American Shorthair should correspond to the body depth.

tail length proportionate to size of body

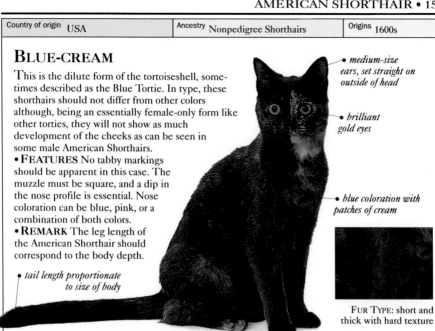

medium-size ears, set straight on outside of head

brilliant gold eyes

blue coloration with patches of cream

FUR TYPE: short and thick with hard texture

Longhair option Blue-cream Maine Coon	Temperament Good-natured

Country of origin USA	Ancestry Nonpedigree Shorthairs	Origins 1600s

DILUTE CALICO

These cats are better known in the United Kingdom as Blue-cream and White. Being a tortoiseshell form, they are available almost exclusively as females; males are likely to be sterile.
• **FEATURES** Patches of blue and cream coloration should be clearly apparent in the coat, with no evidence of brindling. The white areas should predominate on the belly. An area of white on the face is preferable, but there must be no evidence of white hairs in the colored areas of the coat.
• **REMARK** The coat is an important characteristic of the American Shorthair. It should lie close to the body, and there should be no sign of a fluffy undercoat.

clearly defined patches of color

FUR TYPE: short and thick, with hard texture

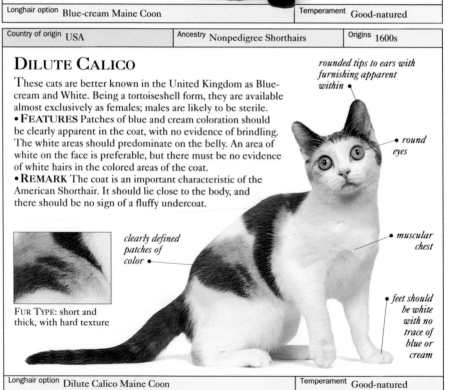

rounded tips to ears with furnishing apparent within

round eyes

muscular chest

feet should be white with no trace of blue or cream

Longhair option Dilute Calico Maine Coon	Temperament Good-natured

Country of origin USA	Ancestry Nonpedigree Shorthairs	Origins 1600s

CREAM CLASSIC TABBY

American Shorthairs are popular in their homeland but are not common elsewhere. The tabby forms were among the notable winners of the 1960s and helped promote the breed.

• **FEATURES** Clear definition is vital: in this case the buff cream markings stand out well against the pale cream ground color. Markings must be symmetrical.

• **REMARK** Having evolved through a process of natural selection, the urge to hunt is still very strong in these cats.

• *orange eyes*

• *widely spaced ears with rounded tips*

• *barring on legs*

• *ground color paler than markings*

• *darker rings on tail*

unbroken "necklaces" on chest •

FUR TYPE: short and thick, with hard texture

Longhair option Cream Classic Tabby Maine Coon	Temperament Good-natured

Country of origin USA	Ancestry Nonpedigree Shorthairs	Origins 1600s

SILVER CLASSIC TABBY

The stunning appearance of these cats results partly from the way in which the coat lies close to the body.

• **FEATURES** The ground color is an attractive silvery white, offset by dense black markings. Great efforts have been made by breeders to eliminate traces of tarnished coloration in these cats.

• **REMARK** The name for this entire group of cats was changed from "Domestic Shorthair" to "American Shorthair" after a Silver Tabby won the US Cat of the Year title in 1965.

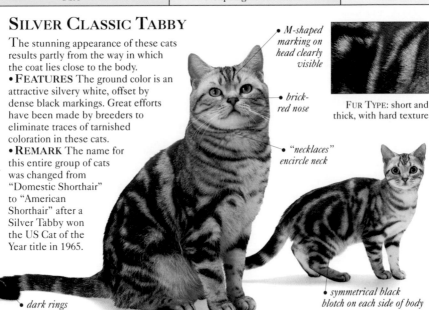

• *M-shaped marking on head clearly visible*

• *brick-red nose*

FUR TYPE: short and thick, with hard texture

• *"necklaces" encircle neck*

• *dark rings*

• *symmetrical black blotch on each side of body*

Longhair option Silver Classic Tabby Maine Coon	Temperament Good-natured

Country of origin	Ancestry	Origins
USA	Nonpedigree Shorthairs	1600s

CHOCOLATE SHADED

Although grooming these cats is straightforward, it should be carried out regularly in order to help emphasize the distinctive markings.
• **FEATURES** The undercoat of the Chocolate Shaded is whitish, with chocolate tipping to the individual hairs creating a variance of shading over the body. The shading is darkest over the back, becoming paler on the flanks, and whitish underneath.
• **REMARK** The coat of the American Shorthair may vary throughout the year, becoming thicker and heavier in winter.

thick, medium-length neck and full, muscular chest •

• *round green eyes, slanted just slightly at outer edges*

FUR TYPE: short and thick with hard texture

• *whitish underparts contrast with chocolate tipping elsewhere on body*

Longhair option	Temperament
Chocolate Shaded Maine Coon	Good-natured

Country of origin	Ancestry	Origins
USA	Nonpedigree Shorthairs	1600s

SHADED SILVER

The presence of more extensive tipping means that the Shaded Silver is darker than the Chinchilla. In this case, a distinctly blackish shade can be seen.
• **FEATURES** The depth of the coloration is most pronounced on the upper parts, shading to white on the lower parts of the body. The eye coloration can be either bluish green or pure green, and the brick-red nose is clearly outlined with a black edging. The pads should be entirely black.
• **REMARK** The short hair of these cats does not allow such a noticeable contrast as in long-haired breeds, but the tipping is still clearly evident.

tipping on face should correspond in depth to that on legs •

• *ears positioned on outside of head; rounded at tips*

muscular body •

under surface of tail white; no tipping evident •

FUR TYPE: short and thick with hard texture

Longhair option	Temperament
Shaded Silver Maine Coon	Good-natured

AMERICAN WIREHAIR

ALTHOUGH CATS with wiry coats were reported in Britain and elsewhere following World War II, none was established, and the origins of today's wirehairs can be traced back to a red and white kitten born on a farm in Verona, New York, in the 1960s. News of this kitten reached a local rex-breeder who obtained both the male kitten and his normally coated sister.

The program then undertaken by the breeder to establish the wire-haired mutation first entailed pairing brother and sister together. It soon emerged that the wirehair characteristic is dominant and, provided one parent is wirehaired, a proportion of wire-haired kittens will occur in the litter. Crossings with American Shorthairs were later used to develop the breed.

Country of origin USA	Ancestry Nonpedigree Shorthairs	Origins 1966

CALICO

The hair of the American Wirehair is crimped, the individual guard hairs being hooked or bent at their ends, even in the ears. The hairs making up the coat are also thinner than normal.

• **FEATURES** The thickness of the coat should result in the appearance of ringlets, which are especially noticeable on the head, as well as a more open wave pattern. Overall, the coats of these cats look and feel rather like lamb's wool, being somewhat less coarse on the underparts, including on the underside of the chin. The whiskers themselves are also normally curled.

• **REMARK** These cats can be bred in any color or pattern, with only the addition of American Shorthairs permitted in their bloodlines. Their eye coloration should always correspond to their coat color. Wire-haired kittens have tight, curly coats at birth, but the full potential of their coats is unlikely to be apparent until they are at least four or five months old.

round, medium-size head, with prominent cheekbones

springy coat

good definition of tortie markings

muscular body

compact feet

hair on tail corresponds to that on body

medium, well-muscled legs

FUR TYPE: medium; crimped and coarse

Longhair option None	Temperament Playful and active

| Country of origin USA | Ancestry Nonpedigree Shorthairs | Origins 1966 |

BROWN MACKEREL TABBY

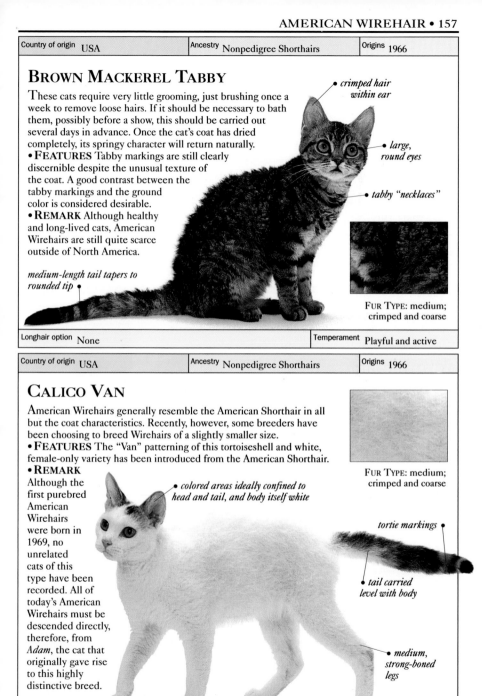

These cats require very little grooming, just brushing once a week to remove loose hairs. If it should be necessary to bath them, possibly before a show, this should be carried out several days in advance. Once the cat's coat has dried completely, its springy character will return naturally.

• **FEATURES** Tabby markings are still clearly discernible despite the unusual texture of the coat. A good contrast between the tabby markings and the ground color is considered desirable.

• **REMARK** Although healthy and long-lived cats, American Wirehairs are still quite scarce outside of North America.

crimped hair within ear

large, round eyes

tabby "necklaces"

medium-length tail tapers to rounded tip

FUR TYPE: medium; crimped and coarse

| Longhair option None | Temperament Playful and active |

| Country of origin USA | Ancestry Nonpedigree Shorthairs | Origins 1966 |

CALICO VAN

American Wirehairs generally resemble the American Shorthair in all but the coat characteristics. Recently, however, some breeders have been choosing to breed Wirehairs of a slightly smaller size.

• **FEATURES** The "Van" patterning of this tortoiseshell and white, female-only variety has been introduced from the American Shorthair.

• **REMARK** Although the first purebred American Wirehairs were born in 1969, no unrelated cats of this type have been recorded. All of today's American Wirehairs must be descended directly, therefore, from *Adam*, the cat that originally gave rise to this highly distinctive breed.

FUR TYPE: medium; crimped and coarse

colored areas ideally confined to head and tail, and body itself white

tortie markings

tail carried level with body

medium, strong-boned legs

oval paws

| Longhair option None | Temperament Playful and active |

AMERICAN CURL

T HE DISTINCTIVE curled ears of this breed are a relatively new mutation in the cat world, having been first documented in 1981. In that year, a long-haired kitten showing this characteristic feature was noticed by Joe and Grace Ruga, of Lakewood, California. In turn, two of this cat's kittens also had curly ears, so it became clear that this was likely to be a dominant mutation, which would occur independent of coat length. The first time that the American Curls were displayed at a show was in 1983, at Palm Springs, California, where they attracted immediate interest. Joe and Grace Ruga, and a friend named Nancy Kiester, set out to establish the breed, which occurs in both a long-haired (*see p.112*) and a short-haired form.

Country of origin USA	Ancestry Nonpedigree Curl	Origins 1981

BROWN CLASSIC TORBIE

The development of the short-haired American Curl has been relatively slow, largely because the original curly eared kittens were long-haired. But they are now gaining in popularity and can be bred in any color, offering great scope for breeders.
• **FEATURES** The extent of the curling of the ears can vary, and those cats showing the greatest degree of curling are preferred, provided that the ears point to the center of the base of the skull. Little emphasis is placed on the color and markings of the coat for judging purposes but, in this case, both tortie and tabby patterning should be clearly apparent.
• **REMARK** Because the American Curl Shorthair has not been established for long, ordinary unregistered cats may feature in some of their pedigrees.

curl extends backward from face •

• *ears firm, and relatively large, with rounded tips*

straight nose •

• *straight legs*

• *relatively long tail*

• *round feet*

hind legs slightly longer than front legs •

moderately long body •

tail tapers along length •

FUR TYPE: short and silky; little undercoat

Longhair option Brown Classic Torbie Long-haired American Curl	Temperament Gentle

| Country of origin USA | Ancestry Nonpedigree Curl | Origins 1981 |

BLACK

American Curls are playful and healthy cats. Grooming requirements are minimal, apart from regular combing in order to remove dead hairs from the coat.
• **FEATURES** Black coloration should be solid, with no white hairs in the coat. The shape of the ears and the proportions of the body are the most significant features. The overall type is semiforeign, with the face of greater length than width. The relatively large eyes are shaped like walnuts, and positioned so that they slant towards the nose.
• **REMARK** The flexible ear tips are able to swivel.

broad-based ears with furnishings within

FUR TYPE: short and silky; little undercoat

smooth coat

tail should correspond to length of body

medium-length legs

medium-size cat

tapering tip

| Longhair option Black Long-haired American Curl | Temperament Gentle |

| Country of origin USA | Ancestry Nonpedigree Curl | Origins 1981 |

SEAL LYNX POINT

The introduction of Siamese color characteristics into the American Curl bloodlines has already taken place, so pointed variants now exist. However, it is important that these cats remain true to their type, midway between that of the Oriental breeds and the cobby outlines of American Shorthairs.
• **FEATURES** The points should show characteristic seal-brown coloration, with tabby markings apparent on the legs and tail. Stripes, notably below the eyes, must also be in evidence.
• **REMARK** Kittens are usually lighter than the adults.

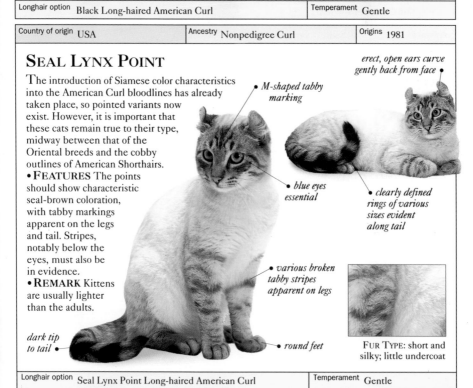

erect, open ears curve gently back from face

M-shaped tabby marking

blue eyes essential

clearly defined rings of various sizes evident along tail

various broken tabby stripes apparent on legs

dark tip to tail

round feet

FUR TYPE: short and silky; little undercoat

| Longhair option Seal Lynx Point Long-haired American Curl | Temperament Gentle |

EUROPEAN SHORTHAIR

I T IS ONLY RECENTLY that moves have been made to establish European Shorthairs as a recognized group in their own right. Before 1982 they were classed alongside British Shorthairs, and even today these two groups of cats are similar in many respects. The divergence in type is becoming more pronounced, however, because the European Shorthairs are now being selectively bred, with no British Shorthair crosses permitted in their pedigrees. However, these cats are available in a similarly wide range of colors, including self, bicolored, tabby, and tortoiseshell forms. Since the European division was first established, such cats have tended to become less cobby than their British relatives, with marginally longer faces.

Country of origin	Italy	Ancestry	Nonpedigree Shorthairs	Origins	1982

CREAM

European Shorthairs are hardy, adaptable cats. Lighter colors, such as the Cream, tend to be quite rare and overall European Shorthairs are far less well known than either their British or American relatives. It is difficult to persuade breeders to support these shorthairs, when similar breeds are already well established.
• **FEATURES** The depth of coloration in the Cream is variable. The "hotter" shades, which show a reddish hue, are frowned upon, as are cats showing clear evidence of tabby markings. This latter fault is very difficult to overcome, however, and even littermates may differ in this respect.
• **REMARK** There is a rare, pure white European Shorthair that is not deaf, in spite of having blue eyes.

rounded face, with relatively small ears and short nose

copper eyes

round tips to ears

even shade of cream, with no trace of white hairs in coat

rounded cheeks

pink nose

strong legs

broad chest and stocky, muscular body of medium size

FUR TYPE: short, very dense, and crisp

Longhair option	Cream Persian	Temperament	Responsive

Country of origin	Ancestry	Origins
Italy	Nonpedigree Shorthairs	1982

RED SHADED CAMEO MACKEREL TABBY

Cats have been kept on mainland Europe for millennia, and a large number of color forms and patterns have arisen without selective breeding. Emphasis is now being placed on establishing a clearly defined type for the European Shorthair.

• **FEATURES** The undercoat in this case is white, with red tipping on the longer guard hairs being most pronounced on the back. The red coloration becomes paler on the sides of the body, and fades out to white on the underparts.

• **REMARK** Like other native breeds, European Shorthairs are hardy, healthy cats.

round tips to ears, which show furnishings inside

well-spaced, large, round eyes

thick tail, broadest at base •

FUR TYPE: short, very dense, and crisp

Longhair option	Temperament
Red Shaded Cameo Mackerel Tabby Persian	Responsive

Country of origin	Ancestry	Origins
Italy	Nonpedigree Shorthairs	1982

TORTIE SMOKE

The Tortoiseshell and Smoke features combine, in this case, to produce a cat showing a good contrast in its outer coloration, but also differing from that of the undercoat.

• **FEATURES** While the undercoat itself should be as white as possible, the cream, red, and black tipping on the guard hairs form the tortoiseshell coloration. These colored areas should be broken into clearly defined, distinct patches.

• **REMARK** If these cats spend long periods outdoors, the black coloration in their patterning may become slightly discolored by the sun, taking on a brownish hue.

round facial shape •

FUR TYPE: short, very dense, and crisp

medium to large body

lighter Smoke coloration most apparent when cat moves

round-tipped, well-proportioned tail •

Longhair option	Temperament
Tortie Smoke Persian	Responsive

Country of origin	Ancestry	Origins
Italy	Nonpedigree Shorthairs	1982

CREAM SHADED CAMEO TABBY

A characteristic type is now apparent in top European Shorthairs, separating them from their British counterparts: the heads of the former are slightly longer, and they are less cobby in overall shape.

FUR TYPE: short, very dense, and crisp

• **FEATURES** The guard hairs are tipped with cream, and superimposed on this light patterning are the tabby markings in a darker shade of cream; both of these contrast with the ground color.

• *M-shaped tabby markings on head*

• *tabby markings in darker shade of cream*

• **REMARK** With their easily cared for short coats and their amenable natures, these cats make a good choice as pets. They do retain a strong hunting instinct, however.

firm, round paws •

Longhair option	Temperament
Cream Shaded Cameo Tabby Persian	Responsive

Country of origin	Ancestry	
Italy	Nonpedigree Shorthairs	1982

RED SILVER MACKEREL TABBY

Tabby combinations are commonly seen in short-haired British and American breeds. European Shorthairs have also been bred in many colors, and in a similarly wide range of tabby patterns.

• *rings on tail*

Mackerel tabby markings on body •

• **FEATURES** The red tabby markings are here set against a silvery ground color, creating an attractive contrast. There must be stripes running back from the corner of each eye, with narrow lines across the cheeks. The ears are the same color as the markings, apart from a central area about the size of a thumbprint, which is silver.

• **REMARK** During shedding, the tabby markings become less distinctive.

• *rings of darker coloration, or "necklaces," around neck*

• *solid colored tip to tail*

• *barring on legs*

FUR TYPE: short, very dense, and crisp

• *medium-long tail*

Longhair option	Temperament
Red Silver Mackerel Tabby Persian	Responsive

Country of origin Italy	Ancestry Nonpedigree Shorthairs	Origins 1982

BLACK SILVER MACKEREL TABBY

• *ear furnishings*

All three basic forms of tabby markings – Classic, Mackerel, and Spotted – occur in the European Shorthair, and do not differ essentially in patterning from those of other related short-haired breeds. The characteristic M-shaped marking on the head is common to all three, while the body patterning serves to distinguish them.

• **FEATURES** The Black Silver is one of the most strikingly marked of all tabbies, its dense black markings contrasting with the silver ground color. There should be a narrow black line running down the center of the back, with broken lines on either side. The vertical stripes radiate from these down the sides of the body. They should be narrow and evenly distributed, with both sides of the body appearing to be symmetrically marked. The tail must be ringed.

• **REMARK** The tabby patterning is usually less apparent in kittens, compared with adult cats, and kittens are also typically darker overall.

strong, round paws •

Mackerel tabby patterning •

muscular neck •

• *well-spaced, large, round, green eyes*

• *barring "bracelets" clearly apparent on legs*

• *dense black markings on silver ground color*

• *narrow stripe running down spine clearly visible*

• *rings on tail may be either complete or broken*

unbroken black "necklaces" present on upper neck and chest •

FUR TYPE: short, very dense, and crisp

firm, tight paws •

black markings on hind legs reach up to hock joint •

black tip to tail •

Longhair option Black Silver Tabby Persian	Temperament Responsive

COLOR POINTED EUROPEAN SHORTHAIR

T HE POINTED APPEARANCE of cats such as the Siamese has been superimposed on European Shorthairs to produce cats that should be identical in terms of type to other European Shorthairs, apart from the coat. As in the Siamese, the production of the color pigment responsible for the coloration of the points is influenced by the temperature; the cat's body is slightly colder at its extremities, and so greater pigment production will occur here. In a warm climate, such as that of southern Europe, it is likely that cats such as these will be slightly paler than those individuals kept farther north.

Country of origin Italy	Ancestry Nonpedigree Shorthairs	Origins 1982

BLUE POINT

Contrast is obviously a significant feature with these cats and, ideally, the points should show an even depth of coloration against the coat. Try to avoid binding the paw if the cat injures it, as the bandage will cause the paw to retain heat and the coloration of the point will be lightened. The body coloration tends to darken with age, so the show career of such cats is usually quite limited, but they will still be valuable afterward for stud purposes.
• **FEATURES** The points, comprising the mask, ears, legs, paws, and tail, should be a light shade of blue, contrasting with the glacial white body coloration, which becomes blue over the back.
• **REMARK** The full range of pointed colors can be developed in these cats.

• blue ears

blue eyes •

blue tail •

shading on back •

FUR TYPE: short, very dense, and crisp

• rounded face

stop between eyes •

medium-length, stocky, well-muscled body •

• even depth of coloration on legs and paws

• thick, medium-length tail

Longhair option Blue Point Himalayan	Temperament Responsive

CHARTREUX

I T IS BELIEVED that this old French breed was developed by Carthusian monks in the monastery of La Grande Chartreuse, near Grenoble. The monastery is believed to date from the 1300s, or even earlier, but the actual origins of the breed are unknown.

Legend has it that such cats were brought back from the Crusades by knights. They passed them to the care of the monks, who controlled the breed by selling only neutered animals. The coloration of these cats is distinctive; indeed, no other colors are recognized.

Country of origin	Ancestry	Origins
France	Nonpedigree Shorthairs	1300s

BLUE-GRAY

The Chartreux used to be bred partly for its unique fur, which would fetch a high price. By the 1920s, however, the breed had declined in numbers; it survived largely through the efforts of two sisters who were attracted by the bluish gray cats they found roaming in hospital grounds at Belle-Ile-sur-Mer, France. These cats formed the nucleus of their breeding program; subsequent crosses involving both nonpedigree and pedigree Blues, and British Shorthairs, were used to maintain and refine the traditional French breed.

• **FEATURES** The solid, bluish gray coat coloration can vary from ash to slate-gray; the silver tipping helps give the coat a sheen.

• **REMARK** This breed was imported to the United States in 1970.

• large, broad, trapezoid head

• coloration should be even in tone

• round paws

• clear, brilliant orange eyes may fade as cat grows older

• blue nose

FUR TYPE: medium-short, dense, and glossy

kitten's eye color changes from blue to brownish-gray, then to orange •

• dense fur with woolly resilient undercoat

blue coat •

• muscular body

medium-length tail with round tip •

Longhair option	Temperament
None	Friendly

CORNISH REX

T HESE CATS originated from a kitten born in Cornwall, England, in 1950. They have since been bred to a relatively foreign, or Oriental, body type in a wide range of colors. The distinctive coat lacks the outer, primary, guard hairs, whereas the remaining, secondary, guard hairs and the down hairs are wavy and reduced in length. Because of their relatively short hair, Cornish Rexes may not be comfortable outdoors if the weather is cold or wet.

Country of origin	Ancestry	Origins
Great Britain	Nonpedigree Shorthairs	1950

WHITE

Named "rex" after a similar mutation found in rabbits, the first rex kitten, *Kallibunker*, was paired back to his mother, and in due course further rexes were produced.
• FEATURES Although *Kallibunker* himself had a reasonably Oriental appearance, the use of short-haired cats in the early breeding program produced a more cobby type, which is now considered to be a fault in this breed.
• REMARK The first Cornish Rexes were exported to the United States in 1957; since then the breed has attracted a substantial following throughout the world.

ears well-covered with fine fur

large ears, wide at base and tapering to rounded tips

long, straight legs give impression of height

Roman nose

oval-shaped eyes

pure white wavy coat

slender, hard, muscular body

long, fine tail, well covered with curly fur

pink pads

FUR TYPE: short, dense, and wavy

Longhair option	Temperament
None	Playful

Country of origin Great Britain	Ancestry Nonpedigree Shorthairs	Origins 1950

CREAM

Cream coloration was apparent almost at the start of the breed's development: *Kallibunker*, the original Cornish Rex, sired two male kittens, one of whom was cream and white.

• **FEATURES** These cats usually have a fairly dense coat, without long guard hairs, but a coat that is shaggy or too short is considered a fault. Whiskers and eyebrows should be crinkled.

• **REMARK** Most Cornish Rex owners groom their pets by stroking them firmly from head to tail. This helps emphasize the distinctive, wavy pattern of the coat.

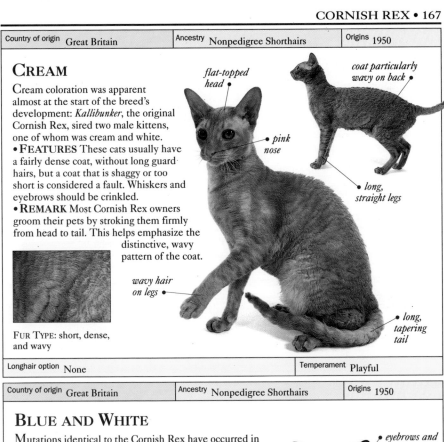

flat-topped head

coat particularly wavy on back

pink nose

long, straight legs

wavy hair on legs

long, tapering tail

FUR TYPE: short, dense, and wavy

Longhair option None	Temperament Playful

Country of origin Great Britain	Ancestry Nonpedigree Shorthairs	Origins 1950

BLUE AND WHITE

Mutations identical to the Cornish Rex have occurred in Germany and in the United States: the German Rex was recorded in 1947 but is now very rare, even in Germany. In North America various rex mutations have been recorded but are not widely kept at present. The Cornish Rex became established in the 1960s and was recognized in 1967.

• **FEATURES** The blue coloration in this case should be even and clearly defined. Breeders often aim to produce a symmetrical pattern of markings, but this is not compulsory.

• **REMARK** Rexes can benefit from a bran bath to remove grease from the coat.

eyebrows and whiskers long and crinkled

good covering of fur over whole body

silky feel to coat

curly or wavy hair

FUR TYPE: short, dense, and wavy

Longhair option None	Temperament Playful

| Country of origin | Great Britain | Ancestry | Nonpedigree Shorthairs | Origins | 1950 |

TORTOISESHELL

The markings of the Tortoiseshell Cornish Rex can vary from one cat to another, but the type should be consistent in every individual.
•**FEATURES** The black patches evident in the coat should be well broken by shades of red, creating good contrast. Younger cats may show traces of gray rather than black hairs but these will usually be replaced when the cat sheds. The coloration within the coat should be evenly distributed. In some cases, a lighter blaze of color may be present on the forehead.
•**REMARK** The short fur covering the underparts should be clearly wavy.

oval eyes

FUR TYPE: short, dense, and wavy

very long legs

arched back and rounded rump

| Longhair option | None | Temperament | Playful |

| Country of origin | Great Britain | Ancestry | Nonpedigree Shorthairs | Origins | 1950 |

CALICO VAN

The somewhat tubular appearance of the Cornish Rex stems from its fine-boned yet muscular body. It stands quite tall, and males are generally larger than females.
•**FEATURES** These cats are predominantly white; the Van pattern is a characteristic of the Turkish Van (*pp.78–79*), with coloration mainly restricted to the tail and odd patches on the head.
•**REMARK** When resting, the Cornish Rex usually curls up the tip of its flexible tail.

tortoiseshell patterning most apparent on head

crinkled whiskers

extremely flexible tail

dainty paws emphasize length of legs

FUR TYPE: short, dense, and wavy

tapering tail

| Longhair option | None | Temperament | Playful |

| Country of origin | Great Britain | Ancestry | Nonpedigree Shorthairs | Origins | 1950 |

CINNAMON SILVER

The quality of the coat is a vital feature in all Cornish Rexes, with no hairless patches or very short areas of fur. The distinctive curly-coated patterning should be evident over the entire body, down to the paws.

• **FEATURES** The coloration consists of a white undercoat with cinnamon ticking. The ticking should be most prominent running from the head to the tail, along the spine and down on to the cat's flanks.

flat skull •

• **REMARK** The cinnamon ticking creates a light, sparkling effect.

• slender, muscular body and arched back

FUR TYPE: short, dense, and wavy

| Longhair option | None | | Temperament | Playful |

| Country of origin | Great Britain | Ancestry | Nonpedigree Shorthairs | Origins | 1950 |

CHOCOLATE POINT SI-REX

The pointed versions of the Cornish Rex are quite a recent development and have yet to receive widespread recognition. In the case of this breed, however, coloration is generally of little significance; the type of these cats and their distinctive coats are important for judging.

• **FEATURES** The body coloration should be basically ivory-white; the relatively little dark shading should correspond to the milk-chocolate-colored points. Nose and pads are of a similar shade.

• **REMARK** Pointed Cornish Rexes should be identical in type to other rexes.

body shading most pronounced over back and flanks •

• chocolate mask

• good quality coat with clear signs of curls, waves, and ripples

FUR TYPE: short, dense, and wavy

long, fine tail, with good covering of curly, milk-chocolate-colored fur •

| Longhair option | None | | Temperament | Playful |

| Country of origin Great Britain | Ancestry Nonpedigree Shorthairs | Origins 1950 |

RED SMOKE

Rexes can be bred in any coat color or pattern, but the most controversial are the Si-rexes, which show Siamese markings.
• **FEATURES** A deep, rich shade of red, free from tabby markings, is desirable, with the lighter Smoke patterning most apparent when the cat moves. The fur itself has a silky texture.
• **REMARK** A shaggy coat is regarded as a serious flaw in this breed, and recent attempts to produce a long-haired form have not met with great interest.

• *ears set high on head*

slender neck •

• *wavy texture clearly visible*

• *even color*

• *long, tapering tail, well covered with fur*

FUR TYPE: short, dense, and wavy

| Longhair option None | Temperament Playful |

| Country of origin Great Britain | Ancestry Nonpedigree Shorthairs | Origins 1950 |

BLUE SMOKE

Cornish Rexes can show a tendency to obesity, which spoils their slender body shape, and may be harmful. It is best, therefore, to avoid overfeeding them.
• **FEATURES** In this case, the blue predominates against a white background. Rex kittens may have a sparse coat, but it usually becomes more profuse as they get older. In adults, however, bare patches are considered to be a serious fault.
• **REMARK** A blue female called *Riovista Kismet* was one of the most famous early rexes, being a direct descendant of the original Cornish Rex *Kallibunker*.

curl, ripple, or wave effect most noticeable over back and tail •

• *long, straight legs*

muscular thighs •

FUR TYPE: short, dense, and wavy

| Longhair option None | Temperament Playful |

| Country of origin | Great Britain | Ancestry | Nonpedigree Shorthairs | Origins | 1950 |

BLUE-CREAM SMOKE

It is said that one of the earliest Cornish Rexes was a Blue-cream male, but this is unlikely as the color is a dilute form of tortoiseshell, and such males are invariably sterile. It is more likely that the individual in question was a Blue Tabby.

• **FEATURES** Although males are larger and heavier than females, they must be lean and muscular in build.

• **REMARK** Cornish Rexes usually prove very healthy, and the females make good mothers.

FUR TYPE: short, dense, and wavy

• *medium blue and pale cream coloration in the coat*

• *fine-boned, well-muscled appearance*

small oval paws •

| Longhair option | None | Temperament | Playful |

| Country of origin | Great Britain | Ancestry | Nonpedigree Shorthairs | Origins | 1950 |

BLACK SMOKE AND WHITE

The quality of the coat, rather than its coloration or markings, is the most important feature of the Cornish Rex. The tight, marcel waves are vital, as is the cat's type. In this case the white markings can be asymmetrical, but they are not allowed in Si-rexes.

• **FEATURES** The silvery undercoat shows clearly in the Smoke Cornish Rexes because of the absence of the long guard hairs. Darker coloration is restricted to the awn hairs, the down being silver.

• **REMARK** The greasy coat of Cornish Rexes can lead to a condition known as stud tail.

• *oval eyes; color in keeping with coat color*

• *length of head one third greater than maximum width*

long slender legs •

• *tail tip carried upward when tail is low*

• *dainty paws*

FUR TYPE: short, dense, and wavy

| Longhair option | None | Temperament | Playful |

DEVON REX

THIS SECOND rex mutation, which appeared in 1960, was originally thought to be a form of the Cornish Rex, but no rex kittens resulted when these cats were mated, confirming that they were genetically different. The coat of the Devon Rex is distinctive, in that both sets of guard hairs and down hairs are present, these being more twisted than in the Cornish mutation.

Country of origin	Great Britain	Ancestry	Nonpedigree Shorthairs	Origins	1960

WHITE

But for the publicity surrounding the appearance of the Cornish Rex at cat shows in 1960, the Devon Rex might have gone unrecorded. A woman in Devon, England, had noticed a large, curly-coated male cat near her home. It mated with her cat, and one of the kittens had a similar, curly coat. Fortunately, having heard about the Cornish Rex, she realized the potential significance of her pet.

• **FEATURES** The coat in this case is pure white, and it may be necessary to wash these particular rexes before a show if the fur becomes dirty. Like all Devon Rexes, they are muscular cats with a distinctly foreign appearance.

• **REMARK** The pixielike ears, which help to distinguish these cats from Cornish Rexes, are large and set low; they need regular cleaning with a cotton swab.

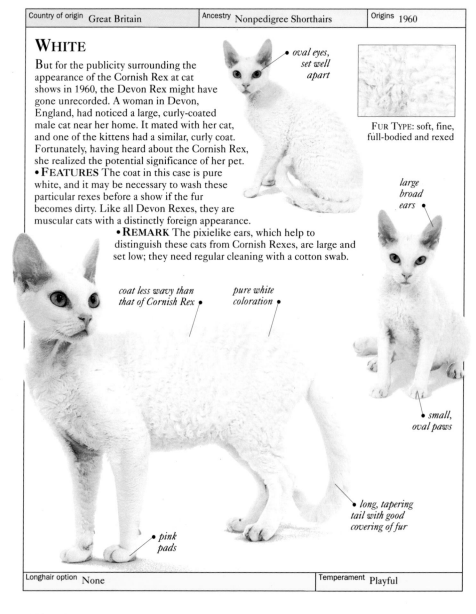

oval eyes, set well apart

FUR TYPE: soft, fine, full-bodied and rexed

large broad ears

coat less wavy than that of Cornish Rex

pure white coloration

small, oval paws

long, tapering tail with good covering of fur

pink pads

Longhair option	None	Temperament	Playful

| Country of origin Great Britain | Ancestry Nonpedigree Shorthairs | Origins 1960 |

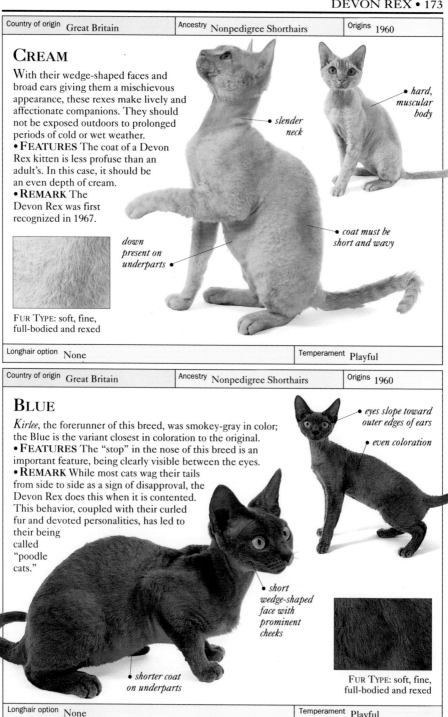

CREAM

With their wedge-shaped faces and broad ears giving them a mischievous appearance, these rexes make lively and affectionate companions. They should not be exposed outdoors to prolonged periods of cold or wet weather.
• **FEATURES** The coat of a Devon Rex kitten is less profuse than an adult's. In this case, it should be an even depth of cream.
• **REMARK** The Devon Rex was first recognized in 1967.

• *slender neck*

• *hard, muscular body*

• *coat must be short and wavy*

down present on underparts •

FUR TYPE: soft, fine, full-bodied and rexed

| Longhair option None | Temperament Playful |

| Country of origin Great Britain | Ancestry Nonpedigree Shorthairs | Origins 1960 |

BLUE

Kirlee, the forerunner of this breed, was smokey-gray in color; the Blue is the variant closest in coloration to the original.
• **FEATURES** The "stop" in the nose of this breed is an important feature, being clearly visible between the eyes.
• **REMARK** While most cats wag their tails from side to side as a sign of disapproval, the Devon Rex does this when it is contented. This behavior, coupled with their curled fur and devoted personalities, has led to their being called "poodle cats."

• *eyes slope toward outer edges of ears*

• *even coloration*

• *short wedge-shaped face with prominent cheeks*

• *shorter coat on underparts*

FUR TYPE: soft, fine, full-bodied and rexed

| Longhair option None | Temperament Playful |

Country of origin Great Britain	Ancestry Nonpedigree Shorthairs	Origins 1960

CREAM LYNX POINT SI-REX

Outcrossings with a range of other breeds, including Burmese, Bombay, and Siamese, have led to the wide range of colors now seen in the Devon Rex. Matings with the Cornish Rex have not been encouraged, since it became clear that the breeds were separate mutations.
• **FEATURES** Coat quality is vitally important in this breed, but kittens do not develop a full coat until they are around 18 months of age. Cream coloration with darker tabby markings on the points distinguishes this variety.
• **REMARK** The Devon Rex is now becoming available worldwide.

FUR TYPE: soft, fine, full-bodied, and rexed

flat skull

small, oval paws

slim legs

coat more profuse in adult

Longhair option None		Temperament Playful

Country of origin Great Britain	Ancestry Nonpedigree Shorthairs	Origins 1960

SILVER TORBIE

One of the many interesting patterned combinations now available, this Devon Rex shows the potential variety within the breed. As with all tortoiseshell forms, these cats are almost invariably female.
• **FEATURES** In Torbies, the tabby markings usually replace the black present in the coat of a tortoiseshell, whereas the white undercoat remains essentially unaffected.
• **REMARK** These cats are sometimes known as "patched tabbies" or "tortie tabbies."

ears set low

strong chin and prominent whisker pads

muscular yet slender body

tail must show no sign of kink

FUR TYPE: soft, fine, full-bodied, and rexed

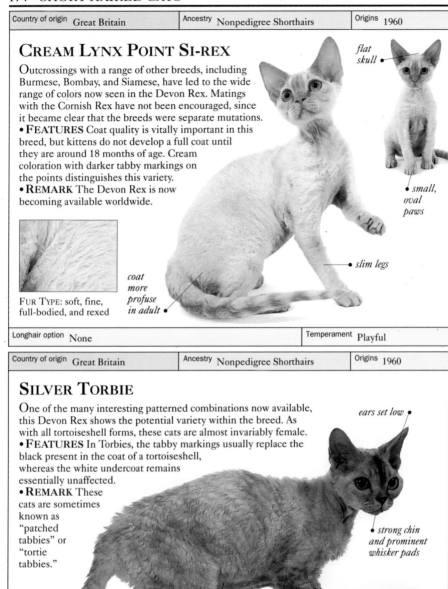

Longhair option None		Temperament Playful

| Country of origin | Great Britain | Ancestry | Nonpedigree Shorthairs | Origins | 1960 |

CREAM AND WHITE

Although bicolor forms of the Devon Rex have not always been popular in show circles, these attractive cats possess the affectionate and devoted nature that is typical of the breed.

• **FEATURES** The distribution of the cream and white patches is less significant than the quality of the coat.

• **REMARK** There should be no tabby markings in the cream areas in adults, although traces may still be visible in the case of kittens.

even cream coloration

FUR TYPE: soft, fine, full-bodied, and rexed

slender oval paws

| Longhair option | None | | Temperament | Playful |

| Country of origin | Great Britain | Ancestry | Nonpedigree Shorthairs | Origins | 1960 |

BLACK AND WHITE SMOKE

Although the mother of the original Devon Rex kitten was a Calico, other bicolor forms have not been generally favored.

• **FEATURES** The ears of the Devon Rex are its most distinctive feature, although the face shape also distinguishes these cats from Cornish Rexes. There should be a good contrast between the white and black areas.

• **REMARK** Breeders have tended to concentrate on improving the quality of the Devon Rex's coat, with less emphasis on the markings, which can be variable.

large ears, well covered with fine fur; may be tufted at tips

hard, slender, muscular body which can be extended in an elongated fashion, as here

white undercoat visible in black areas

good covering of fur on tail

FUR TYPE: soft, fine, full-bodied, and rexed

| Longhair option | None | | Temperament | Playful |

| Country of origin Great Britain | Ancestry Nonpedigree Shorthairs | Origins 1960 |

DILUTE CALICO

short muzzle

As a member of the tortoiseshell group, the blue-cream and white Devon Rex is essentially a female-only variant; any males are likely to be sterile.
- **FEATURES** While baldness is a serious fault in these cats, it is accepted that their whiskers are fragile and may therefore break off quite easily.
  - **REMARK** Devon Rexes may shed a considerable amount of fur when shedding, resulting in bald patches. This is not a cause for concern, but an isolated area of hair loss at other times might indicate the presence of a ringworm infection.

long tail

characteristic stop in facial profile

long hind legs

body carried high on legs

FUR TYPE: soft, fine, full-bodied, and rexed

| Longhair option None | Temperament Playful |

| Country of origin Great Britain | Ancestry Nonpedigree Shorthairs | Origins 1960 |

BLACK SMOKE

The coat of the Devon Rex has a slightly coarser feel than that of its Cornish relative, as well as being less consistent in both the length of the hair and its wavy patterning.
- **FEATURES** Although coloration is not considered to be as significant in the Smoke as type and quality of the coat, the Black is often preferred because of its striking contrasts. In some cats the front legs may appear to be bowed but this is an illusion, resulting from the broad chest, rather than being due to an inherent weakness.
- **REMARK** Grooming by hand, and using a piece of silk, help emphasize the arrangement of the hairs.

fur-covered ears

wavy coat

tail well covered with fur, but not bushy

FUR TYPE: soft, fine, full-bodied, and rexed

| Longhair option None | Temperament Playful |

Country of origin Great Britain	Ancestry Nonpedigree Shorthairs	Origins 1960

RED SILVER TABBY

Stroking these cats by hand is one of the best ways to groom their distinctive coats; using a piece of silk will ensure an even better gloss.
• **FEATURES** Grooming helps emphasize the natural waviness of the coat. Coloration should be a deep, rich shade of red in this case. Whiskers are brittle and break easily, as in this individual.
• **REMARK** A warm bran bath suits these cats well; rubbed roughly into the coat, it helps absorb the grease. The bran must then be brushed out and the coat polished well.

FUR TYPE: soft, fine, full-bodied, and rexed

• *good depth of coloration*

• *wavy, rippling coat, especially over back and sides*

• *long, muscular, hind limbs*

tabby markings •

Longhair option None	Temperament Playful

Country of origin Great Britain	Ancestry Nonpedigree Shorthairs	Origins 1960

BROWN TABBY

Although rexes have emerged in various countries, including Germany, the Netherlands, Great Britain, and the United States, there is no clear genetic similarity between all of them.
• **FEATURES** Devon Rexes have wide cheeks and short muzzles. The darker tabby markings are most likely to be evident on the head, legs, and tail. The relatively short fur emphasizes the body shape, which should be of medium length, slender, and muscular.
• **REMARK** If you are planning to exhibit a Devon Rex, try to prevent it from being soaked in heavy rain as this will flatten the curly coat for a time, detracting somewhat from its usually buoyant appearance.

• *fragile, crinkled whiskers*

• *broad chest*

• *darker tabby markings*

soft, curly fur •

FUR TYPE: soft, fine, full-bodied, and rexed

long tail showing tabby markings •

Longhair option None	Temperament Playful

SPHYNX

THE SPHYNX may not appeal to everyone, but it always attracts attention. Some cat organizations do not recognize the breed, believing that the lack of hair may be potentially harmful to the cats' well-being. This is not unique, however; similar mutations have occurred in dogs and in mice.

Country of origin Canada	Ancestry Nonpedigree Shorthairs	Origins 1966

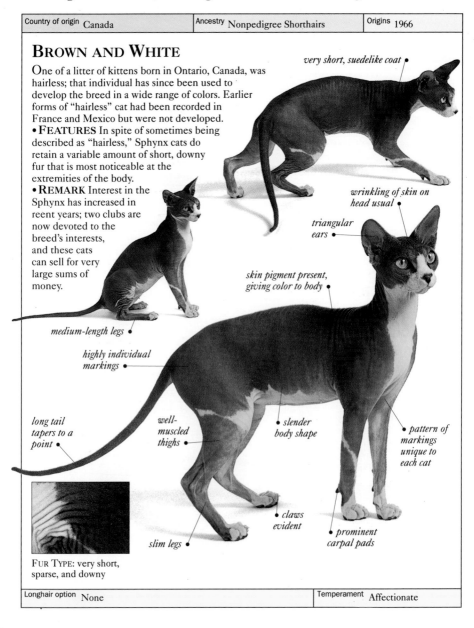

BROWN AND WHITE

One of a litter of kittens born in Ontario, Canada, was hairless; that individual has since been used to develop the breed in a wide range of colors. Earlier forms of "hairless" cat had been recorded in France and Mexico but were not developed.

• **FEATURES** In spite of sometimes being described as "hairless," Sphynx cats do retain a variable amount of short, downy fur that is most noticeable at the extremities of the body.

• **REMARK** Interest in the Sphynx has increased in reent years; two clubs are now devoted to the breed's interests, and these cats can sell for very large sums of money.

very short, suedelike coat •

wrinkling of skin on head usual •

triangular ears •

skin pigment present, giving color to body •

medium-length legs •

highly individual markings •

long tail tapers to a point •

well-muscled thighs •

slender body shape •

pattern of markings unique to each cat

claws evident

slim legs •

prominent carpal pads

FUR TYPE: very short, sparse, and downy

Longhair option None	Temperament Affectionate

Country of origin Canada	Ancestry Nonpedigree Shorthairs	Origins 1966

BLACK AND WHITE

The first Sphynx was actually born to a Black and White cat. Now, however, the breed has been developed in a wide range of colors and markings. In all cases, eye coloration should correspond with that of the body. The relative lack of coat means that these cats are not only vulnerable to the cold, but are also at risk in hot weather, the white areas being susceptible to sunburn.

• **FEATURES** The coloration of each individual cat is evident from its skin; this color is also emphasized by the sparse coating of fur. Kittens are usually born with a denser covering of fur, which becomes thinner as they grow older.

• **REMARK** It is now clear that the Sphynx's lack of hair is a recessive mutation, which means these cats need to be paired together in order to ensure that the offspring will have a similar "hairless" appearance.

ears rounded at tip •

whiskers may be absent •

rounded, barrel-shaped chest •

• body typically feels warm to touch

• characteristic stance with front paw raised and curled back under body

• clear contrast between white and black areas

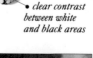

• face slightly angular, with broad ears

• body muscular, and not excessively wrinkled

FUR TYPE: very short, sparse, and downy

• powerful paws

"lion tail" of slightly longer hair close to tip •

Longhair option None	Temperament Affectionate

SELKIRK REX

T HERE IS ALWAYS the possibility that new mutations will arise unexpectedly and, if there is sufficient interest, breeds may be developed from them. The Selkirk Rex is one of the latest additions to the list of cat breeds and originated in the United States in 1987. In that year, Peggy Voorhees, of the Bozeman Humane Society, saw a blue-cream and white kitten in a litter of nonpedigree cats born in Wyoming. The kitten had green eyes, the hair was curly, as were the whiskers, and the ear furnishings resembled steel wool.

Country of origin USA	Ancestry Nonpedigree Shorthairs	Origins 1987

BLUE-CREAM

The original curly-coated kitten was mated at 14 months of age with a pedigree Black Persian, owned by Jeri Newman, a breeder of Persians. Of the six kittens that resulted, three had curly coats like that of their mother.

• **FEATURES** There is no restriction on color in this breed; the coat is a much more significant feature for exhibition purposes. The clarity of coloration is important, however, with the eye color matching that of the coat. In this case, the coat is blue and cream; the eyes can vary from deep gold to copper.

• **REMARK** The curly coat indicates that this is a rex-type breed, but it differs from the previously established forms, being a genetically dominant feature.

curls most evident around neck •

• rounded head

• medium-size ears with rounded tips, well spaced on head

• large paws

• rectangular, muscular body, showing good color

medium-length, thick tail, tapering to tip •

• loose curls clearly apparent on tail

• well-boned, muscular legs, contributing to somewhat bulky appearance

FUR TYPE: thick, plush, and curly

Longhair option Blue-cream Long-haired Selkirk Rex	Temperament Friendly

Country of origin USA	Ancestry Nonpedigree Shorthairs	Origins 1987

TORTOISESHELL

Although kittens are born with the curled type of coat, these hairs are shed around the age of six months and the coat then becomes rather sparse and wiry for a period. Not until they are between eight and ten months old will these rexes develop their characteristically thick, plush coats.
• **FEATURES** The curling effect is evident both in the rather coarse outer guard hairs and in the underlying down and awn hairs. The whiskers are also curled.
• **REMARK** The distribution of tortoiseshell patterning is random, as is the case in other breeds.

• rounded head with full cheeks and short, square muzzle

FUR TYPE: thick, plush, and curly

• body rises slightly in height to hindquarters

• coat hangs in loose, single curls over body

coat shows good density and soft texture •

• distinctive tortoiseshell patterning

Longhair option Tortoiseshell Long-haired Selkirk Rex	Temperament Friendly

Country of origin USA	Ancestry Nonpedigree Shorthairs	Origins 1987

BLACK TORTIE SMOKE

Various breeds are being used as outcrosses in the development of the Selkirk Rex, including British, American, and Exotic Shorthairs, as well as Persians. The use of other rexes, such as the Cornish or Devon forms, is not permitted. In August 1990, two American cat associations agreed to accept the breed; its supporters had formed the Selkirk Rex Society to guide its development.
• **FEATURES** The white undercoat contrasts with black tipping and tortie areas in the coat.
• **REMARK** Both sexes have jowls.

• ear tuft

• furnishings visible in well-spaced ears

• round, widely separated eyes

FUR TYPE: thick, plush, and curly

• females invariably smaller than males

kitten's coat develops from eight to ten months •

• rounded tip to tail •

Longhair option Black Tortie Smoke Long-haired Selkirk Rex	Temperament Friendly

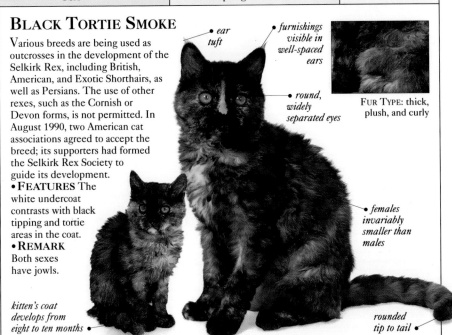

RUSSIAN SHORTHAIR

THESE CATS were originally known as "Archangel Blues" after the Russian port from which they were first brought to Britain, perhaps as early as the 1600s. They were exhibited at the early cat shows in the same class as the Blue British Shorthair, but from 1912 were grouped separately as "Foreign Blues." First registered in the United States in 1900, black and white forms have been developed in recent years, mainly in Australia and New Zealand.

Country of origin Russian	Ancestry Nonpedigree Shorthairs	Origins 1800s

BLUE

The numbers of Russian Blues declined drastically after World War II. In order to preserve the breed, crosses involving Blue Point Siamese were used, but this resulted in these cats developing a more foreign type. In recent years, breeders have worked hard to reestablish their distinctive traditional appearance.

• **FEATURES** The fur of the Russian Shorthair has a unique, seallike texture. It should be a solid, medium shade of blue with a distinctive silvery sheen. The nose and paw pads are also blue, except in the case of kittens, while the almond-shaped eyes should be a vivid emerald-green.

• **REMARK** Russian breeders are now hoping to reestablish these cats in their homeland, using stock obtained from Britain and elsewhere.

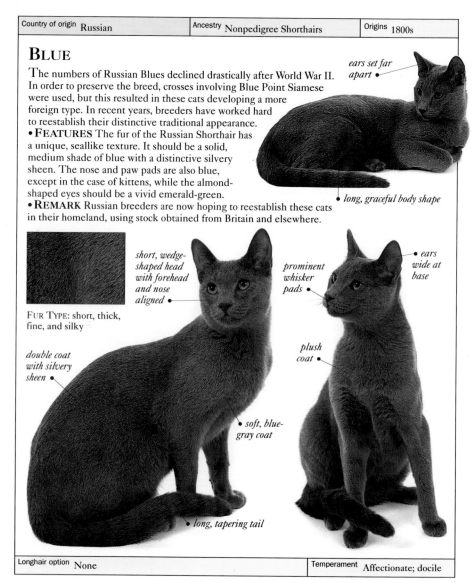

ears set far apart

long, graceful body shape

FUR TYPE: short, thick, fine, and silky

short, wedge-shaped head with forehead and nose aligned

prominent whisker pads

ears wide at base

double coat with silvery sheen

plush coat

soft, blue-gray coat

long, tapering tail

Longhair option None	Temperament Affectionate; docile

KORAT

NAMED AFTER the province of Korat, in northeast Thailand, these cats appear to have a very long history in that part of the world. The breed was first seen in the West in 1896, with modern bloodlines dating from as recently as 1959 when an American breeder obtained a pair. These were bred together, and others followed, and now Korats are kept by cat fanciers around the world. A breed association was established in 1965.

Country of origin	Thailand	Ancestry	Unknown	Origins	1300–1700s

BLUE

This breed has been prized in Thailand for centuries, and is recorded in the *Cat Book Poems* of the Ayutthaya kingdom (1350–1767).
• **FEATURES** In the *Cat Book Poems*, the Korat is described as having "smooth hairs with tips like clouds and roots like silver and eyes that shine like dewdrops on a lotus leaf." Since its introduction to the West, breeders have been careful to preserve the traditional appearance of the Korat.
• **REMARK** Although the Korat was recognized in the United States in 1966, this was not achieved in Great Britain until 1975.

• *round, luminous, green eyes*

• *medium legs, with small, oval paws*

large, round-tipped ears •

• *heart-shaped head*

• *broad forehead with gently curving face*

tapering tail, heavier at base •

• *medium-length tail with round tip*

silvery sheen to coat •

• *medium-size, muscular body*

FUR TYPE: short, fine, and close-lying

Longhair option	None	Temperament	Playful

SIAMESE / COLORPOINT SHORTHAIR

W ITH THEIR ANGULAR FACES and svelte outlines, these are among the best known of pedigree cats although, ironically, they seem to have lost some popularity to the newer breeds that have been developed from them in recent years. In the United States, only the four "pure" colors are described as Siamese, other colors being known as Colorpoint Shorthairs.

Country of origin Thailand	Ancestry Nonpedigree Asiatics	Origins 1300s

CREAM POINT

The temperature at which these cats are kept has a direct influence on their pigmentation: relatively warm surroundings are likely to result in paler coloration of the points. All Siamese are born pure white; the darker shade of the points becomes apparent only gradually, and the full contrast is not apparent until they are one year old.

- **FEATURES** The back and sides of the body are pale cream in this case, the remainder of the body being white. The points are a darker shade of cream, most notably on the ears, mask, and tail.
- **REMARK** Slight signs of darker freckling on the pink coloration of the nose and pads are not penalized. Cream points breed true when they are mated together.

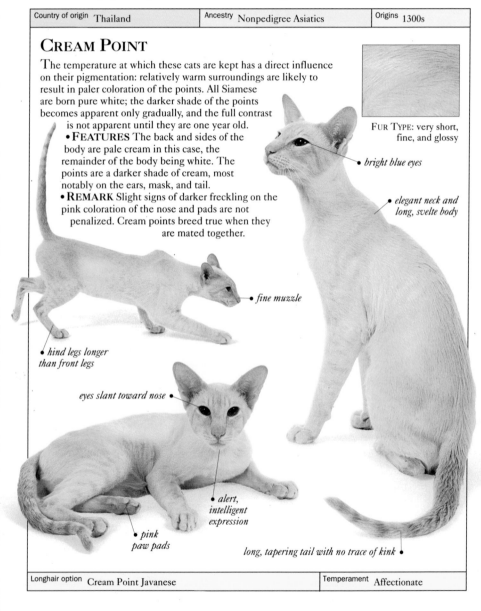

FUR TYPE: very short, fine, and glossy

• *bright blue eyes*

• *elegant neck and long, svelte body*

• *fine muzzle*

• *hind legs longer than front legs*

eyes slant toward nose •

• *alert, intelligent expression*

• *pink paw pads*

long, tapering tail with no trace of kink •

Longhair option Cream Point Javanese	Temperament Affectionate

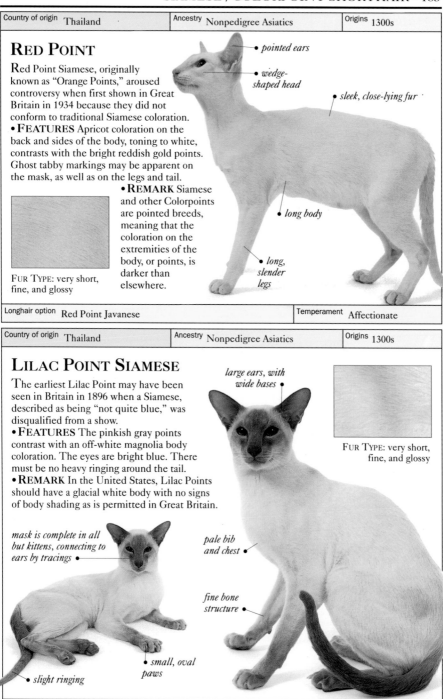

| Country of origin | Thailand | Ancestry | Nonpedigree Asiatics | Origins | 1300s |

RED POINT

Red Point Siamese, originally known as "Orange Points," aroused controversy when first shown in Great Britain in 1934 because they did not conform to traditional Siamese coloration.
• FEATURES Apricot coloration on the back and sides of the body, toning to white, contrasts with the bright reddish gold points. Ghost tabby markings may be apparent on the mask, as well as on the legs and tail.
• REMARK Siamese and other Colorpoints are pointed breeds, meaning that the coloration on the extremities of the body, or points, is darker than elsewhere.

pointed ears •

• wedge-shaped head

• sleek, close-lying fur

• long body

• long, slender legs

FUR TYPE: very short, fine, and glossy

| Longhair option | Red Point Javanese | Temperament | Affectionate |

| Country of origin | Thailand | Ancestry | Nonpedigree Asiatics | Origins | 1300s |

LILAC POINT SIAMESE

The earliest Lilac Point may have been seen in Britain in 1896 when a Siamese, described as being "not quite blue," was disqualified from a show.
• FEATURES The pinkish gray points contrast with an off-white magnolia body coloration. The eyes are bright blue. There must be no heavy ringing around the tail.
• REMARK In the United States, Lilac Points should have a glacial white body with no signs of body shading as is permitted in Great Britain.

large ears, with wide bases •

FUR TYPE: very short, fine, and glossy

mask is complete in all but kittens, connecting to ears by tracings •

pale bib and chest •

fine bone structure •

• slight ringing

• small, oval paws

| Longhair option | Lilac Point Balinese | Temperament | Affectionate |

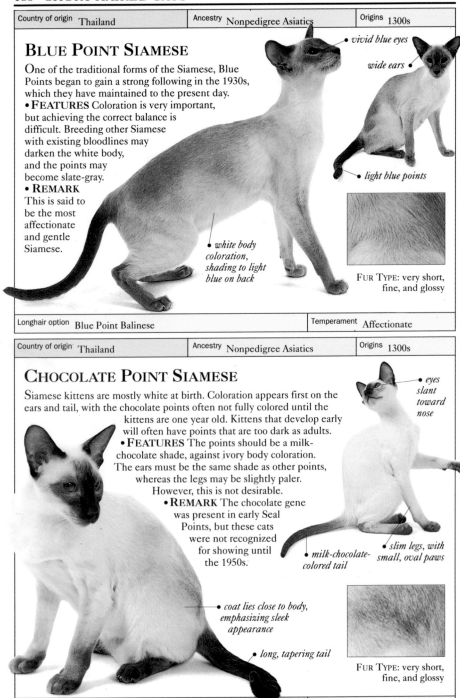

| Country of origin Thailand | Ancestry Nonpedigree Asiatics | Origins 1300s |

BLUE POINT SIAMESE

One of the traditional forms of the Siamese, Blue Points began to gain a strong following in the 1930s, which they have maintained to the present day.
• **FEATURES** Coloration is very important, but achieving the correct balance is difficult. Breeding other Siamese with existing bloodlines may darken the white body, and the points may become slate-gray.
• **REMARK** This is said to be the most affectionate and gentle Siamese.

• vivid blue eyes

wide ears •

• light blue points

• white body coloration, shading to light blue on back

FUR TYPE: very short, fine, and glossy

| Longhair option Blue Point Balinese | Temperament Affectionate |

| Country of origin Thailand | Ancestry Nonpedigree Asiatics | Origins 1300s |

CHOCOLATE POINT SIAMESE

Siamese kittens are mostly white at birth. Coloration appears first on the ears and tail, with the chocolate points often not fully colored until the kittens are one year old. Kittens that develop early will often have points that are too dark as adults.
• **FEATURES** The points should be a milk-chocolate shade, against ivory body coloration. The ears must be the same shade as other points, whereas the legs may be slightly paler. However, this is not desirable.
• **REMARK** The chocolate gene was present in early Seal Points, but these cats were not recognized for showing until the 1950s.

• eyes slant toward nose

• slim legs, with small, oval paws

• milk-chocolate-colored tail

• coat lies close to body, emphasizing sleek appearance

• long, tapering tail

FUR TYPE: very short, fine, and glossy

| Longhair option Chocolate Point Balinese | Temperament Affectionate |

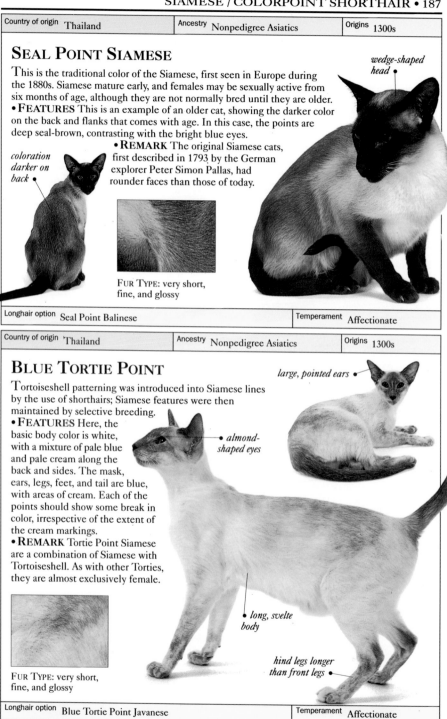

| Country of origin | Thailand | Ancestry | Nonpedigree Asiatics | Origins | 1300s |

SEAL POINT SIAMESE

This is the traditional color of the Siamese, first seen in Europe during the 1880s. Siamese mature early, and females may be sexually active from six months of age, although they are not normally bred until they are older.
• **FEATURES** This is an example of an older cat, showing the darker color on the back and flanks that comes with age. In this case, the points are deep seal-brown, contrasting with the bright blue eyes.
• **REMARK** The original Siamese cats, first described in 1793 by the German explorer Peter Simon Pallas, had rounder faces than those of today.

wedge-shaped head

coloration darker on back

FUR TYPE: very short, fine, and glossy

| Longhair option | Seal Point Balinese | Temperament | Affectionate |

| Country of origin | Thailand | Ancestry | Nonpedigree Asiatics | Origins | 1300s |

BLUE TORTIE POINT

Tortoiseshell patterning was introduced into Siamese lines by the use of shorthairs; Siamese features were then maintained by selective breeding.
• **FEATURES** Here, the basic body color is white, with a mixture of pale blue and pale cream along the back and sides. The mask, ears, legs, feet, and tail are blue, with areas of cream. Each of the points should show some break in color, irrespective of the extent of the cream markings.
• **REMARK** Tortie Point Siamese are a combination of Siamese with Tortoiseshell. As with other Torties, they are almost exclusively female.

large, pointed ears

almond-shaped eyes

long, svelte body

hind legs longer than front legs

FUR TYPE: very short, fine, and glossy

| Longhair option | Blue Tortie Point Javanese | Temperament | Affectionate |

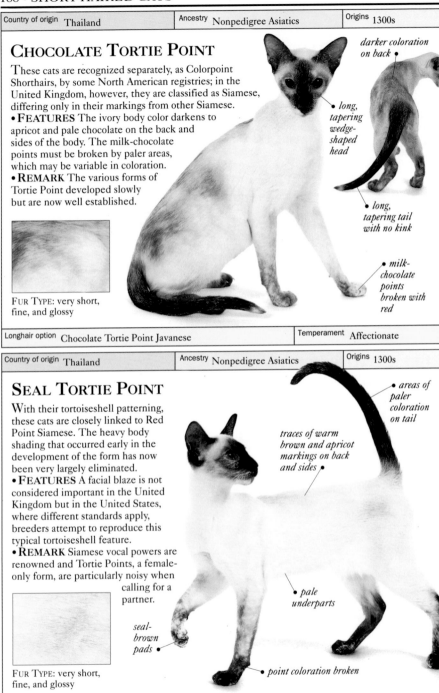

Country of origin Thailand	Ancestry Nonpedigree Asiatics	Origins 1300s

CHOCOLATE TORTIE POINT

These cats are recognized separately, as Colorpoint Shorthairs, by some North American registries; in the United Kingdom, however, they are classified as Siamese, differing only in their markings from other Siamese.
• **FEATURES** The ivory body color darkens to apricot and pale chocolate on the back and sides of the body. The milk-chocolate points must be broken by paler areas, which may be variable in coloration.
• **REMARK** The various forms of Tortie Point developed slowly but are now well established.

darker coloration on back

long, tapering wedge-shaped head

long, tapering tail with no kink

milk-chocolate points broken with red

FUR TYPE: very short, fine, and glossy

Longhair option Chocolate Tortie Point Javanese	Temperament Affectionate

Country of origin Thailand	Ancestry Nonpedigree Asiatics	Origins 1300s

SEAL TORTIE POINT

With their tortoiseshell patterning, these cats are closely linked to Red Point Siamese. The heavy body shading that occurred early in the development of the form has now been very largely eliminated.
• **FEATURES** A facial blaze is not considered important in the United Kingdom but in the United States, where different standards apply, breeders attempt to reproduce this typical tortoiseshell feature.
• **REMARK** Siamese vocal powers are renowned and Tortie Points, a female-only form, are particularly noisy when calling for a partner.

areas of paler coloration on tail

traces of warm brown and apricot markings on back and sides

pale underparts

seal-brown pads

point coloration broken

FUR TYPE: very short, fine, and glossy

Longhair option Seal Tortie Point Javanese	Temperament Affectionate

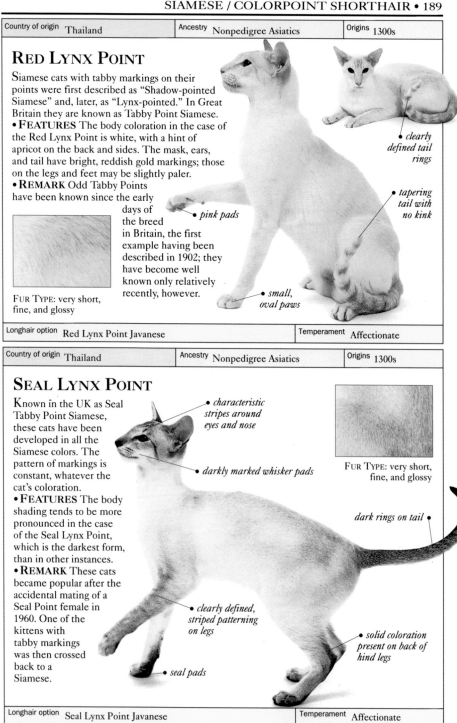

| Country of origin | Thailand | Ancestry | Nonpedigree Asiatics | Origins | 1300s |

RED LYNX POINT

Siamese cats with tabby markings on their points were first described as "Shadow-pointed Siamese" and, later, as "Lynx-pointed." In Great Britain they are known as Tabby Point Siamese.
• **FEATURES** The body coloration in the case of the Red Lynx Point is white, with a hint of apricot on the back and sides. The mask, ears, and tail have bright, reddish gold markings; those on the legs and feet may be slightly paler.
• **REMARK** Odd Tabby Points have been known since the early days of the breed in Britain, the first example having been described in 1902; they have become well known only relatively recently, however.

clearly defined tail rings

tapering tail with no kink

pink pads

small, oval paws

FUR TYPE: very short, fine, and glossy

| Longhair option | Red Lynx Point Javanese | Temperament | Affectionate |

| Country of origin | Thailand | Ancestry | Nonpedigree Asiatics | Origins | 1300s |

SEAL LYNX POINT

Known in the UK as Seal Tabby Point Siamese, these cats have been developed in all the Siamese colors. The pattern of markings is constant, whatever the cat's coloration.
• **FEATURES** The body shading tends to be more pronounced in the case of the Seal Lynx Point, which is the darkest form, than in other instances.
• **REMARK** These cats became popular after the accidental mating of a Seal Point female in 1960. One of the kittens with tabby markings was then crossed back to a Siamese.

characteristic stripes around eyes and nose

darkly marked whisker pads

FUR TYPE: very short, fine, and glossy

dark rings on tail

clearly defined, striped patterning on legs

solid coloration present on back of hind legs

seal pads

| Longhair option | Seal Lynx Point Javanese | Temperament | Affectionate |

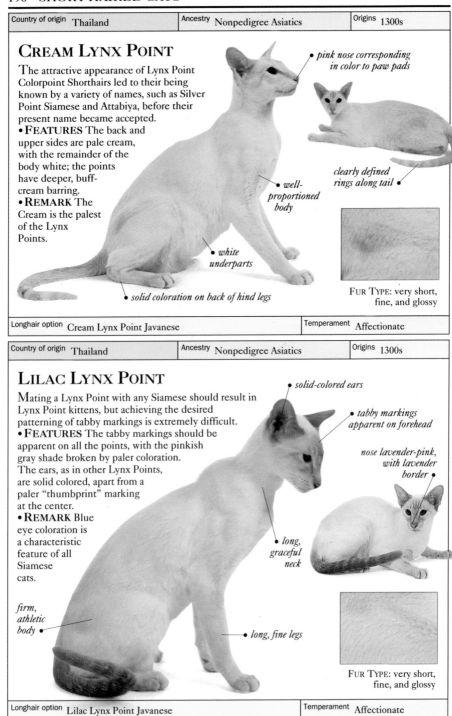

| Country of origin | Thailand | Ancestry | Nonpedigree Asiatics | Origins | 1300s |

CREAM LYNX POINT

The attractive appearance of Lynx Point
Colorpoint Shorthairs led to their being
known by a variety of names, such as Silver
Point Siamese and Attabiya, before their
present name became accepted.
• **FEATURES** The back and
upper sides are pale cream,
with the remainder of the
body white; the points
have deeper, buff-
cream barring.
• **REMARK** The
Cream is the palest
of the Lynx
Points.

*pink nose corresponding
in color to paw pads*

*clearly defined
rings along tail*

*well-
proportioned
body*

*white
underparts*

solid coloration on back of hind legs

FUR TYPE: very short,
fine, and glossy

| Longhair option | Cream Lynx Point Javanese | Temperament | Affectionate |

| Country of origin | Thailand | Ancestry | Nonpedigree Asiatics | Origins | 1300s |

LILAC LYNX POINT

Mating a Lynx Point with any Siamese should result in
Lynx Point kittens, but achieving the desired
patterning of tabby markings is extremely difficult.
• **FEATURES** The tabby markings should be
apparent on all the points, with the pinkish
gray shade broken by paler coloration.
The ears, as in other Lynx Points,
are solid colored, apart from a
paler "thumbprint" marking
at the center.
• **REMARK** Blue
eye coloration is
a characteristic
feature of all
Siamese
cats.

solid-colored ears

*tabby markings
apparent on forehead*

*nose lavender-pink,
with lavender
border*

*long,
graceful
neck*

*firm,
athletic
body*

long, fine legs

FUR TYPE: very short,
fine, and glossy

| Longhair option | Lilac Lynx Point Javanese | Temperament | Affectionate |

Country of origin	Thailand	Ancestry	Nonpedigree Asiatics	Origins	1300s

BLUE LYNX POINT

Once the Lynx Point feature was established, it was not difficult to combine this with all the point colors of the Siamese. Good contrast is most likely in the darker pointed forms, although excessive shading can also then be apparent.

• **FEATURES** The body coloration varies from bluish white to platinum-gray, the underparts being much lighter. The points should be blue-gray, broken by paler areas.

• **REMARK** As Lynx Points grow older, body coloration is likely to shows markings such as large spots or wide bands.

long, tapering tail

slightly convex profile; long nose with no break

clearly defined striping on legs

solid coloration at back of hind legs

FUR TYPE: very short, fine, and glossy

Longhair option	Blue Lynx Point Javanese	Temperament	Affectionate

Country of origin	Thailand	Ancestry	Nonpedigree Asiatics	Origins	1300s

CHOCOLATE LYNX POINT

large ears

pinkish nose, edged by chocolate

The unmistakable M-shaped tabby marking on the head is a feature of all Lynx Points, but it is most prominent in cats with the darker colored points. Other tabby characteristics must also be apparent, such as the "pencil" lines on either side of the face, extending from the eyes.

• **FEATURES** The ivory-colored body may darken with age. The points, in this case, are a warm, milk-chocolate color broken by lighter coloration, and take the form of striped legs and rings around the tail. The eyes are a brilliant clear blue, with dark rims.

• **REMARK** Lynx Points were recognized as Siamese in Great Britain in 1966.

tabby markings and point colors not evident in young kitten

tinted ivory on back and sides of body

markings on legs paler than on other points

FUR TYPE: very short, fine, and glossy

dark tip to tail

Longhair option	Chocolate Lynx Point Javanese	Temperament	Affectionate

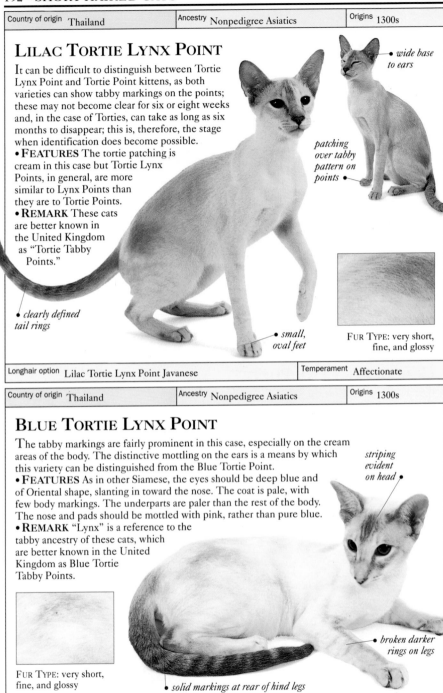

| Country of origin | Thailand | Ancestry | Nonpedigree Asiatics | Origins | 1300s |

LILAC TORTIE LYNX POINT

It can be difficult to distinguish between Tortie
Lynx Point and Tortie Point kittens, as both
varieties can show tabby markings on the points;
these may not become clear for six or eight weeks
and, in the case of Torties, can take as long as six
months to disappear; this is, therefore, the stage
when identification does become possible.

• **FEATURES** The tortie patching is
cream in this case but Tortie Lynx
Points, in general, are more
similar to Lynx Points than
they are to Tortie Points.

• **REMARK** These cats
are better known in
the United Kingdom
as "Tortie Tabby
Points."

*• wide base
to ears*

*patching
over tabby
pattern on
points •*

*• clearly defined
tail rings*

*• small,
oval feet*

FUR TYPE: very short,
fine, and glossy

| Longhair option | Lilac Tortie Lynx Point Javanese | Temperament | Affectionate |

| Country of origin | Thailand | Ancestry | Nonpedigree Asiatics | Origins | 1300s |

BLUE TORTIE LYNX POINT

The tabby markings are fairly prominent in this case, especially on the cream
areas of the body. The distinctive mottling on the ears is a means by which
this variety can be distinguished from the Blue Tortie Point.

• **FEATURES** As in other Siamese, the eyes should be deep blue and
of Oriental shape, slanting in toward the nose. The coat is pale, with
few body markings. The underparts are paler than the rest of the body.
The nose and pads should be mottled with pink, rather than pure blue.

• **REMARK** "Lynx" is a reference to the
tabby ancestry of these cats, which
are better known in the United
Kingdom as Blue Tortie
Tabby Points.

*striping
evident
on head •*

*• broken darker
rings on legs*

FUR TYPE: very short,
fine, and glossy

• solid markings at rear of hind legs

| Longhair option | Blue Tortie Lynx Point Javanese | Temperament | Affectionate |

Country of origin	Thailand	Ancestry	Nonpedigree Asiatics	Origins	1300s

Chocolate Tortie Lynx Point

These cats are precocious, like other Siamese, and may be sexually mature by six months of age. Females make good mothers, but do not like unnecessary disturbance, especially cats that have not bred before.
• **FEATURES** The warm, chocolate markings associated with the tabby are broken by characteristic red or cream mottling on the points. The basic body shade is ivory, with some shading. As in other cases, there should be a paler thumbprint of color in the center of the ears, which is more prominent in this darker form.
• **REMARK** In the UK these cats are included in the Siamese grouping, whereas in the US they are regarded as Colorpoint Shorthairs.

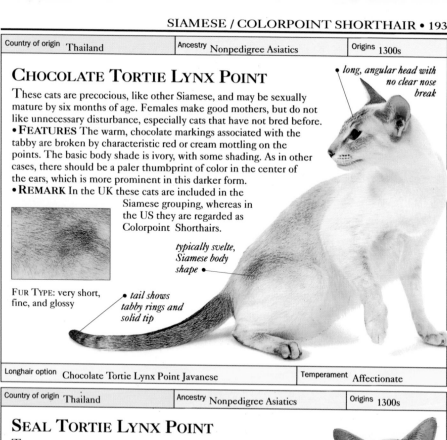

long, angular head with no clear nose break

typically svelte, Siamese body shape

FUR TYPE: very short, fine, and glossy

tail shows tabby rings and solid tip

Longhair option	Chocolate Tortie Lynx Point Javanese	Temperament	Affectionate

Country of origin	Thailand	Ancestry	Nonpedigree Asiatics	Origins	1300s

Seal Tortie Lynx Point

The sleek appearance of Siamese is easily maintained; brushing and combing about twice a week is adequate, while rubbing the coat occasionally with a chamois cloth emphasizes its natural gloss. Torbie Points are often quieter and less demanding than traditional forms, making them a good choice of pet.
• **FEATURES** As with other Siamese, the markings of these cats tend to be highly individual, with none showing identical patterning. The tabby pattern on the points is broken with cream. The body coloration in the Seal is more pronounced than in the lighter forms.
• **REMARK** The appearance of this form resulted from combining Lynx Point and Tortie Point with Seal Point coloration.

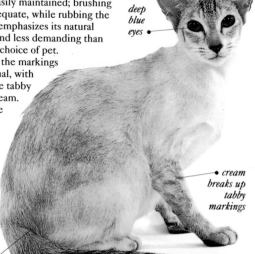

deep blue eyes

cream breaks up tabby markings

darker shading on body and flanks

FUR TYPE: very short, fine, and glossy

Longhair option	Seal Tortie Lynx Point Javanese	Temperament	Affectionate

BURMESE / MALAYAN

T HE COMPACT SHAPE of these cats, coupled with their good nature, has ensured their popularity. Some US registries recognize only the sable brown coloration as Burmese; other colors are described as Malayan. North American Burmese have a more stocky build than their British counterparts. This has led to the development of a Foreign Burmese category here.

Country of origin Thailand	Ancestry Nonpedigree Shorthairs	Origins 1400s

CREAM

Young Burmese kittens of all varieties tend to be quite pale in color and may also display slight tabby markings. In the case of adult Cream Burmese, some tabby traces may still be apparent on the face. Other slight markings are permitted, provided they are not on the sides of the body or the underparts; a white patch is considered a serious flaw.

FUR TYPE: short and glossy, with satin feel

• **FEATURES** Adults should be a rich shade of cream. The ears should be slightly darker in coloration than the back.

• **REMARK** An unplanned mating in 1964 between a Red Tabby and a Blue Burmese began the breeding program that led to the development of these cats. They finally achieved recognition in Great Britain in 1970.

• *outer line of ear continues that of face*

• *large, wide-set eyes with rounded aperture*

• *strong, rounded chest*

• *slender legs*

well-spaced, golden yellow eyes •

muscular body •

straight tail tapering to tip •

hind legs slightly longer than front legs •

pink pads •

Longhair option Cream Tiffany	Temperament Playful

Country of origin Thailand	Ancestry Nonpedigree Shorthairs	Origins 1400s

RED

The Red has yet to achieve widespread recognition in North America, even in the Malayan category, but in Great Britain its development has forged ahead.
• **FEATURES** The coat color should be a light tangerine shade with traces of tabby face markings accepted.
• **REMARK** These elegant cats, of foreign type, should display neither the extreme svelte type of the Siamese, nor the cobby shape of the British Shorthair.

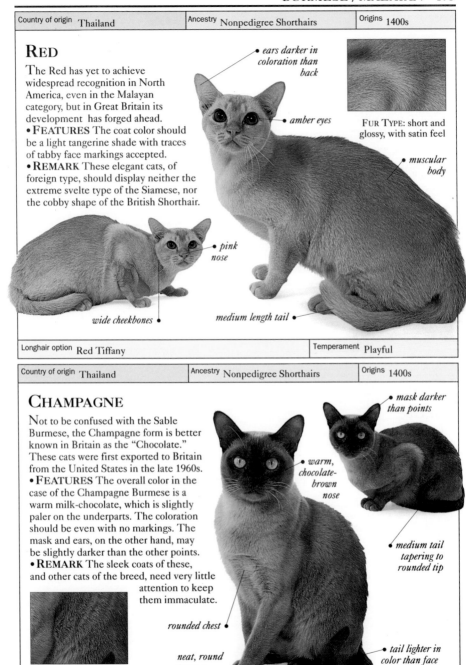

ears darker in coloration than back

amber eyes

FUR TYPE: short and glossy, with satin feel

muscular body

pink nose

wide cheekbones

medium length tail

Longhair option Red Tiffany	Temperament Playful

Country of origin Thailand	Ancestry Nonpedigree Shorthairs	Origins 1400s

CHAMPAGNE

Not to be confused with the Sable Burmese, the Champagne form is better known in Britain as the "Chocolate." These cats were first exported to Britain from the United States in the late 1960s.
• **FEATURES** The overall color in the case of the Champagne Burmese is a warm milk-chocolate, which is slightly paler on the underparts. The coloration should be even with no markings. The mask and ears, on the other hand, may be slightly darker than the other points.
• **REMARK** The sleek coats of these, and other cats of the breed, need very little attention to keep them immaculate.

mask darker than points

warm, chocolate-brown nose

medium tail tapering to rounded tip

rounded chest

neat, round paws

tail lighter in color than face

FUR TYPE: short and glossy, with satin feel

Longhair option Chocolate Tiffany	Temperament Playful

Country of origin	Thailand	Ancestry	Nonpedigree Shorthairs	Origins	1400s

PLATINUM

Champagne and Sable Burmese were imported from the United States to Britain in 1969, laying the foundations for the development of this form.
• **FEATURES** Pale as kittens, these cats gradually change color to a delicate shade of dove-gray. The pads change from shell-pink to lavender-pink. The ears and mask may show deeper coloration than the rest of the body.
• **REMARK** These cats are known in Great Britain as Lilac Burmese.

round-tipped ears tilt slightly forward

• muscular, yet elegant neck

• pink pads

FUR TYPE: short and glossy, with satin feel

hind legs slightly longer than front legs •

Longhair option	Lilac Tiffany	Temperament	Playful

Country of origin	Thailand	Ancestry	Nonpedigree Shorthairs	Origins	1400s

BLUE

The appearance of this color in a litter of Burmese in 1955 aroused considerable interest, the kitten herself being appropriately named *Sealcoat Blue Surprise*.
• **FEATURES** The blue coloration in Burmese is actually a soft shade of silvery gray, sometimes spoken of as being "antique silver." The silvery sheen should be most pronounced on the feet, face, and ears. A slightly darker shade is permitted on the back and tail.
• **REMARK** Recognized in Britain in 1970, Blues were slower to gain a following in the United States.

• glossy coat indicates good health

• silvery sheen on feet

• high, wide cheekbones taper to form short, blunt wedge

FUR TYPE: short and glossy, with satin feel

dark gray nose •

Longhair option	Blue Tiffany	Temperament	Playful

| Country of origin | Thailand | Ancestry | Nonpedigree Shorthairs | Origins | 1400s |

SABLE BURMESE

Although cats with a similar appearance to the Burmese have been known in Thailand for centuries, the development of the line in the West began with the mating of *Wong Mau*, a brown cat brought from Burma (Myanmar) to the United States in 1930, with a Siamese male.

- **FEATURES** Mature cats should be a rich, warm shade of seal-brown, and just slightly paler on the underparts.
- **REMARK** This is the original form of the Burmese, known in Great Britain as the Brown.

mask and ears slightly darker than body

even depth of coloration

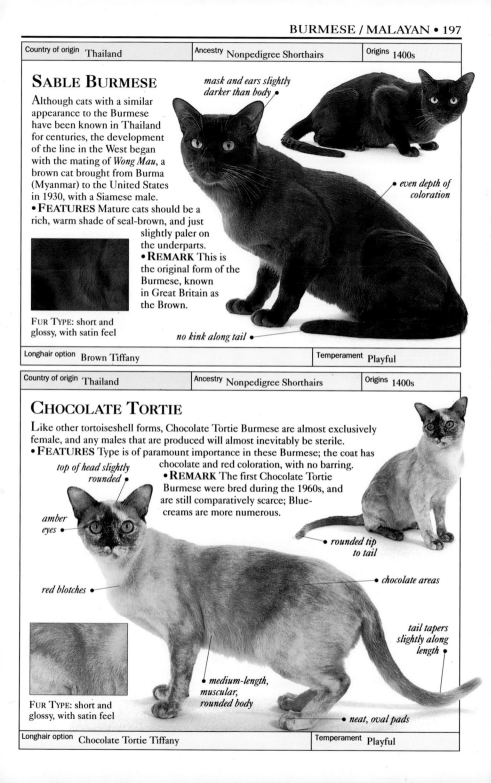

FUR TYPE: short and glossy, with satin feel

no kink along tail

| Longhair option | Brown Tiffany | Temperament | Playful |

| Country of origin | Thailand | Ancestry | Nonpedigree Shorthairs | Origins | 1400s |

CHOCOLATE TORTIE

Like other tortoiseshell forms, Chocolate Tortie Burmese are almost exclusively female, and any males that are produced will almost inevitably be sterile.

- **FEATURES** Type is of paramount importance in these Burmese; the coat has chocolate and red coloration, with no barring.
- **REMARK** The first Chocolate Tortie Burmese were bred during the 1960s, and are still comparatively scarce; Blue-creams are more numerous.

top of head slightly rounded

amber eyes

red blotches

rounded tip to tail

chocolate areas

tail tapers slightly along length

FUR TYPE: short and glossy, with satin feel

medium-length, muscular, rounded body

neat, oval pads

| Longhair option | Chocolate Tortie Tiffany | Temperament | Playful |

Country of origin Thailand	Ancestry Nonpedigree Shorthairs	Origins 1400s

LAVENDER-CREAM

In this case, as with other Malayan, the underparts are a lighter shade than the coloration on the back. Although odd white hairs in the cat's coat may be overlooked by judges, any real evidence of white patches is deemed a serious fault. The coat itself is naturally glossy and helps emphasize the elegant outline of the Malayan.

• **FEATURES** The coloration of the Lavender-cream should be a combination of lilac and cream, which gives rise to its description in the UK of Lilac-cream. There should be no trace of barring on the coat, but considerable variation is permitted in terms of the coloration itself. As with other tortoiseshell forms, the variance in shades may make the coat appear to consist of several distinct colors.

• **REMARK** Less emphasis is placed on coloration in the Tortie Malayan than on the type.

• head slightly rounded on top

• well-spaced eyes, with upper lid slanting toward nose; lower lid rounded

FUR TYPE: short and glossy, with satin feel

• medium-length, muscular body

straight tail with no kink •

• attractive intermingling of colors

round ear tips •

• nose break clearly visible in profile

medium-length tail •

• relatively long neck

• wide cheekbones, narrowing to short wedge

sleek coat •

• strong, rounded chest

• slender legs

tail tapers along length to rounded tip •

hind legs longer than front •

• neat, oval paws

Longhair option Lilac-cream Tiffany	Temperament Playful

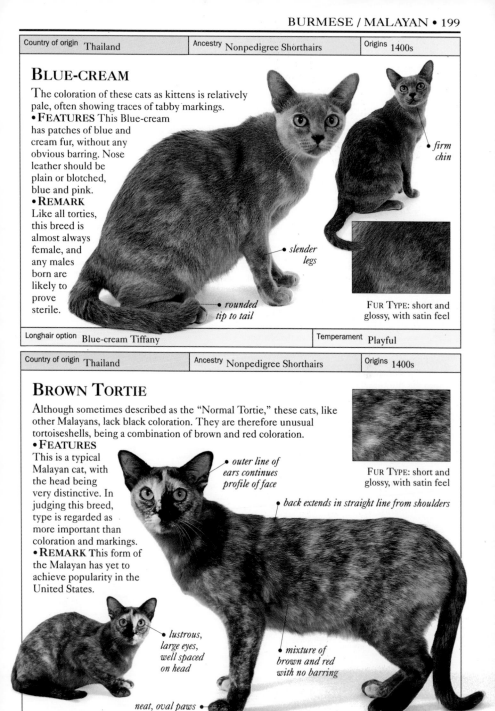

| Country of origin | Thailand | Ancestry | Nonpedigree Shorthairs | Origins | 1400s |

BLUE-CREAM

The coloration of these cats as kittens is relatively pale, often showing traces of tabby markings.

• **FEATURES** This Blue-cream has patches of blue and cream fur, without any obvious barring. Nose leather should be plain or blotched, blue and pink.

• **REMARK** Like all torties, this breed is almost always female, and any males born are likely to prove sterile.

firm chin

slender legs

rounded tip to tail

FUR TYPE: short and glossy, with satin feel

| Longhair option | Blue-cream Tiffany | Temperament | Playful |

| Country of origin | Thailand | Ancestry | Nonpedigree Shorthairs | Origins | 1400s |

BROWN TORTIE

Although sometimes described as the "Normal Tortie," these cats, like other Malayans, lack black coloration. They are therefore unusual tortoiseshells, being a combination of brown and red coloration.

• **FEATURES** This is a typical Malayan cat, with the head being very distinctive. In judging this breed, type is regarded as more important than coloration and markings.

• **REMARK** This form of the Malayan has yet to achieve popularity in the United States.

outer line of ears continues profile of face

FUR TYPE: short and glossy, with satin feel

back extends in straight line from shoulders

lustrous, large eyes, well spaced on head

mixture of brown and red with no barring

neat, oval paws

| Longhair option | Brown Tortie Tiffany | Temperament | Playful |

TONKINESE

T HERE IS EVIDENCE to suggest that the first Tonkinese seen in the West was actually accepted as the founder of the Burmese line. There is certainly a close relationship between Tonkinese and Burmese, the Tonkinese being accepted as a Burmese x Siamese hybrid. In the 1960s, during the early development of the Tonkinese, they became known as Golden Siamese because they had the distinctive golden bronze-sepia coloration of the Burmese, offset against the point patterning of the Siamese. The Tonkinese was first recognized in Canada and then later accepted in the United States in 1972.

Country of origin Burma (Myanmar)	Ancestry Burmese x Siamese	Origins 1930s

HONEY MINK

The breeding of these cats now revolves around Tonkinese bloodlines, and a percentage of both Burmese and Siamese kittens can be anticipated in each litter. The Tonkinese is now accepted by all registering bodies in the United States.

• **FEATURES** There is considerable variation in the acceptance of colors. In Great Britain, for instance, the Cat Association has now chosen to accept Tonkinese in the range of colors that already exist within the Burmese breed.

• **REMARK** The points are slightly darker than the body.

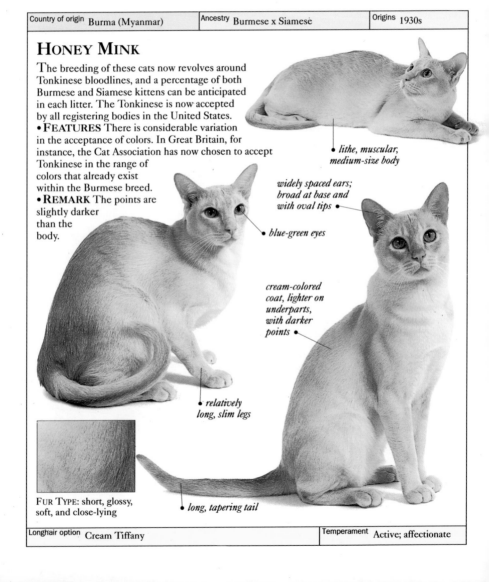

lithe, muscular, medium-size body

widely spaced ears; broad at base and with oval tips

blue-green eyes

cream-colored coat, lighter on underparts, with darker points

relatively long, slim legs

long, tapering tail

FUR TYPE: short, glossy, soft, and close-lying

Longhair option Cream Tiffany	Temperament Active; affectionate

Country of origin Burma (Myanmar)	Ancestry Burmese x Siamese	Origins 1930s

PLATINUM MINK

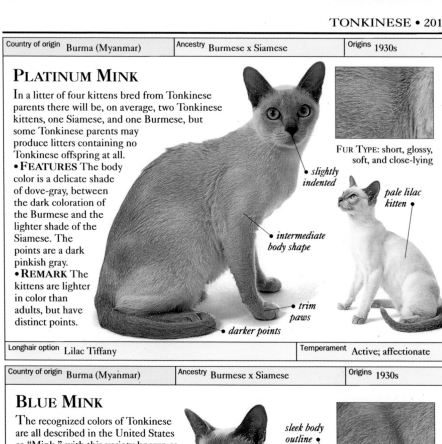

In a litter of four kittens bred from Tonkinese parents there will be, on average, two Tonkinese kittens, one Siamese, and one Burmese, but some Tonkinese parents may produce litters containing no Tonkinese offspring at all.

• **FEATURES** The body color is a delicate shade of dove-gray, between the dark coloration of the Burmese and the lighter shade of the Siamese. The points are a dark pinkish gray.

• **REMARK** The kittens are lighter in color than adults, but have distinct points.

slightly indented

intermediate body shape

FUR TYPE: short, glossy, soft, and close-lying

pale lilac kitten

trim paws

darker points

Longhair option Lilac Tiffany	Temperament Active; affectionate

Country of origin Burma (Myanmar)	Ancestry Burmese x Siamese	Origins 1930s

BLUE MINK

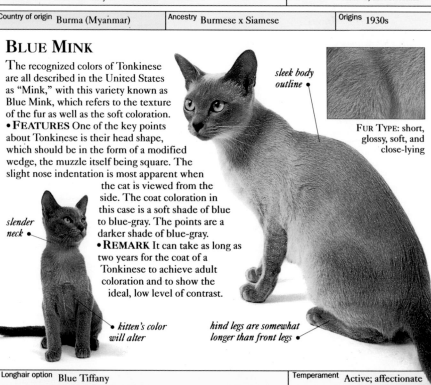

The recognized colors of Tonkinese are all described in the United States as "Mink," with this variety known as Blue Mink, which refers to the texture of the fur as well as the soft coloration.

• **FEATURES** One of the key points about Tonkinese is their head shape, which should be in the form of a modified wedge, the muzzle itself being square. The slight nose indentation is most apparent when the cat is viewed from the side. The coat coloration in this case is a soft shade of blue to blue-gray. The points are a darker shade of blue-gray.

• **REMARK** It can take as long as two years for the coat of a Tonkinese to achieve adult coloration and to show the ideal, low level of contrast.

sleek body outline

FUR TYPE: short, glossy, soft, and close-lying

slender neck

kitten's color will alter

hind legs are somewhat longer than front legs

Longhair option Blue Tiffany	Temperament Active; affectionate

| Country of origin Burma (Myanmar) | Ancestry Burmese x Siamese | Origins 1930s |

NATURAL MINK

Better known in Great Britain as the Brown, these and other Tonkinese make good pets. Their tendency to wander can be dangerous in urban locations.
• **FEATURES** The warm brown body color in this case is offset against the dark chocolate points.
• **REMARK** The body shape of these cats is intermediate between the svelte outline of the Siamese and the stronger-set Burmese.

FUR TYPE: short, glossy, soft, and close-lying

almond-shaped eyes

dark chocolate-colored tail

body coloration typically darkens in older cats

| Longhair option Brown Tiffany | Temperament Active; affectionate |

| Country of origin Burma (Myanmar) | Ancestry Burmese x Siamese | Origins 1930s |

CHAMPAGNE MINK

Grooming these cats is straightforward, and stroking the fur will help impart a good gloss. Polishing with a silk cloth is ideal just before a show.
• **FEATURES** The body coloration of the Champagne is basically a milk-chocolate shade, offset against chocolate points. Coloration on the head may be darker than on other points.
• **REMARK** The coloration is unaffected by variations in temperature.

oval-tipped ears

FUR TYPE: short, glossy, soft, and close-lying

no kinks in tail

chocolate kitten

medium-size, well-muscled body

rounded oval paws

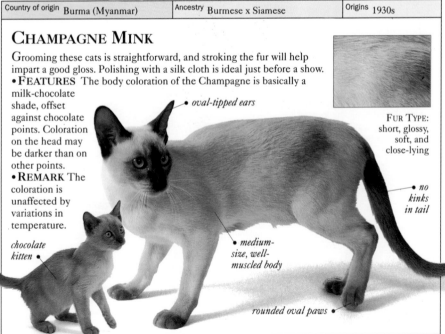

| Longhair option Chocolate Tiffany | Temperament Active; affectionate |

Country of origin Burma (Myanmar)	Ancestry Burmese x Siamese	Origins 1930s

LAVENDER TORTIE

One of the most distinctive features of the Tonkinese is their eye coloration, which should ideally be of a blue-green shade, referred to as aquamarine.

• **FEATURES** In these cats, the lilac points are broken by cream markings, which vary considerably in size and extent. There should be no sign of a facial blaze.

• **REMARK** Depth of color, clarity, and brilliance are important factors in assessing the eye coloration in these cats.

straight tail

oval tips to ears

eyes rounded at lower edge, slanting toward outer corner of ear

FUR TYPE: short, glossy, soft, and close-lying

Longhair option Lavender Tortie Tiffany	Temperament Active; affectionate

Country of origin Burma (Myanmar)	Ancestry Burmese x Siamese	Origins 1930s

BROWN TORTIE

Although Tonkinese may appear light, they are much heavier than their Siamese relatives. There must be a clear distinction between the points and the body coloration. Kittens do not reach their true adult coloration until they are about one year old.

• **FEATURES** The coloration on the body should be an even shade of warm brown; the points are slightly darker, broken by cream patches.

• **REMARK** Barring is most likely in the case of young cats, and should disappear within one year. Kittens also lack the tracings that link the mask and ears in adults.

elegant, well-muscled body

high cheekbones

tight abdomen

oval, dainty feet

fairly long tail, tapering toward tip

FUR TYPE: short, glossy, soft, and close-lying

Longhair option Brown Tortie Tiffany	Active; affectionate

BURMILLA

THIS FAIRLY RECENT introduction to the cat scene is best known in Great Britain, where its development began during the 1980s. It is an agouti breed, and is bred in both silver and golden forms, with tipping or shading on the coat. Careful inbreeding has emphasized the short, dense, soft coat.

Country of origin Great Britain	Ancestry Burmese x Chinchilla Persian	Origins 1981

CHOCOLATE TIPPED

The kittens produced from the unplanned mating of a Silver Chinchilla Persian with a Lilac Burmese formed the original stock for the Burmilla. Their owner, Baroness Miranda von Kirchberg, developed a breeding program with the aim of producing cats with the type of the Burmese and the tipping of the Silver Chinchilla. Burmillas first appeared at a Cat Association show in 1983.
• **FEATURES** The tipping in this case is chocolate, with a silver undercoat. The deepest coloration should be along the back, continuing down the tail, and becoming paler on the flanks.
• **REMARK** Some light spotting on the belly of these cats is permitted.

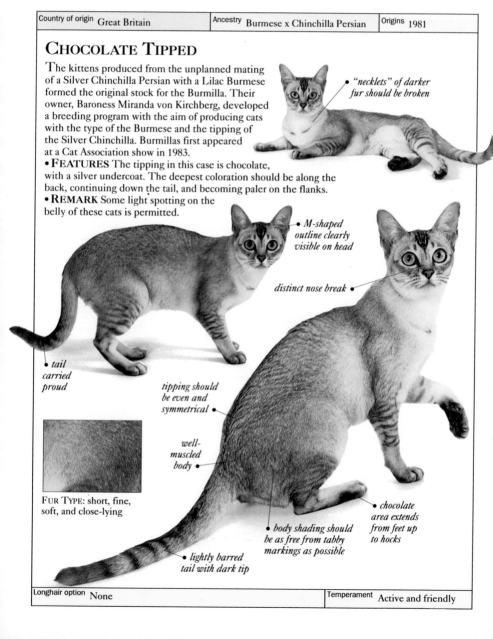

"necklets" of darker fur should be broken

M-shaped outline clearly visible on head

distinct nose break

tail carried proud

tipping should be even and symmetrical

well-muscled body

FUR TYPE: short, fine, soft, and close-lying

chocolate area extends from feet up to hocks

body shading should be as free from tabby markings as possible

lightly barred tail with dark tip

Longhair option None	Temperament Active and friendly

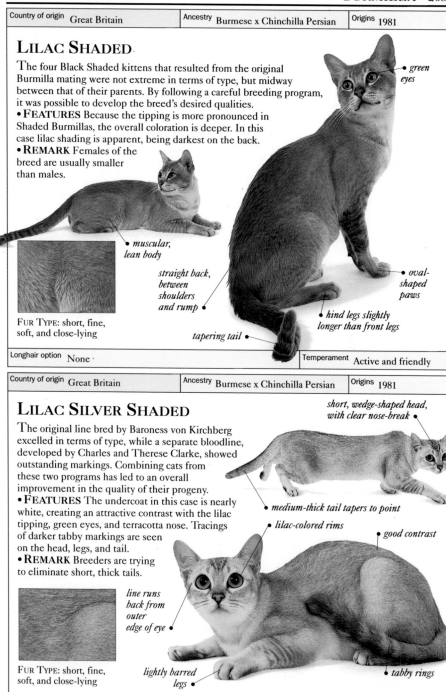

Country of origin Great Britain	Ancestry Burmese x Chinchilla Persian	Origins 1981

LILAC SHADED

The four Black Shaded kittens that resulted from the original Burmilla mating were not extreme in terms of type, but midway between that of their parents. By following a careful breeding program, it was possible to develop the breed's desired qualities.
• **FEATURES** Because the tipping is more pronounced in Shaded Burmillas, the overall coloration is deeper. In this case lilac shading is apparent, being darkest on the back.
• **REMARK** Females of the breed are usually smaller than males.

green eyes

• *muscular, lean body*

straight back, between shoulders and rump •

• *oval-shaped paws*

• *hind legs slightly longer than front legs*

FUR TYPE: short, fine, soft, and close-lying

tapering tail •

Longhair option None	Temperament Active and friendly

Country of origin Great Britain	Ancestry Burmese x Chinchilla Persian	Origins 1981

LILAC SILVER SHADED

The original line bred by Baroness von Kirchberg excelled in terms of type, while a separate bloodline, developed by Charles and Therese Clarke, showed outstanding markings. Combining cats from these two programs has led to an overall improvement in the quality of their progeny.
• **FEATURES** The undercoat in this case is nearly white, creating an attractive contrast with the lilac tipping, green eyes, and terracotta nose. Tracings of darker tabby markings are seen on the head, legs, and tail.
• **REMARK** Breeders are trying to eliminate short, thick tails.

short, wedge-shaped head, with clear nose-break •

• *medium-thick tail tapers to point*

• *lilac-colored rims*

• *good contrast*

line runs back from outer edge of eye •

FUR TYPE: short, fine, soft, and close-lying

lightly barred legs •

• *tabby rings*

Longhair option None	Temperament Active and friendly

| Country of origin | Great Britain | Ancestry | Burmese x Chinchilla Persian | Origins | 1981 |

LIGHT CHOCOLATE TIPPED

The depth of tipping (or shading) is not a consistent feature throughout the cat's life, the coloration tending to darken as the cat matures.
• **FEATURES** The shape of the eyes is an important characteristic; they must be of intermediate shape between round and almond. They are set rather like those of an Oriental, with a slight slope towards the nose. The tipping in this case corresponds to the rich chocolate coloration of the Burmese.
• **REMARK** Burmilla kittens are relatively light in coloration at birth.

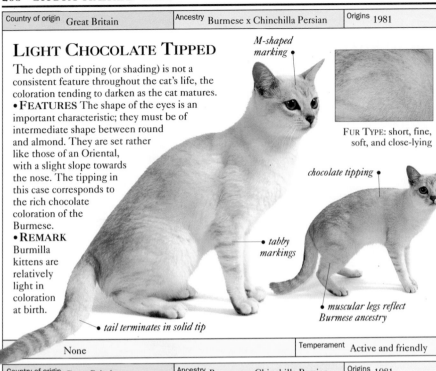

M-shaped marking

FUR TYPE: short, fine, soft, and close-lying

chocolate tipping

tabby markings

muscular legs reflect Burmese ancestry

tail terminates in solid tip

| | None | Temperament | Active and friendly |

| Country of origin | Great Britain | Ancestry | Burmese x Chinchilla Persian | Origins | 1981 |

BROWN TIPPED

One of the most important features of the Asian group, including the Burmilla, is temperament, and this is reflected in the breed standards used for judging purposes – a relatively new departure for the cat fancy.
• **FEATURES** Brown tipping, offset against the silver undercoat, typifies these cats. The depth of tipping is not especially significant, provided that it is even. Very pale tipping is considered undesirable, as it results in a virtually white appearance.
• **REMARK** The Burmilla was granted recognition in Great Britain in November 1983, and in the United States in 1990.

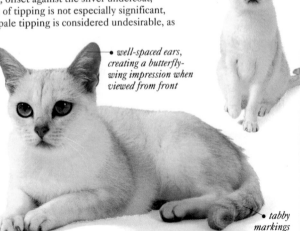

green eyes

well-spaced ears, creating a butterfly-wing impression when viewed from front

tabby markings

FUR TYPE: short, fine, soft, and close-lying

| Longhair option | None | Temperament | Active and friendly |

ASIAN

T HE DESCRIPTION "Asian" is used to describe cats of traditional Burmese type that differ in terms of coloration, patterning, or coat length. However the name itself is used only for the Asian Smokes and Tabbies, which have been developed in Classic, Mackerel, Spotted, and Ticked forms; in contrast the Asian group, as drawn up by the GCCF in Britain, includes a much wider range of breeds, including the Burmilla, Bombay, and Tiffany, which are all of similar type to these other Asians. The Singapura may be added to the group once these cats are more widely established.

Country of origin Great Britain	Ancestry Burmese x Chinchilla Persian	Origins 1981

BROWN MACKEREL TABBY

There is tremendous potential for breeders within the Asian tabby group, for such cats can be bred in all four tabby patterns, and a wide range of colours; even a variety of tortie combinations are possible.

• **FEATURES** The Asian Mackerel Tabby has more discrete markings than the Classic form. Like the latter it shows a line running down the back to the tip of the tail, but in this case, narrow vertical lines also extend down the sides of the body, with no blotches on the flanks. Asian Ticked Tabbies show a great reduction in the number of markings on their coat, their fur being mainly ticked, while the Spotted form can similarly be distinguished quite easily.

• **REMARK** Good contrast between the black tabby markings and the lighter ground color is important in this Asian Mackerel Tabby.

ears tilt slightly forward

well-spaced eyes

distinct nose break

M-shaped marking on head

oval paws

medium-length body

elegant, medium-thick tail

tail carried proud

neat, tight paws

hind legs longer than front legs

FUR TYPE: short, fine, soft, and close-lying

Longhair option Brown Mackerel Tabby Tiffany	Temperament Active and friendly

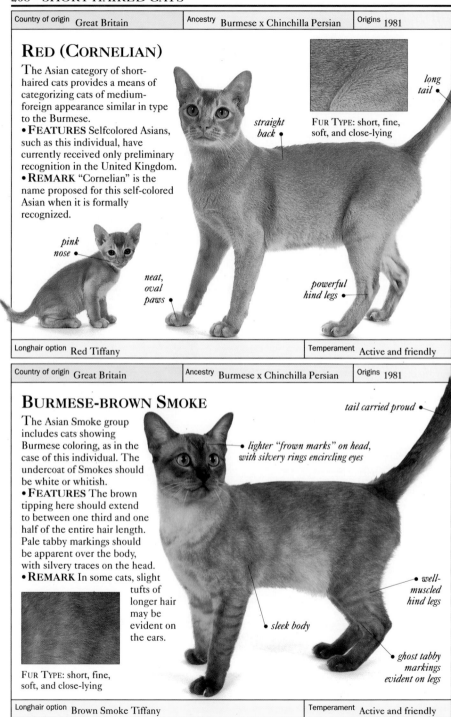

| Country of origin | Great Britain | Ancestry | Burmese x Chinchilla Persian | Origins | 1981 |

RED (CORNELIAN)

The Asian category of short-haired cats provides a means of categorizing cats of medium-foreign appearance similar in type to the Burmese.

• **FEATURES** Selfcolored Asians, such as this individual, have currently received only preliminary recognition in the United Kingdom.

• **REMARK** "Cornelian" is the name proposed for this self-colored Asian when it is formally recognized.

long tail

straight back

FUR TYPE: short, fine, soft, and close-lying

pink nose

neat, oval paws

powerful hind legs

| Longhair option | Red Tiffany | Temperament | Active and friendly |

| Country of origin | Great Britain | Ancestry | Burmese x Chinchilla Persian | Origins | 1981 |

BURMESE-BROWN SMOKE

The Asian Smoke group includes cats showing Burmese coloring, as in the case of this individual. The undercoat of Smokes should be white or whitish.

• **FEATURES** The brown tipping here should extend to between one third and one half of the entire hair length. Pale tabby markings should be apparent over the body, with silvery traces on the head.

• **REMARK** In some cats, slight tufts of longer hair may be evident on the ears.

tail carried proud

lighter "frown marks" on head, with silvery rings encircling eyes

well-muscled hind legs

sleek body

ghost tabby markings evident on legs

FUR TYPE: short, fine, soft, and close-lying

| Longhair option | Brown Smoke Tiffany | Temperament | Active and friendly |

Country of origin	Great Britain	Ancestry	Burmese x Chinchilla Persian	Origins	1981

CHOCOLATE SMOKE

These Asian breeds tend to be slightly quieter by nature than their Burmese relatives, but their voices can still be quite loud; this is especially true when a female in oestrus is calling for a mate.

• **FEATURES** The contrast in this case between the chocolate outer coat and the whitish ground color can be seen when the fur is parted. Very slight tabby markings are apparent on the coat. The relatively large, widely spaced eyes add to the appealing appearance of these friendly cats.

• **REMARK** Paler areas in the coat are acceptable but actual white areas are viewed as a fault.

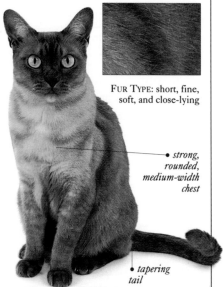

FUR TYPE: short, fine, soft, and close-lying

• *strong, rounded, medium-width chest*

contrast of Smoke patterning becomes more evident as cat walks

• *tapering tail*

Longhair option	Chocolate Smoke Tiffany	Temperament	Active and friendly

Country of origin	Great Britain	Ancestry	Burmese x Chinchilla Persian	Origins	1981

BLACK SMOKE

Contrast between the different colors in the coat is most pronounced in this Smoke variety. As in other Asians, the coloration of the nose, pads, and eye-rims matches the color of the outer coat.

• **FEATURES** The Smoke effect, created by the contrast between the whitish ground color and the jet-black hair, is clearly discernible. The pale tabby markings should give the shimmering effect of watered silk over the body.

• **REMARK** The silvery markings around the eyes of Asians are known as "clown marks," because of their resemblance to the makeup of circus clowns.

• *gently rounded skull between large ears*

• *medium-thick tapering tail*

• *lighter undercoat less apparent along back than on underparts*

FUR TYPE: short, fine, soft, and close-lying

oval-shaped paws •

Longhair option	Black Smoke Tiffany	Temperament	Active and friendly

BOMBAY

T HIS HIGHLY DISTINCTIVE breed was created in 1958 by Nikki Horner of Kentucky. The intention was to produce a cat that resembled a miniature black panther. The breed is of intermediate type, but a noticeable difference is now emerging between the original cats, developed in the United States, and those being bred in Britain, resulting from the difference in type of their Burmese ancestors. First recognized in the United States in 1976, the Bombay has yet to receive universal recognition. The GCCF include it in the Asian group because of its similarity in type to the Burmese.

Country of origin USA	Ancestry Burmese x American Shorthair	Origins 1950s

BLACK

The Bombay is a cat that craves human attention, as well as being tolerant of children and dogs. It is therefore ideal as a family pet.

• **FEATURES** The short, "patent-leather" coat is a distinctive feature of the breed, and is offset by the brightly colored eyes. Kittens may prove quite slow to develop, with tabby markings often present in their coat. Their eyes are blue at first, like those of all kittens. They then turn gray, and finally turn a gold or deep copper color.

• **REMARK** The Bombay was developed from the combination of a Sable Burmese and a Black American Shorthair. Today, while the breed retains the coloration of the American Shorthair, it also closely resembles the Burmese in type.

FUR TYPE: short and sleek; discernible sheen

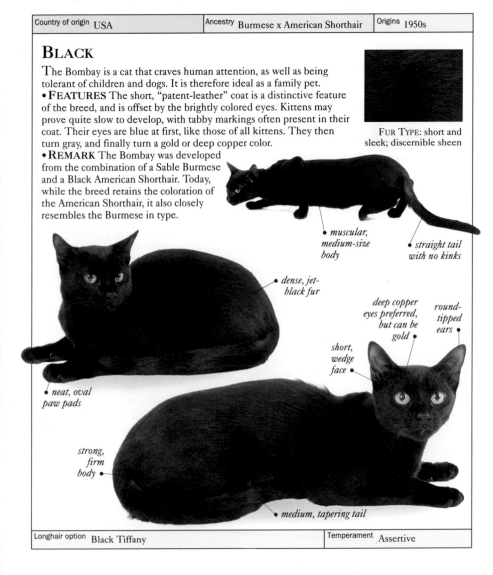

muscular, medium-size body

straight tail with no kinks

dense, jet-black fur

deep copper eyes preferred, but can be gold

round-tipped ears

short, wedge face

neat, oval paw pads

strong, firm body

medium, tapering tail

Longhair option Black Tiffany	Temperament Assertive

SINGAPURA

T HE NAME "SINGAPURA" originates from the Malaysian name for Singapore, where development of this breed began during the mid-1970s. The ancestors of these cats, living feral lives in southeastern Asia, and known as the "Drain Cats of Singapore," show an Abyssinian-type coat pattern.

Country of origin	Singapore	Ancestry	Nonpedigree Ticked Shorthairs	Origins	1965

SEPIA AGOUTI

Tommy Meadow took five of the local Singapore cats back to the United States in 1975. These five cats, plus another individual taken out of the Singapore SPCA in 1980, provided the foundation for the breed.
• FEATURES The Singapura is a small breed, and may weigh less than 6 lb (2.7 kg). Traditionally sable-brown in color with warm brown, wavy ticking over much of the body and the muzzle, the chin and chest are usually lighter.
• REMARK The Singapura was first exhibited in the United States during 1975, and the breed was awarded championship status there soon afterward.

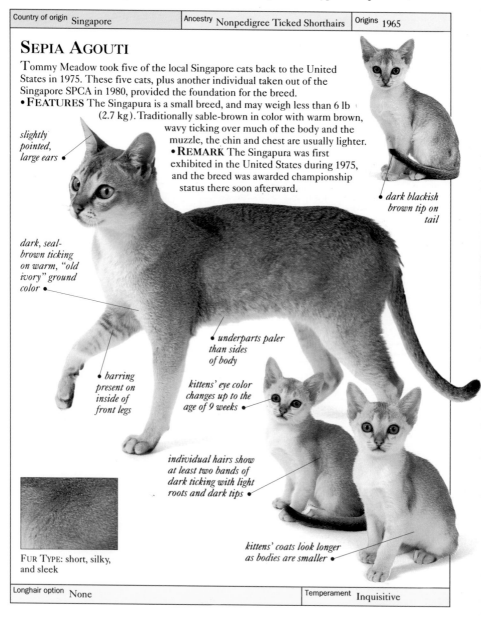

slightly pointed, large ears

dark blackish brown tip on tail

dark, seal-brown ticking on warm, "old ivory" ground color

underparts paler than sides of body

barring present on inside of front legs

kittens' eye color changes up to the age of 9 weeks

individual hairs show at least two bands of dark ticking with light roots and dark tips

FUR TYPE: short, silky, and sleek

kittens' coats look longer as bodies are smaller

Longhair option	None	Temperament	Inquisitive

ORIENTAL SHORTHAIR

SOME OF THE FIRST Siamese cats seen in the West had a solid body color and no Siamese markings. These cats gradually died out, however, as only typical Siamese with blue eyes were recognized for exhibiting at that time. Successful attempts to recreate the type began in the 1950s. The category includes both self colors and marked varieties such as the tabbies; they can be bred in any color and with any markings except in a pointed form.

Country of origin Great Britain	Ancestry Siamese crosses	Origins 1950s

WHITE

Following the successful development of the Havana (*p.216*), the quest for this color began in Britain by crossing Siamese with short-haired whites. This led to white cats with either orange or blue eyes, and the breed was then developed by mating those with blue eyes back to Siamese. Although two of the three original lines had problems with deafness, this has now been eliminated.

• **FEATURES** In type, these cats are now indistinguishable from their Siamese ancestors in all but fur coloration.

• **REMARK** This breed was accepted for show purposes in Britain under the name of Foreign White, but it has become better known internationally as the Oriental White.

blue eyes •

FUR TYPE: short, fine, and glossy

• *long, slender legs terminate in small, oval paws*

very long, thin, tapering tail •

• *pure white coat emphasizes svelte shape*

• *pink nose with no trace of darker markings*

• *pink pads on feet*

Longhair option White Oriental Longhair	Temperament Lively

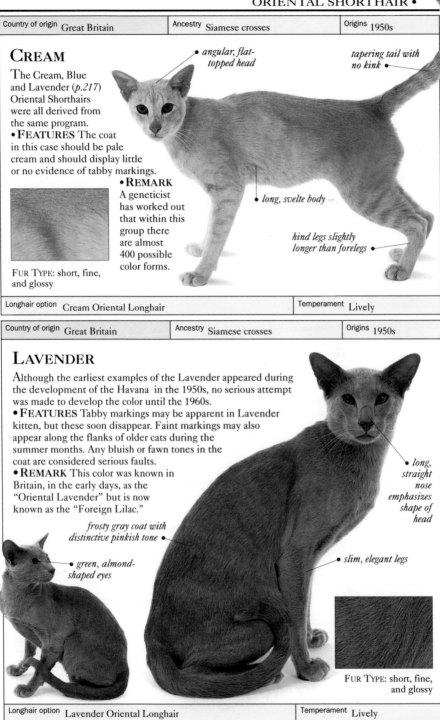

Country of origin	Great Britain	Ancestry	Siamese crosses	Origins	1950s

CREAM

The Cream, Blue and Lavender (*p.217*) Oriental Shorthairs were all derived from the same program.
• **FEATURES** The coat in this case should be pale cream and should display little or no evidence of tabby markings.

angular, flat-topped head

tapering tail with no kink

• **REMARK** A geneticist has worked out that within this group there are almost 400 possible color forms.

long, svelte body

hind legs slightly longer than forelegs

FUR TYPE: short, fine, and glossy

Longhair option	Cream Oriental Longhair	Temperament	Lively

Country of origin	Great Britain	Ancestry	Siamese crosses	Origins	1950s

LAVENDER

Although the earliest examples of the Lavender appeared during the development of the Havana in the 1950s, no serious attempt was made to develop the color until the 1960s.
• **FEATURES** Tabby markings may be apparent in Lavender kitten, but these soon disappear. Faint markings may also appear along the flanks of older cats during the summer months. Any bluish or fawn tones in the coat are considered serious faults.
• **REMARK** This color was known in Britain, in the early days, as the "Oriental Lavender" but is now known as the "Foreign Lilac."

long, straight nose emphasizes shape of head

frosty gray coat with distinctive pinkish tone

green, almond-shaped eyes

slim, elegant legs

FUR TYPE: short, fine, and glossy

Longhair option	Lavender Oriental Longhair	Temperament	Lively

Country of origin Great Britain	Ancestry Siamese crosses	Origins 1950s

RED

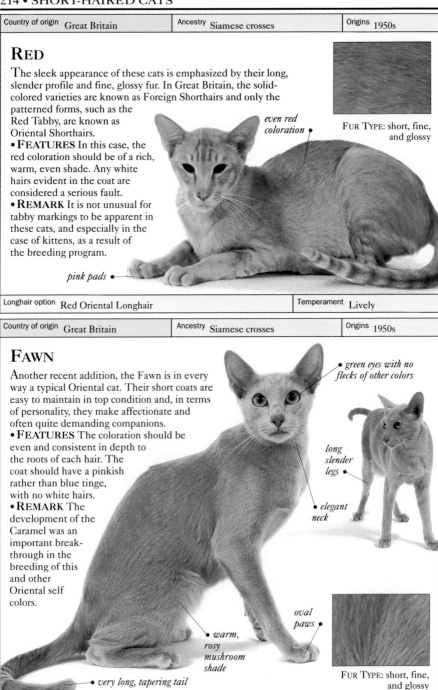

The sleek appearance of these cats is emphasized by their long, slender profile and fine, glossy fur. In Great Britain, the solid-colored varieties are known as Foreign Shorthairs and only the patterned forms, such as the Red Tabby, are known as Oriental Shorthairs.

even red coloration

FUR TYPE: short, fine, and glossy

• **FEATURES** In this case, the red coloration should be of a rich, warm, even shade. Any white hairs evident in the coat are considered a serious fault.
• **REMARK** It is not unusual for tabby markings to be apparent in these cats, and especially in the case of kittens, as a result of the breeding program.

pink pads

Longhair option Red Oriental Longhair	Temperament Lively

Country of origin Great Britain	Ancestry Siamese crosses	Origins 1950s

FAWN

Another recent addition, the Fawn is in every way a typical Oriental cat. Their short coats are easy to maintain in top condition and, in terms of personality, they make affectionate and often quite demanding companions.

green eyes with no flecks of other colors

• **FEATURES** The coloration should be even and consistent in depth to the roots of each hair. The coat should have a pinkish rather than blue tinge, with no white hairs.
• **REMARK** The development of the Caramel was an important break-through in the breeding of this and other Oriental self colors.

long slender legs

elegant neck

warm, rosy mushroom shade

oval paws

very long, tapering tail

FUR TYPE: short, fine, and glossy

Longhair option Fawn Oriental Longhair	Temperament Lively

Country of origin Great Britain	Ancestry Siamese crosses	Origins 1950s

RED AND WHITE

There is tremendous scope within the Oriental group, with the possibility of superimposing virtually any color or pattern onto cats of Oriental type.

• **FEATURES** In this breed, poise and balance are significant with all parts of the body in proportion. The head should take the form of a well-balanced triangle.

• **REMARK** This kitten is going to be used in the development of a new British breed, the Seychellois.

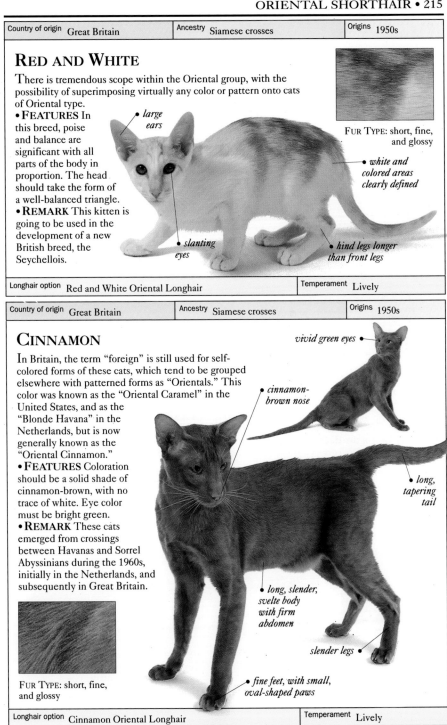

large ears

FUR TYPE: short, fine, and glossy

white and colored areas clearly defined

slanting eyes

hind legs longer than front legs

Longhair option Red and White Oriental Longhair	Temperament Lively

Country of origin Great Britain	Ancestry Siamese crosses	Origins 1950s

CINNAMON

In Britain, the term "foreign" is still used for self-colored forms of these cats, which tend to be grouped elsewhere with patterned forms as "Orientals." This color was known as the "Oriental Caramel" in the United States, and as the "Blonde Havana" in the Netherlands, but is now generally known as the "Oriental Cinnamon."

• **FEATURES** Coloration should be a solid shade of cinnamon-brown, with no trace of white. Eye color must be bright green.

• **REMARK** These cats emerged from crossings between Havanas and Sorrel Abyssinians during the 1960s, initially in the Netherlands, and subsequently in Great Britain.

vivid green eyes

cinnamon-brown nose

long, tapering tail

long, slender, svelte body with firm abdomen

slender legs

fine feet, with small, oval-shaped paws

FUR TYPE: short, fine, and glossy

Longhair option Cinnamon Oriental Longhair	Temperament Lively

Country of origin Great Britain	Ancestry Siamese crosses	Origins 1950s

CARAMEL

These cats emerged during the development of Oriental Shaded cats and have contributed in turn to newer self colors such as the Apricot.
• FEATURES With a typical Siamese profile, these cats are entirely bluish fawn in color; the coloration extends to nose, pads and eye rims.
• REMARK This variety originated from the mating of a Silver Chinchilla Persian and a Siamese.

angular head

medium-size body

pure green eyes

FUR TYPE: short, fine, and glossy

small oval paws

Longhair option Caramel Oriental Longhair	Temperament Lively

Country of origin Great Britain	Ancestry Siamese crosses	Origins 1950s

HAVANA BROWN

In Great Britain, this breed was known as the Chestnut Brown Foreign Shorthair until 1970, when it was renamed the Havana.
• FEATURES The individual shown here is a British Havana; it is more similar to the Oriental Self Brown being bred in North America than to the American form of the Havana Brown. The latter is of discernible Siamese type, with a head longer than it is wide, and narrowing to a rounded muzzle.
• REMARK The development of the Havana in Britain began with the mating of a Chocolate Point Siamese and a black nonpedigree cat.

vivid green eyes

rich, warm, chestnut-brown coloration

distinctive muzzle

FUR TYPE: short, fine, and glossy

long, slim legs

slender, medium-length tail

Longhair option Brown Oriental Longhair	Temperament Lively

| Country of origin Great Britain | Ancestry Siamese crosses | Origins 1950s |

BLUE

These and other Orientals tend to be somewhat quieter than their Siamese ancestors, yet they can be just as affectionate and demanding.
• **FEATURES** Pure blue coloration without any traces of white is required. The eyes must be entirely green with no flecking.
• **REMARK** Blue cats of foreign type cropped up occasionally in litters of Siamese but did not attract great attention until the development of the Havana Brown and Lavender.

FUR TYPE: short, fine, and glossy

eyes slant toward nose

color consistent to base of hairs

| Longhair option Blue Oriental Longhair | Temperament Lively |

| Country of origin Great Britain | Ancestry Siamese crosses | Origins 1950s |

EBONY

Also known as the "Black," this is the oldest of the Oriental forms now being bred. It came to prominence in the 1980s.
• **FEATURES** The coloration in this case must be pure black with no hint of a rusty hue in adults.
• **REMARK** The first Ebony Orientals were bred from Siamese mated to Russian Blues during the development of the Havana. Their sleek, glossy coats give them a very striking appearance.

wedge-shaped head

long nose with no stop

large, pricked ears

shiny, jet-black coat

long, slender legs

fur lies close to body, emphasizing sleek shape

very long, tapering tail

FUR TYPE: short, fine, and glossy

| Black Oriental Longhair | Temperament Lively |

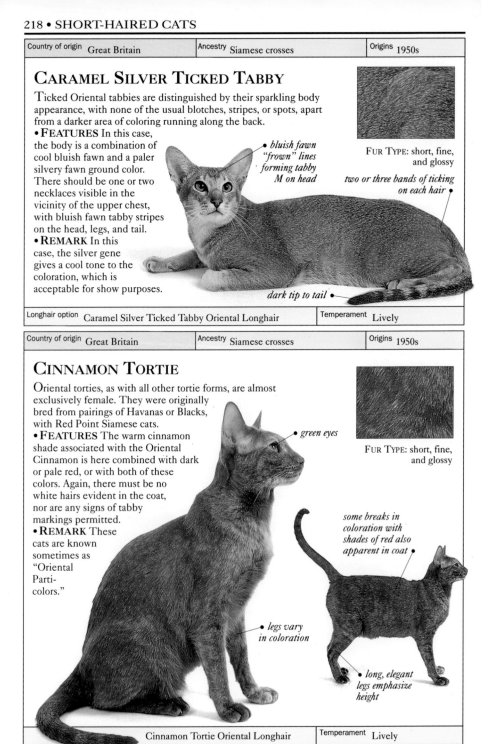

| Country of origin | Great Britain | Ancestry | Siamese crosses | Origins | 1950s |

CARAMEL SILVER TICKED TABBY

Ticked Oriental tabbies are distinguished by their sparkling body appearance, with none of the usual blotches, stripes, or spots, apart from a darker area of coloring running along the back.

• **FEATURES** In this case, the body is a combination of cool bluish fawn and a paler silvery fawn ground color. There should be one or two necklaces visible in the vicinity of the upper chest, with bluish fawn tabby stripes on the head, legs, and tail.

• **REMARK** In this case, the silver gene gives a cool tone to the coloration, which is acceptable for show purposes.

bluish fawn "frown" lines forming tabby M on head

FUR TYPE: short, fine, and glossy

two or three bands of ticking on each hair

dark tip to tail

| Longhair option | Caramel Silver Ticked Tabby Oriental Longhair | Temperament | Lively |

| Country of origin | Great Britain | Ancestry | Siamese crosses | Origins | 1950s |

CINNAMON TORTIE

Oriental torties, as with all other tortie forms, are almost exclusively female. They were originally bred from pairings of Havanas or Blacks, with Red Point Siamese cats.

• **FEATURES** The warm cinnamon shade associated with the Oriental Cinnamon is here combined with dark or pale red, or with both of these colors. Again, there must be no white hairs evident in the coat, nor are any signs of tabby markings permitted.

• **REMARK** These cats are known sometimes as "Oriental Parti-colors."

green eyes

FUR TYPE: short, fine, and glossy

some breaks in coloration with shades of red also apparent in coat

legs vary in coloration

long, elegant legs emphasize height

| | Cinnamon Tortie Oriental Longhair | Temperament | Lively |

Country of origin	Great Britain	Ancestry	Siamese crosses.	Origins	1950s

CHESTNUT TORTIE

The pattern of markings in these cats is entirely random but it is nevertheless important that the colored areas on the head, body, and extremities show the characteristic tortie markings.
• **FEATURES** The basic appearance of these cats is a warm shade of chestnut-brown, offset by either dark or pale red patterning, or a combination of both colors. A red facial blaze, although not considered essential, is preferred.
• **REMARK**
Green eyes are characteristic of all Oriental torties.

chocolate and red coloration •

• *slender neck*

fine muzzle •

• *broken coloration*

• *underparts as mottled as mantle*

FUR TYPE: short, fine, and glossy

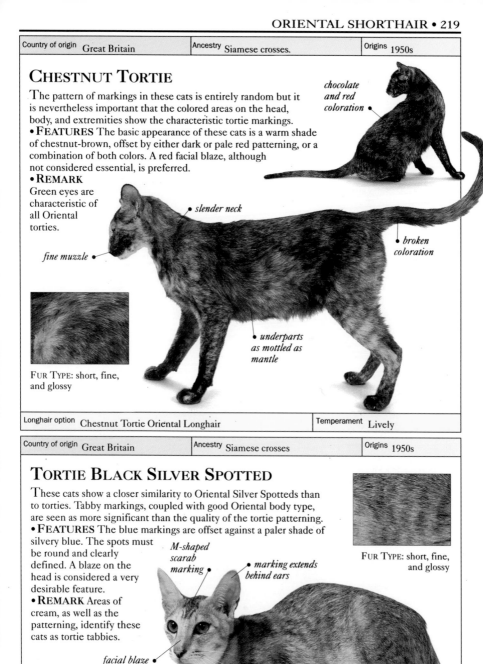

Longhair option	Chestnut Tortie Oriental Longhair	Temperament	Lively

Country of origin	Great Britain	Ancestry	Siamese crosses	Origins	1950s

TORTIE BLACK SILVER SPOTTED

These cats show a closer similarity to Oriental Silver Spotteds than to torties. Tabby markings, coupled with good Oriental body type, are seen as more significant than the quality of the tortie patterning.
• **FEATURES** The blue markings are offset against a paler shade of silvery blue. The spots must be round and clearly defined. A blaze on the head is considered a very desirable feature.
• **REMARK** Areas of cream, as well as the patterning, identify these cats as tortie tabbies.

M-shaped scarab marking •

• *marking extends behind ears*

FUR TYPE: short, fine, and glossy

facial blaze •

bars apparent on legs •

Longhair option	Tortie Black Silver Spotted Oriental Longhair	Temperament	Lively

Country of origin Great Britain	Ancestry Siamese crosses	Origins 1950s

CHESTNUT SPOTTED

Once known in Britain as "Egyptian Maus," the name was changed to avoid confusion with a different breed known by that name in the United States.
• **FEATURES** The spotting is the result of rich shades of chocolate-brown, with lighter tones being preferred. The spotted markings should stand out clearly against the bronze agouti ground color. The spots must be rounded and evenly spaced.
• **REMARK** While kittens may have a solid spinal line, in adult cats this is seen as a serious fault.

ears emphasize wedge-shaped head

FUR TYPE: short, fine, and glossy

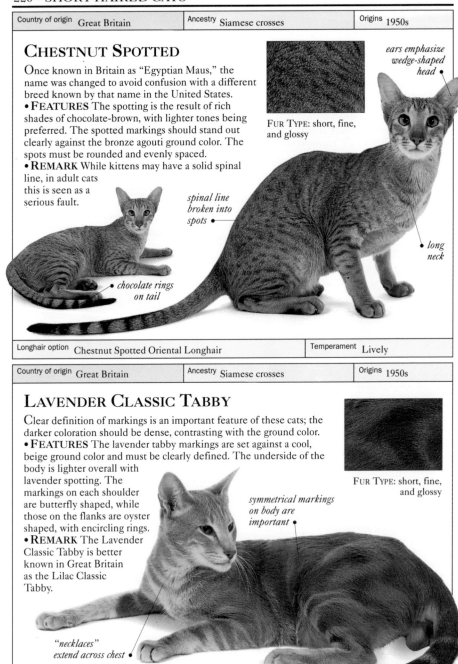

spinal line broken into spots

long neck

chocolate rings on tail

Longhair option Chestnut Spotted Oriental Longhair	Temperament Lively

Country of origin Great Britain	Ancestry Siamese crosses	Origins 1950s

LAVENDER CLASSIC TABBY

Clear definition of markings is an important feature of these cats; the darker coloration should be dense, contrasting with the ground color.
• **FEATURES** The lavender tabby markings are set against a cool, beige ground color and must be clearly defined. The underside of the body is lighter overall with lavender spotting. The markings on each shoulder are butterfly shaped, while those on the flanks are oyster shaped, with encircling rings.
• **REMARK** The Lavender Classic Tabby is better known in Great Britain as the Lilac Classic Tabby.

FUR TYPE: short, fine, and glossy

symmetrical markings on body are important

"necklaces" extend across chest

lilac tip to tail

Longhair option Lavender Classic Tabby Oriental Longhair	Temperament Lively

Country of origin Great Britain	Ancestry Siamese crosses	Origins 1950s

BLACK SMOKE

These cats result from matings between Siamese and Chinchilla Persians with the use of Blacks and Havanas to establish type. A Red Point Siamese bred to a Silver Shaded Persian produced the first Oriental Smoke during the 1970s.

• **FEATURES** The black appearance is belied by the white undercoat, which should be approximately one third of the total hair length. An even Smoke effect is desirable, without prominent silver brindling.

• **REMARK** Ghost tabby markings are often apparent on Oriental Smokes, giving a watered silk effect to the cat's appearance.

white undercoat evident as cat moves

green eyes

slim legs

the Smoke effect on body should correspond to that on head

shadowy tabby markings apparent

color of pads matches basic color

FUR TYPE: short, fine, and glossy

long, tapering tail

Longhair option Black Smoke Oriental Longhair	Temperament Lively

Country of origin Great Britain	Ancestry Siamese crosses	Origins 1950s

BLACK SMOKE AND WHITE

Any color is accepted in the Oriental Smoke category, a group that has developed rapidly in recent years. This is one of the first bicolors to be bred.

• **FEATURES** The undercoat is pure white and the topcoat is heavily tipped with black, giving the impression of a black and white bicolor. The distribution of black and white patches varies according to the individual.

• **REMARK** The bicolored Oriental has arisen from the Seychellois breeding program, which is aiming for mainly white bicolors.

large, wide ears continue line of head

FUR TYPE: short, fine, and glossy

clear definition between white and black Smoke areas of fur

restricted white markings

small, oval paws

Longhair option Black Smoke and White Oriental Longhair	Temperament Lively

Country of origin Great Britain	Ancestry Siamese crosses	Origins 1950s

RED TICKED TABBY

The Ticked Tabbies can be distinguished by the lack of patterning in their coats, compared with the other three tabby variants established in Orientals.
• **FEATURES** There should be two, and ideally three, bands of darker red coloration on the individual hairs. Contrast here is based on the warm, rich red banding on a lighter, bright apricot ground color.
• **REMARK** There should be no solid spinal line down the back, but tabby stripes should be apparent on the face, legs, and tail.

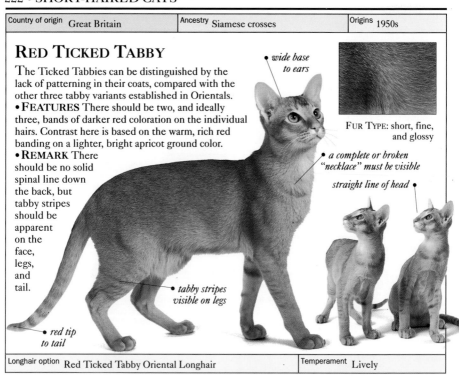

• *wide base to ears*

FUR TYPE: short, fine, and glossy

• *a complete or broken "necklace" must be visible*

straight line of head •

• *tabby stripes visible on legs*

• *red tip to tail*

Longhair option Red Ticked Tabby Oriental Longhair	Temperament Lively

Country of origin Great Britain	Ancestry Siamese crosses	Origins 1950s

LAVENDER TICKED TABBY

Contrast is a key feature of the Ticked Tabbies, but any sign of traditional tabby patterning on the body is penalized. Darker shading may, however, be apparent on the back.
• **FEATURES** In this case, the lavender ticking is displayed against a cool beige color. The nose, pads, and eye rims are of a faded lavender shade, although some pinkish coloration may be seen on the nose and pads. The eyes should be green, with no flecks of any other color apparent.
• **REMARK** There may well be evidence of tabby markings on the underside of the body.

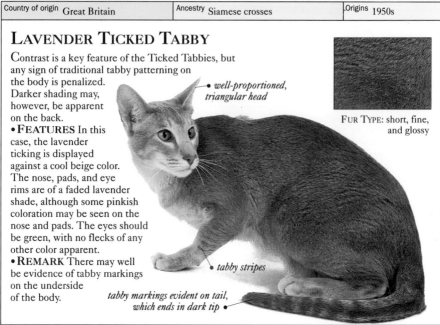

• *well-proportioned, triangular head*

FUR TYPE: short, fine, and glossy

• *tabby stripes*

tabby markings evident on tail, which ends in dark tip •

Longhair option Lavender Ticked Tabby Oriental Longhair	Temperament Lively

Country of origin Great Britain	Ancestry Siamese crosses	Origins 1950s

CARAMEL TICKED TABBY

The sparkling effect of the coat results from the ticking on individual hairs, which should have two or three bands of color along their length.
• **FEATURES** The cool, bluish fawn markings contrast with a beige agouti ground color. There should be no blotches, stripes, or spots, but traces of tabby markings are permitted on the undersides. The darker caramel color must extend up the hind legs and should be present at the tip of the tail.
• **REMARK** Although the fur is darker along the back, any trace of a solid line here is a flaw.

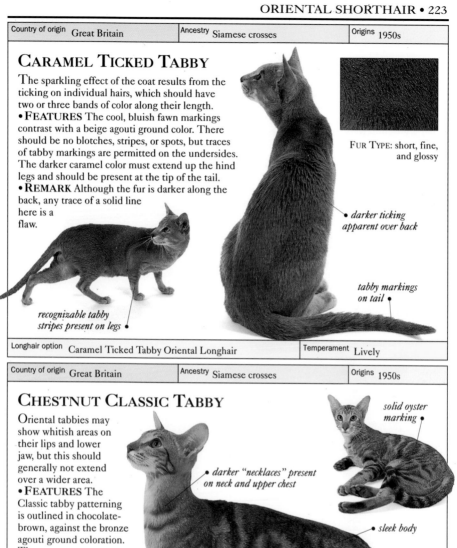

FUR TYPE: short, fine, and glossy

darker ticking apparent over back

tabby markings on tail

recognizable tabby stripes present on legs

Longhair option Caramel Ticked Tabby Oriental Longhair	Temperament Lively

Country of origin Great Britain	Ancestry Siamese crosses	Origins 1950s

CHESTNUT CLASSIC TABBY

Oriental tabbies may show whitish areas on their lips and lower jaw, but this should generally not extend over a wider area.
• **FEATURES** The Classic tabby patterning is outlined in chocolate-brown, against the bronze agouti ground coloration. The eyes are green.
• **REMARK** The eye rims are chocolate-brown, offset by the green eye color.

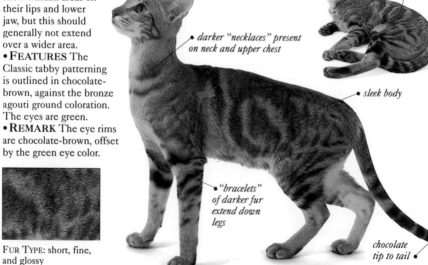

solid oyster marking

darker "necklaces" present on neck and upper chest

sleek body

"bracelets" of darker fur extend down legs

chocolate tip to tail

FUR TYPE: short, fine, and glossy

Longhair option Chestnut Classic Tabby Oriental Longhair	Temperament Lively

Country of origin Great Britain	Ancestry Siamese crosses	Origins 1950s

CHESTNUT TICKED TABBY

The origin of today's Oriental tabbies can be traced back to the breeding of tabby-pointed Siamese, at a time when Siamese were mated with nonpedigree tabbies. Later refinement of the breed occurred with the pairing of Havanas and tabby-pointed Siamese.
• **FEATURES** The chocolate ticking contrasts with the bronze agouti ground color on the body, creating a sparkling effect. The tipping at the end of the hairs is darkest. In this example, typical tabby markings are confined to the head, legs, and tail.
• **REMARK** This, as well as other Chestnut Oriental varieties, is better known in Great Britain as "Chocolate." Eye coloration in this group of cats, as in the majority of Oriental tabbies, should be pure green, with no flecks of other colors visible.

green eyes characterize this and many other Oriental tabbies

svelte body

long tail

clear signs of tabby markings must be apparent on head

small paws

darker shading on back

long, wedge-shaped head with straight nose

at least one "necklace" around neck

chocolate markings extend up back of both hind legs

even ticking

FUR TYPE: short, fine, and glossy

Longhair option Chestnut Ticked Tabby Oriental Longhair	Temperament Lively

Country of origin Great Britain	Ancestry Siamese crosses	Origins 1950s

BLACK SILVER SPOTTED

This is one of the most striking of the Oriental Spotted group, with a vivid contrast between coat and markings.
• **FEATURES** While the head markings resemble those of the Classic tabby, the body markings consist of a series of spots of varying size that should be well distributed over the coat, and not overlapping or forming blotches.
• **REMARK** Two rows of spots should be apparent on the underside, with spotted patterning in place of a solid line along the back.

typical M-shaped tabby marking on head •

long, svelte body shape •

FUR TYPE: short, fine, and glossy

spots or bars permitted on legs •

Longhair option Black Silver Spotted Oriental Longhair	Temperament Lively

Country of origin Great Britain	Ancestry Siamese crosses	Origins 1950s

CHESTNUT SILVER CLASSIC TABBY

The contrast between the ground color and the markings is most apparent in the darker forms, such as the Chocolate.
• **FEATURES** In this color form, the chocolate markings are offset against a paler silvery chocolate ground color. The wedge-shaped, triangular face of Oriental cats is distinctive.
• **REMARK** The intelligent and playful nature of these cats, plus the wide range of colors and patterns in which they are now being bred, have ensured their popularity.

Oriental-shaped eyes, slanting toward nose •

silvery white coloration may extend to throat in Silver Tabbies

long, slender neck •

slim legs with small, oval paws •

good contrast between markings and ground color

long, tapering tail showing tabby markings •

FUR TYPE: short, fine, and glossy

sleek appearance, with healthy gloss on coat •

Longhair option Chestnut Silver Tabby Oriental Longhair	Temperament Lively

EGYPTIAN MAU

THIS GROUP of spotted cats has been developed in the United States from European stock. They show a striking similarity to the cats of ancient Egypt, featured on tomb paintings and papyrus scrolls dating back thousands of years. The Egyptian Mau is a relatively scarce breed, even today, but attempts have been made in Europe to create cats that look similar. This bloodline was originally based on tabbies produced during the breeding of the Lynx Point Siamese. Such cats are now described as Oriental Spotted Tabbies, rather than as Egyptian Maus, in order to prevent any confusion.

Country of origin Egypt	Ancestry Nonpedigree Shorthairs	Origins 1950s

SILVER

The development of this breed in North America had its roots in the Mediterranean area. Having fallen in love with cats showing these markings, the Princess Troubetskoy obtained a specimen from Cairo and mated her with an Italian cat, producing two kittens. In 1956, the Princess took her Egyptian Maus to the United States, where the breed was registered and exhibited for the first time the following year.

• **FEATURES** These cats are intermediate between the cobby outline of the American Shorthair and the svelte profile of Oriental breeds. The wedge-shaped head is gently rounded; the muzzle should not be pointed. The angle changes from the cat's forehead down to the nose.

• **REMARK** Females tend to be slightly smaller than males.

- large, pointed ears
- gooseberry-green eyes
- "mascara" line extends from outer corner of eye, joined by second line starting at center of cheek
- tail thick at base, tapering along length
- characteristic M-shaped marking
- black patterning on silver ground color
- dorsal stripe along body, with well-formed spots on flanks
- heavily banded tail, with dark tip
- muscular body

FUR TYPE: dense, fine, silky, and resilient

Longhair option None	Temperament Lively; responsive

Country of origin Egypt	Ancestry Nonpedigree Shorthairs	Origins 1950s

BRONZE

There are only three color forms of the Egyptian Mau, all of which have the usual spotted patterning associated with tabbies. The spots themselves must be clearly defined. The ground color is made up of banded hairs with black tips. At least two bands, if not more, should be apparent on each hair.
• **FEATURES** The spots should be round and evenly distributed over the body. There are also so-called "vest buttons" of spots on the underside. In newly born kittens the spots tend to be less clearly defined.
• **REMARK** While shedding, the spotting becomes less distinct.

arched neck

black barring on bronze ground color

medium-length hair with distinctive ticking

FUR TYPE: dense, fine, silky, and resilient

dainty, oval paws

Longhair option None	Temperament Lively; responsive

Country of origin Egypt	Ancestry Nonpedigree Shorthairs	Origins 1950s

BLACK SMOKE

The contrast in the coloration of these cats takes up to two years to develop fully. There is no ticking apparent; the hairs have whitish roots and black tips, creating a contrast as the cat moves.
• **FEATURES** The eyes are very large, oval in shape, and slanting. The distinctive green coloration can be relatively slow to develop and, in later life, the eyes tend to become paler green.
• **REMARK** Egyptian Maus are quiet cats, compared to Oriental breeds. The black coloration may become bleached a lighter brown if the cat is exposed to bright sunlight.

characteristic green eyes

broad forehead gives width between ears

jet-black spots on dark gray ground color

muscular neck

FUR TYPE: dense, fine, silky, and resilient

very long toes on hind feet

tail equal to body length

Longhair option None	Temperament Lively; responsive

ABYSSINIAN

SIMILAR IN APPEARANCE to the cats of ancient Egypt, the Abyssinian is believed, by some, to be one of the oldest breeds of domestic cat. The first cats of this type were brought to Britain by soldiers returning home from the Abyssinian War in 1868. Attempts to develop the breed in Great Britain, by crossings involving British Shorthairs, modified the appearance and coloration of the Abyssinian. Although slow to breed, not being particularly prolific, the Abyssinian was finally recognized as a breed in its own right in 1882.

Country of origin Great Britain	Ancestry Nonpedigree Ticked Shorthairs	Origins 1860s

LAVENDER

There has been considerable development of the range of available Abyssinian colors in recent years, and the Lavender is now quite common. Abyssinians in general display an intelligent and often demonstrative temperament.
• **FEATURES** Abyssinians have a lithe, muscular body. The head is wedge shaped, with a slight indentation on the nose; the eyes are large and almond shaped. In the case of the Lavender Abyssinian, the body is a warm shade of pale ivory, with darker ticking of the same color. The underparts and insides of the legs are paler in coloration.
• **REMARK** At present the Lavender, and other new Abyssinian colors, has received only limited worldwide recognition.

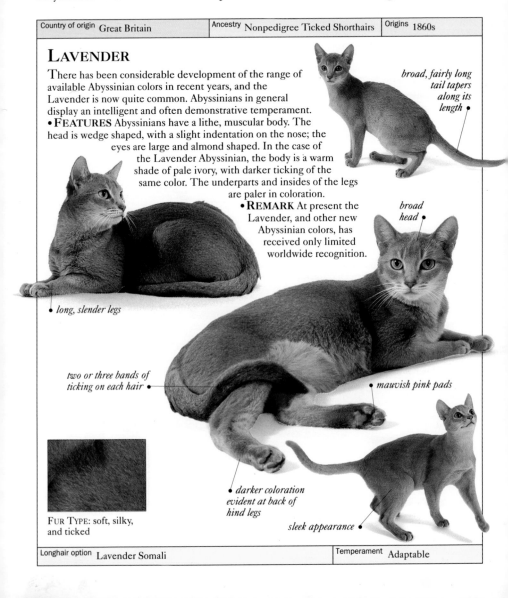

broad, fairly long tail tapers along its length

broad head

long, slender legs

two or three bands of ticking on each hair

mauvish pink pads

darker coloration evident at back of hind legs

sleek appearance

FUR TYPE: soft, silky, and ticked

Longhair option Lavender Somali	Temperament Adaptable

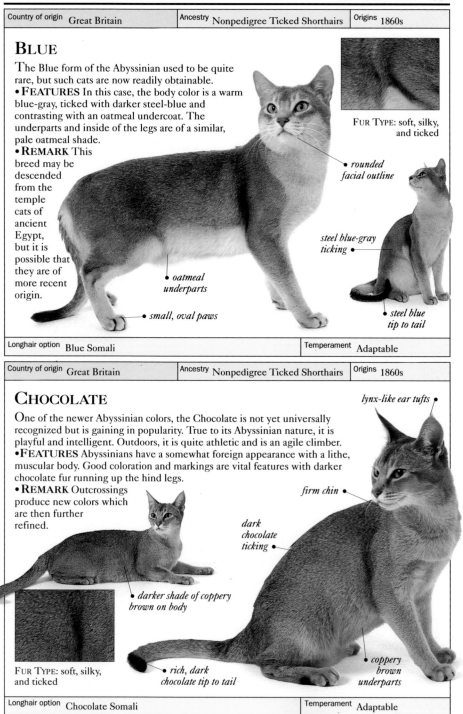

| Country of origin Great Britain | Ancestry Nonpedigree Ticked Shorthairs | Origins 1860s |

BLUE

The Blue form of the Abyssinian used to be quite rare, but such cats are now readily obtainable.
• **FEATURES** In this case, the body color is a warm blue-gray, ticked with darker steel-blue and contrasting with an oatmeal undercoat. The underparts and inside of the legs are of a similar, pale oatmeal shade.
• **REMARK** This breed may be descended from the temple cats of ancient Egypt, but it is possible that they are of more recent origin.

FUR TYPE: soft, silky, and ticked

rounded facial outline

steel blue-gray ticking

oatmeal underparts

small, oval paws

steel blue tip to tail

| Longhair option Blue Somali | Temperament Adaptable |

| Country of origin Great Britain | Ancestry Nonpedigree Ticked Shorthairs | Origins 1860s |

CHOCOLATE

lynx-like ear tufts

One of the newer Abyssinian colors, the Chocolate is not yet universally recognized but is gaining in popularity. True to its Abyssinian nature, it is playful and intelligent. Outdoors, it is quite athletic and is an agile climber.
• **FEATURES** Abyssinians have a somewhat foreign appearance with a lithe, muscular body. Good coloration and markings are vital features with darker chocolate fur running up the hind legs.
• **REMARK** Outcrossings produce new colors which are then further refined.

firm chin

dark chocolate ticking

darker shade of coppery brown on body

FUR TYPE: soft, silky, and ticked

rich, dark chocolate tip to tail

coppery brown underparts

| Longhair option Chocolate Somali | Temperament Adaptable |

Country of origin Great Britain	Ancestry Nonpedigree Ticked Shorthairs	Origins 1860s

BLACK SILVER

Several forms of the Silver Abyssinian are recognized, including Black (shown here), Sorrel, and Blue, but in each case the undercoat must be white.
• **FEATURES** Here, the shading over the spine is black, as are the tip of the tail and the solid coloration on the hind legs. Traces of yellow in the coat are considered undesirable.
• **REMARK** The Silver form has been developed to a high standard in both Britain and New Zealand during recent years.

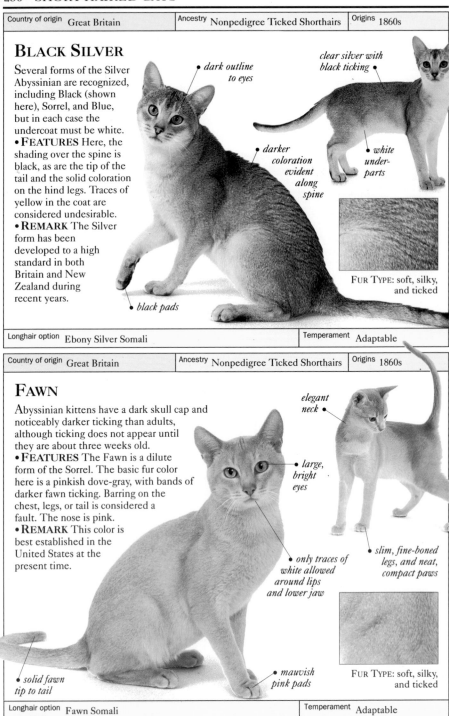

• *dark outline to eyes*

clear silver with black ticking •

• *darker coloration evident along spine*

• *white under-parts*

• *black pads*

FUR TYPE: soft, silky, and ticked

Longhair option Ebony Silver Somali	Temperament Adaptable

Country of origin Great Britain	Ancestry Nonpedigree Ticked Shorthairs	Origins 1860s

FAWN

Abyssinian kittens have a dark skull cap and noticeably darker ticking than adults, although ticking does not appear until they are about three weeks old.
• **FEATURES** The Fawn is a dilute form of the Sorrel. The basic fur color here is a pinkish dove-gray, with bands of darker fawn ticking. Barring on the chest, legs, or tail is considered a fault. The nose is pink.
• **REMARK** This color is best established in the United States at the present time.

elegant neck •

• *large, bright eyes*

• *slim, fine-boned legs, and neat, compact paws*

• *only traces of white allowed around lips and lower jaw*

• *solid fawn tip to tail*

• *mauvish pink pads*

FUR TYPE: soft, silky, and ticked

Longhair option Fawn Somali	Temperament Adaptable

Country of origin Great Britain	Ancestry Nonpedigree Ticked Shorthairs	Origins 1860s

SORREL

Few cats are more elegant in appearance than the Abyssinian, and one advantage is the ease with which they may be groomed. They have never been prolific breeders, and only rarely produce more than three or four kittens per litter.
• **FEATURES** The base hair here is deep apricot with the body coloration slightly darker. The ticking is chocolate.
• **REMARK** The Sorrel was once known as the Red, but now attempts are being made to develop a genuine red.

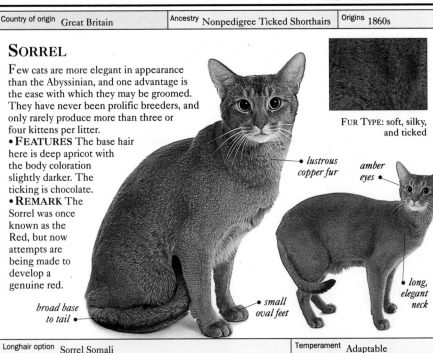

FUR TYPE: soft, silky, and ticked

lustrous copper fur

amber eyes

long, elegant neck

broad base to tail

small oval feet

Longhair option Sorrel Somali	Temperament Adaptable

Country of origin Great Britain	Ancestry Nonpedigree Ticked Shorthairs	Origins 1860s

RUDDY

There is some difference in type between Abyssinians in Europe and those in North America. The latter may have a more rounded and shorter head shape whereas in Europe the breed has developed a foreign appearance. It is hoped, however, that any further lengthening of the face can be prevented by means of the breed standard.
• **FEATURES** In Great Britain this color form is known as the Usual. Its ruddy colored hair is usually most apparent on the tail. Body color is a rich golden brown.
• **REMARK** This breed was recognized in Great Britain in 1882.

large, pricked ears

black tip to tail

medium-length body

FUR TYPE: soft, silky, and ticked

ticking clearly visible

long, slender legs

Longhair option Ruddy Somali	Temperament Adaptable

| Country of origin Great Britain | Ancestry Nonpedigree Ticked Shorthairs | Origins 1860s |

SORREL SILVER

The Abyssinian patterning is equivalent to that of the Ticked Tabby, but selective breeding has led to the disappearance of markings on the legs and tail, as well as of the "necklaces" of darker fur encircling the neck in this case. Any of these traits are now considered serious flaws in the Abyssinian. Another problem that has proved harder to eradicate is the presence of white fur: any white areas, apart from those around the lips and lower jaw, are regarded as faults.

• FEATURES These cats are distinguished by a white undercoat. Their body coloration is silvery peach, with chocolate ticking. Both the pads and the nose should be pink, and there must be a line of dark pigment encircling the eyes. Eye coloration of amber, green, or hazel is acceptable.

• REMARK The only clearly distinctive tabby markings are those present on the heads of these cats.

large, widely spaced ears; broad at base •

• lithe, muscular body with no tendency to cobby shape

tufted ears preferred •

slanting eyes •

• spinal shading may be present

tapering tail •

• two or three bands of ticking on each individual hair

tip of tail matches ticking •

• fine-boned, slim legs terminating in small, oval feet

M-shaped tabby marking clearly apparent, with darker pencil lines also evident •

• broad, tapering, wedge-shaped head with slight nose break

• medium-length body

• compact paws

• darker hair extends up back of hind legs

FUR TYPE: soft, silky, and ticked

| Longhair option Sorrel Silver Somali | Temperament Adaptable |

WILD ABYSSINIAN

DURING RECENT YEARS, cat fanciers have given a great deal of attention to cats with Abyssinian-type coat patterning. Already the Singapura is quite well known, and enthusiasts of the Wild Abyssinian hope that their cats will follow suit. It is thought to be similar in its markings to the early Abyssinians seen in Victorian Britain, but is not a hybrid developed from crossing wild and domestic cats as its name might suggest. A third member of this group, the Ceylonese, is somewhat similar to the Wild Abyssinian and was developed as a result of the endeavors of the Cat Club of Ceylon (now Sri Lanka). The Wild Abyssinian is now being bred in Italy and elsewhere.

Country of origin Singapore	Ancestry Nonpedigree Shorthairs	Origins 1980s

RUDDY

The ancestors of these cats, which had been living wild in Singapore, were taken to the United States where Tord Svenson and other breeders are now developing the breed. In order to maintain their original "wild" appearance, and to minimize the detrimental effects of inbreeding, it has been decided that within the pedigree of each cat there should be at least one imported individual shown within five generations.
• **FEATURES** Larger than the Abyssinian itself, these cats at present exist only in the Ruddy (or Usual) form; their coloration is a rich shade of golden brown, with a ruddy-orange undercoat. Black ticking is visible on the coat and, in contrast to the Abyssinian, barring is visible on the legs; the tail has a series of distinctive black rings.
• **REMARK** Selective breeding of the Abyssinian, which is actually a ticked tabby, has eliminated the normal tabby barring, so that the coat is simply ticked. This is seen as a distinctive characteristic of the Wild Abyssinian.

FUR TYPE: short, fine, dense, and close-lying

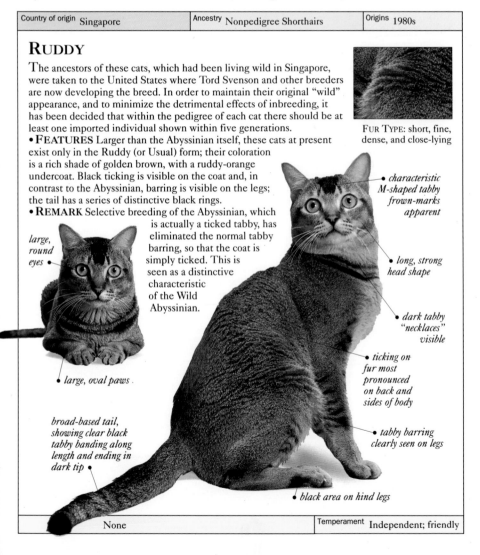

• characteristic M-shaped tabby frown-marks apparent

large, round eyes •

• long, strong head shape

• dark tabby "necklaces" visible

• ticking on fur most pronounced on back and sides of body

• large, oval paws

• tabby barring clearly seen on legs

broad-based tail, showing clear black tabby banding along length and ending in dark tip •

• black area on hind legs

None	Temperament Independent; friendly

OCICAT

T HIS RELATIVELY RECENT addition to the cat world appeared in 1964 after a chance mating between a male Chocolate Point Siamese and a female Abyssinian x Seal Point Siamese. The owner of these cats, Virginia Daly, who was living in Michigan, was attracted to the wild-cat appearance of the resulting kitten, which she called *Dalai Talua*. She repeated the mating and another breeder, Tom Brown, subsequently helped develop the bloodline.

Country of origin USA	Ancestry Siamese x Siamese / Abyssinian	Origins 1964

CHOCOLATE

In the United States, American Shorthairs were used to increase the size and range of colors in these cats. Development in Europe from separate stock began quite recently, the first kitten being born in 1984.
• **FEATURES** These are large cats, with a well-designed pattern of spots. There is no link between coat and eye color; blue eyes are not permitted. An impression of power and strength is an important feature of this breed. Newborn kittens have a cublike appearance.
• **REMARK** The name combines two previous names: "Ocelette" for the similarity to the ocelot, and "Accicat" as the breed arose from an accidental mating.

FUR TYPE: short, soft, and lustrous

• *longish tail*

• *rise from bridge of nose to brow apparent*

• *clear contrast between markings and ground color*

• *clearly defined spots*

• *powerful, muscular legs with sturdy, oval paws*

Longhair option None	Temperament Friendly and alert

| Country of origin USA | Ancestry Siamese x Siamese / Abyssinian | Origins 1964 |

TAWNY

The Ocicat is of intermediate type, neither cobby nor Oriental overall. The entire coat, apart from the tip of the tail, consists of banded hairs, and spotting is evident over the cat's body.
• **FEATURES** Lighter coloration is present around the eyes, chin, and lower jaw as well as underneath the body. The markings on the head, legs, and tail areas are typically darker in color than those on the body.
• **REMARK** During the shedding period, the clarity of the spotted markings is often reduced.

M-shaped tabby marking extends over top of head •

FUR TYPE: short, soft, and lustrous

patterned tail, terminating in black tip •

• *long legs*

| Longhair option None | Temperament Friendly and alert |

| Country of origin USA | Ancestry Siamese x Siamese / Abyssinian | Origins 1964 |

SILVER

A distinctive feature of the Ocicat is that the dark lines around the neck and on the legs should be broken up into spots. The lines that extend along the spine will be replaced by spots as the cat matures.
• **FEATURES** The contrast is provided by a pattern of black spots on a silvery white ground color. The pads should be black; the brick-red nose is edged with black.
• **REMARK** American Shorthairs were used in breeding to introduce the silver gene.

"mascara" lines extend from eyes to cheeks

large, almond-shaped eyes slant toward ears •

• *large ears, preferably tufted*

tail tapers slightly along length •

• *spots on flanks about size and shape of thumbprint*

FUR TYPE: short, soft, and lustrous

• *strong, neat paws*

| Longhair option None | Temperament Friendly and alert |

CALIFORNIA SPANGLED

T HE CALIFORNIA SPANGLED was launched in a blaze of publicity through the 1986 Christmas mail-order catalog of a well-known American store. The breed was the creation of a California scriptwriter, Paul Casey, who assembled a variety of cat breeds from around the world, including a Spotted Manx, Silver Spotted Tabby Persian, Seal Point Siamese, and British and American Shorthairs. He also used street cats from Cairo, and other nonpedigree cats from Asia, to produce a spotted cat with the look of its wild relatives.

Country of origin USA	Ancestry Pedigree and Nonpedigree cats	Origins 1971

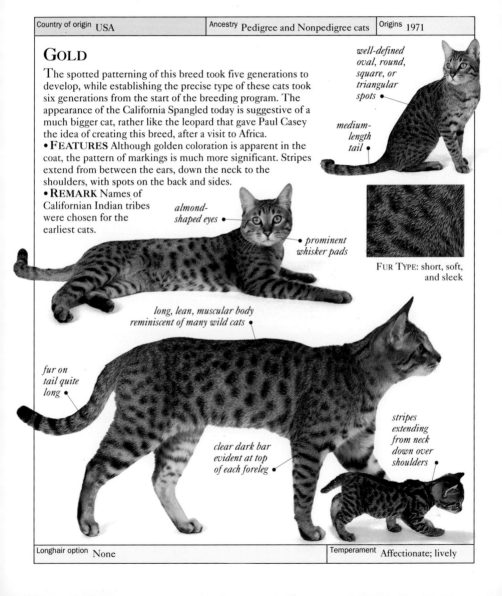

GOLD

The spotted patterning of this breed took five generations to develop, while establishing the precise type of these cats took six generations from the start of the breeding program. The appearance of the California Spangled today is suggestive of a much bigger cat, rather like the leopard that gave Paul Casey the idea of creating this breed, after a visit to Africa.

• FEATURES Although golden coloration is apparent in the coat, the pattern of markings is much more significant. Stripes extend from between the ears, down the neck to the shoulders, with spots on the back and sides.

• REMARK Names of Californian Indian tribes were chosen for the earliest cats.

well-defined oval, round, square, or triangular spots

medium-length tail

almond-shaped eyes

prominent whisker pads

FUR TYPE: short, soft, and sleek

long, lean, muscular body reminiscent of many wild cats

fur on tail quite long

clear dark bar evident at top of each foreleg

stripes extending from neck down over shoulders

Longhair option None	Temperament Affectionate; lively

Country of origin USA	Ancestry Pedigree and Nonpedigree cats	Origins 1971

SILVER

The "natural" appearance of these cats was achieved without any recourse to wild cats and did not entail any inbreeding; it was based on eight separate bloodlines. Such was the interest in the California Spangled that there is still invariably a waiting list for kittens from the relatively few breeders with stock.
• **FEATURES** The black markings are set against a silvery ground color; this contrast is considered an important aspect of the cat's patterning.
• **REMARK** This is one of Paul Casey's own kittens at the age of ten months.

more than two dark rings should be present at end of tail

rounded ears

muscular thighs

prominent cheekbones

longer fur on underparts

markings clearly apparent

large paws

FUR TYPE: short, soft, and sleek

Longhair option None		Temperament Affectionate; lively

Country of origin USA	Ancestry Pedigree and Nonpedigree cats	Origins 1971

BLUE

Since the California Spangled breed was devised to be an environmental symbol for the protection of endangered species of spotted wild cat, it is hardly surprising that considerable emphasis is placed on the quality of its patterning.
• **FEATURES** Only the coloration of these cats differs, as their names indicate. The pattern of markings is identical in all cases, except for the Snow Leopard variety, whose kittens are born white, and who only develop their markings gradually over 18 months.
• **REMARK** Paul Casey's aim has not been to popularize this breed, but to use it as a focus for the link between domestic cat breeds and the endangerment of many of their wild relatives.

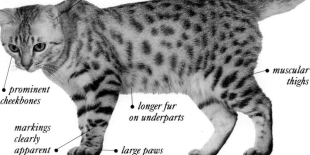

FUR TYPE: short, soft, and sleek

complete dark neckband extends across throat, sometimes scalloping up at center

ears set well back on head, away from face

muscular body

kittens are lively and playful

agile paws

Longhair option None		Temperament Affectionate; lively

Country of origin USA	Ancestry Pedigree and Nonpedigree cats	Origins 1971

CHARCOAL

It is not just the appearance of these cats that is important. They must also be intelligent and fit, and they benefit from climbing frames and other toys that keep them occupied. Sociable by nature, they get on well with other cats, and even dogs, and become devoted to their owners.
• **FEATURES** Good contrast is a feature of the Charcoal.
• **REMARK** The expressive face highlights the breed's individual nature.

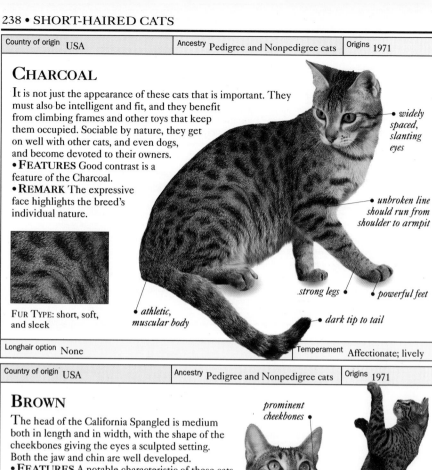

• *widely spaced, slanting eyes*

• *unbroken line should run from shoulder to armpit*

strong legs •   • *powerful feet*

FUR TYPE: short, soft, and sleek

• *athletic, muscular body*

• *dark tip to tail*

Longhair option None		Temperament Affectionate; lively

Country of origin USA	Ancestry Pedigree and Nonpedigree cats	Origins 1971

BROWN

The head of the California Spangled is medium both in length and in width, with the shape of the cheekbones giving the eyes a sculpted setting. Both the jaw and chin are well developed.
• **FEATURES** A notable characteristic of these cats is the way the body remains close to the ground when they walk, in spite of their relatively long legs. This is a result of their angled joints – the forelegs, for example, almost make a right angle to the elbow and, as a result, they are effectively slung backward beneath the body when the cat is walking.
• **REMARK** The hind legs of this breed are developed in a similar way, extending well back beyond the body when the cat is stalking.

prominent cheekbones •

• *spots on back and sides*

• *small white bib marking allowed on throat*

FUR TYPE: short, soft, and sleek

• *patterning continues on tail*

Longhair option None		Temperament Affectionate; lively

BENGAL

CROSSINGS BETWEEN small wild cats and domestic cats have been documented for more than a century, and some of the resulting hybrids were exhibited at cat shows in Victorian times. At least ten species have been used, and such matings became popular again during the 1960s. The Bengal evolved from an American breeding program, begun in 1963, in which a geneticist named Jean Sugden crossed a male domestic cat with a female Asian leopard cat, attempting to transfer the wild cat's markings to a domestic breed.

Country of origin USA	Ancestry Asian leopard cat crosses	Origins 1963

LEOPARD

One kitten, christened *Kinkin*, was produced and fostered alongside a litter of domestic cats. In due course she was mated back to her father and produced both self and spotted kittens. In 1981, Jean Mill (*née* Sugden) and Dr Willard Centerwall, another geneticist, both began work in earnest on the development of the Bengal.
• **FEATURES** The Bengal's spotted patterning is highly distinctive and quite unlike that of a Spotted Tabby. The large spots are arranged horizontally, ideally showing signs of developing into rosettes. Sound temperament is a vital feature of the breed, due to its wild origins.
• **REMARK** Sorrel (light orange with brown spotting) and Mink (black markings on rich mahogany) varieties have also now been produced.

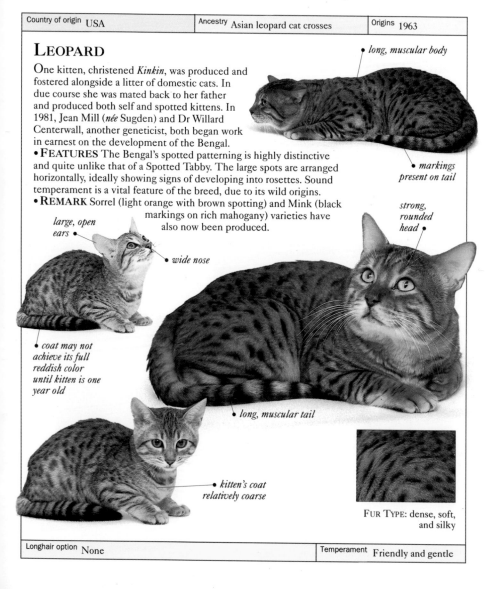

• *long, muscular body*

• *markings present on tail*

strong, rounded head •

large, open ears •

• *wide nose*

• *coat may not achieve its full reddish color until kitten is one year old*

• *long, muscular tail*

• *kitten's coat relatively coarse*

FUR TYPE: dense, soft, and silky

Longhair option None	Temperament Friendly and gentle

NONPEDIGREE

HESE ARE PROBABLY the most common cats in the world; they are often known simply as "moggies." They can be found in the full range of colors and patterns, although the bi-colors tend to predominate and the "foreign" colors, such as chocolate, are quite scarce. These colors can be produced, however, by unplanned matings with a pedigree partner. Although Nonpedigree cats, by definition, are not of recognizable type, they can evolve into a distinctive form through repeated matings of similar cats. These shorthairs tend to be of cobby shape with rather rounded faces.

Country of origin Egypt	Ancestry African wild cat	Origins 1500 BC

BLUE AND WHITE

It is from cats such as these that Victorian breeders began to develop the British Shorthair breed. It was necessary to eliminate the white markings, however, in order to produce the solid-colored cats, such as the Blue, associated with this breed today. The lack of selection in pairings of nonpedigree shorthairs means that white markings are still conspicuous in most of these cases.

• **FEATURES** In nonpedigree cats, white and blue hairs may intermingle. There may also be some signs of darker tabby barring.

• **REMARK** Selective breeding of pedigree cats has concentrated on developing certain specific features present in the non-pedigree population.

FUR TYPE: short, dense, and crisp

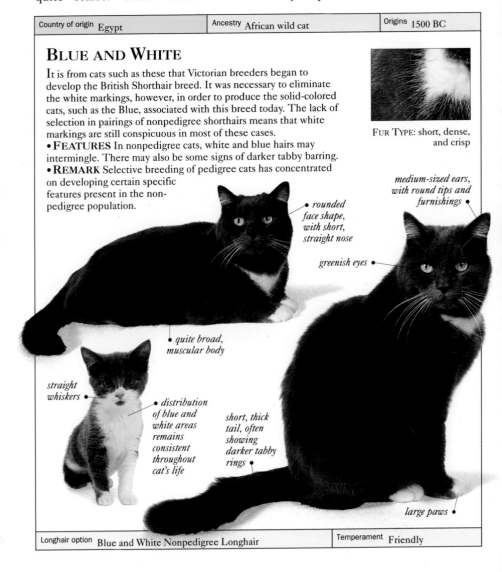

medium-sized ears, with round tips and furnishings •

• rounded face shape, with short, straight nose

greenish eyes •

• quite broad, muscular body

straight whiskers •

• distribution of blue and white areas remains consistent throughout cat's life

short, thick tail, often showing darker tabby rings •

large paws •

Longhair option Blue and White Nonpedigree Longhair	Temperament Friendly

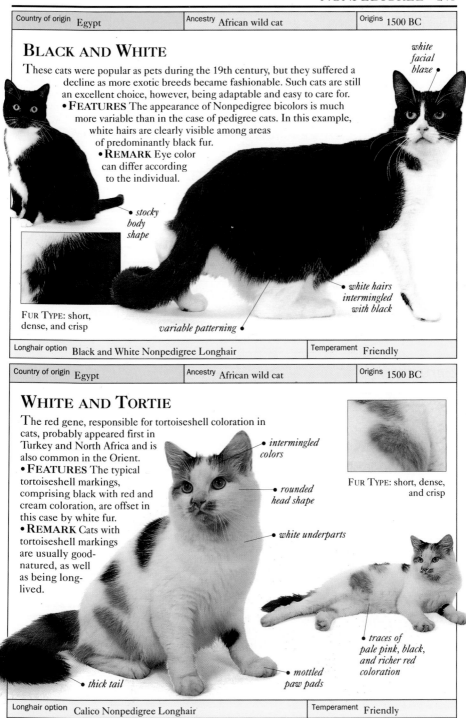

Country of origin Egypt	Ancestry African wild cat	Origins 1500 BC

BLACK AND WHITE

These cats were popular as pets during the 19th century, but they suffered a decline as more exotic breeds became fashionable. Such cats are still an excellent choice, however, being adaptable and easy to care for.
• **FEATURES** The appearance of Nonpedigree bicolors is much more variable than in the case of pedigree cats. In this example, white hairs are clearly visible among areas of predominantly black fur.
• **REMARK** Eye color can differ according to the individual.

white facial blaze

stocky body shape

white hairs intermingled with black

FUR TYPE: short, dense, and crisp

variable patterning

Longhair option Black and White Nonpedigree Longhair	Temperament Friendly

Country of origin Egypt	Ancestry African wild cat	Origins 1500 BC

WHITE AND TORTIE

The red gene, responsible for tortoiseshell coloration in cats, probably appeared first in Turkey and North Africa and is also common in the Orient.
• **FEATURES** The typical tortoiseshell markings, comprising black with red and cream coloration, are offset in this case by white fur.
• **REMARK** Cats with tortoiseshell markings are usually good-natured, as well as being long-lived.

intermingled colors

rounded head shape

white underparts

FUR TYPE: short, dense, and crisp

traces of pale pink, black, and richer red coloration

thick tail

mottled paw pads

Longhair option Calico Nonpedigree Longhair	Temperament Friendly

| Country of origin Egypt | Ancestry African wild cat | Origins 1500 BC |

BLUE-CREAM

Blue-creams typically
result from the mating of
a cream and a blue cat.
They are the dilute form
of the Tortoiseshell.
• **FEATURES** In Britain,
(standards differ in the
United States) a pedigree
Blue-cream should have
well-mixed blue and
cream hairs. In a
Nonpedigree, however,
distinct patches of blue
and cream color are more
likely to be seen.
• **REMARK** Male blue and
cream cats can only be
produced if they have a
rare extra chromosome in
their genetic makeup.

legs usually quite short •

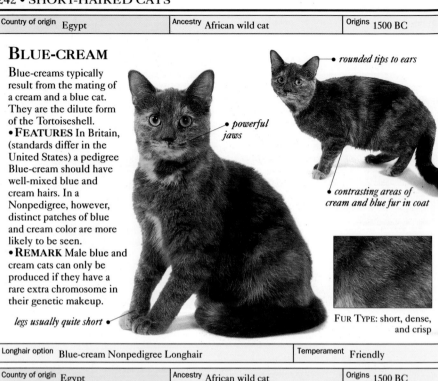

• *rounded tips to ears*

• *powerful jaws*

• *contrasting areas of cream and blue fur in coat*

FUR TYPE: short, dense, and crisp

| Longhair option Blue-cream Nonpedigree Longhair | Temperament Friendly |

| Country of origin Egypt | Ancestry African wild cat | Origins 1500 BC |

CALICO

Even if the mother is attractively marked, it is impossible to predict
the likely markings of tortoiseshell kittens; they are always variable.
• **FEATURES** In this case the characteristic tortoiseshell colors, rather
than the areas of white fur, predominate in the cat's coat.
• **REMARK** Tortoiseshell patterning occurs as the result of a gradual
shutdown of one of the female's paired sex
chromosomes during an early stage of embryonic
growth, when coloration corresponds to genes on
one chromosone or the other. The
red gene chromosome
switches off in
some cells;
in others
it is the
black.

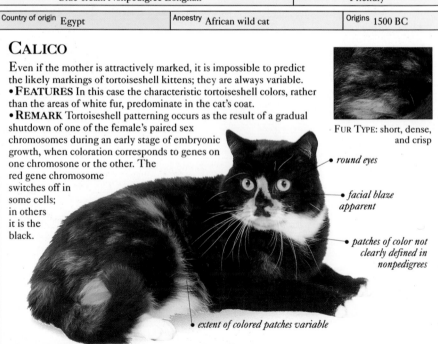

FUR TYPE: short, dense, and crisp

• *round eyes*

• *facial blaze apparent*

• *patches of color not clearly defined in nonpedigrees*

• *extent of colored patches variable*

| Longhair option Calico Nonpedigree Longhair | Temperament Friendly |

Country of origin Egypt	Ancestry African wild cat	Origins 1500 BC

RED CLASSIC TABBY AND WHITE

Nonpedigree cats of this color are sometimes known as "ginger and white" because of the rather orange tinge to their red fur. The tabby markings are a darker shade of red.

• **FEATURES** The white fur is distributed entirely randomly, and some overlap between white and colored areas is not unusual. In type, these cats show a similarity to the British Shorthair, but they are usually smaller in size.

• **REMARK** The tabby markings are not as well-ordered in this case as they are in a pedigree tabby.

• *darker frown lines apparent on head*

FUR TYPE: short, dense, and crisp

• *variable markings*

white paws •

• *broad tail with rounded tip* •

Longhair option Red Classic Tabby and White Nonpedigree Longhair	Temperament Friendly

Country of origin Egypt	Ancestry African wild cat	Origins 1500 BC

BLUE MACKEREL TABBY AND WHITE

Tabby markings in cats have been known for centuries; this Mackerel form originated in Britain, possibly during the 17th century.

• **FEATURES** Not only do the markings vary from cat to cat, but the depth of blue coloration is not entirely consistent. In some cases, the contrast between the ground coloration and the tabby markings is less pronounced than in others.

• **REMARK** The relative size and distribution of the white patches will not alter from the kitten stage.

• *pure white areas contrast with blue*

FUR TYPE: short, dense, and crisp

• *rounded head with relatively small ears*

tabby markings clearly discernible •

Longhair option Blue Mackerel Tabby & White Nonpedigree Longhair	Temperament Friendly

Country of origin Egypt	Ancestry African wild cat	Origins 1500 BC

BROWN CLASSIC TABBY AND WHITE

The disruptive coat markings that result from the darker tabby patterning
help these cats to conceal themselves quite effectively when hunting.
• **FEATURES** The dark
tabby markings are clearly
contrasted here with the
lighter brown body
coloration. White
areas in this case are
very restricted.
• **REMARK** This
placid tabby is
probably the most
common cat in Britain.

ringed tail •

round head set on short,
muscular neck •

straight
tail •

patching
clearly
apparent on
side of body

barring
present
on legs

short,
powerful legs •

FUR TYPE: short, dense,
and crisp

Longhair option Brown Classic Tabby and White Nonpedigree Longhair	Temperament Friendly

Country of origin Egypt	Ancestry African wild cat	Origins 1500 BC

BROWN SPOTTED

One of the reasons that tabby
markings are so common amongst
ordinary household cats is that such
patterning is genetically dominant.
Since many nonpedigree cats are
the result of random matings,
tabby genes have become widely
distributed and are often evident in
most countries' cat populations.
• **FEATURES** This tabby has a
Mackerel-type coat pattern, although
some of the vertical lines are broken.
• **REMARK** Selective breeding has
enabled this patterning to be developed
into the
symmetrical,
balanced markings
associated with
pedigree Mackerel
tabbies today.

M-shaped tabby
marking •

thick,
unbroken
"bracelet"
around
neck •

striped patterning
running vertically
down sides of body

black
stripes

heavy
black
line

bars
on legs •

FUR TYPE: short, dense,
and crisp

Longhair option Brown Spotted Nonpedigree Longhair	Temperament Friendly

| Country of origin Egypt | Ancestry African wild cat | Origins 1500 BC |

WHITE AND BROWN TABBY

Tabby markings do not
extend over areas of
white fur, as is clearly
shown in this cat.
• **FEATURES** This
amount of white would
not be acceptable in the
equivalent pedigree
shorthair. Although the
tabby markings are
restricted, it is clear that
this is a Blotched rather
than a Mackerel tabby.
• **REMARK** A study of
nonpedigree cat populations in
countries such as Australia has
shown that tabbies are more
common in the newer cities,
resulting from the cats taken
overseas by immigrants.

pure white fur

• white facial blaze between eyes

odd white hairs may be present in tabby areas •

FUR TYPE: short, dense, and crisp

no tabby markings on white legs •

• thick tail

| Longhair option White and Brown Tabby Nonpedigree Longhair | Temperament Friendly |

| Country of origin Egypt | Ancestry African wild cat | Origins 1500 BC |

BROWN MACKEREL TABBY

Although the chin area is usually whitish
in these tabbies, in the example shown
the white areas are more widespread and
extend to the nose and above the jaws.
• **FEATURES** The markings are not
especially even, so that black areas are
more prominent in some parts of
the coat than in others. The
bands on the cat's tail are
also irregular.
• **REMARK** Tabby
patterning is a
dominant trait, so
a number of
tabby kittens
will always be
produced in a
tabbie litter.

furnishing of hair within ears •

FUR TYPE: short, dense, and crisp

• pinkish red nose with darker border

large black blotch on hind foot •

• irregular tabby patterning extends along length of tail

| Longhair option | Brown Tabby Nonpedigree Longhair | Temperament Friendly |

CAT CREDITS

We are indebted and immensely grateful to the many owners and breeders who brought their cats from far and wide to be photographed for this book; without their help and enthusiastic cooperation, it could not have been produced. The cats, along with the names of their owners and breeders, are listed in page order, with references to indicate the exact position of each cat on the page.

KEY TO ABBREVIATIONS

Page numbers, in bold type, are followed by position references:
b   bottom
c   center
l   left
r   right
t   top

The cats' names are prefixed by an abbreviated reference to their current championship status:
GrPr   Grand Premier
Pr   Premier
GrCh   Grand Champion
Ch   Champion
EurCh   European Champion
IntCh   International Champion
GrEurCh   Grand European Champion
SupGrCh   Supreme Grand Champion
SupGrPr   Supreme Grand Premier

• **1 c** *Midamist Shynal* J Bright (C Bone)
• **2 tl (grandmother)** *Ch Fleic Mimosa Magic* P & J Choppen (P & J Choppen); **tc (great grandfather)** *GrCh Fleic Chocolate Imperial* P & J Choppen (P & J Choppen); **tr (mother)** *Ch Jasrobinka Angelique* P & J Choppen (P & J Choppen); **bl (kitten)** *Jasrobinka Annamonique* P & J Choppen (P & J Choppen)
• **3 c** *Pandapaws Mr Biggs* S Ward-Smith (J Varley & J Dicks)
• **5 b** *Skogens Volla* A S Watt (A Moss & J Higgins); **cl** *Bealltainn Bezique* T Stracstone (T Stracstone); **tr** *UK GrCh Nobilero Loric Vilesilensa* AE & RE Hobson (M Reed)
• **8 br** *Marble Masquerade* F Wagner (B Street & G Pascoe); **cl** *Kajenka Juniper* K Jenkins (J North)
• **9 bc & tr** *IntGrCh Gardenia du Vaumichon* G Bock (J Simonnet); **bl (kitten)** *IntCh Giroflée du Bois de Meudon* G Bock (G Bock)
• **11 br** *Friskie* (Bethlehem Cat Sanctuary)
• **12-13 c** *GrCh Aerostar Spectre* J E D Mackie (S Callen & I Hotten)
• **13 cl (white)** *Ch Miletree Memories* R Towse (P Kratz); **rc (ruff)** *Sitah Orllando* M Harvey (M Harvey)
• **16 bc (kitten)** *Sheephouse Diamond Lil* J Bradley (J Bradley); **bl (adult)**

Ch Lancendel Santa Claw P Ross (G Ellins & B Hollandt); **br (kitten)** *Sheephouse Precious Pearl* J Bradley (J Bradley); **cl** *Satinmist Charlie Brown* I Worsley-Waring (I Worsley-Waring); **cr (kitten)** L Berry *Kavida Amethyst* (L Berry); **cr (kitten)** L Berry *Kavida Cadberry* L Berry (L Berry); **cr (kitten)** *Kavida Primetime* L Berry (L Berry); **lc (adult)** *Adixish Talisman* M Acton (M Acton); **t (kitten)** *Lipema Monty Moon* P Brown (P Brown); **t (kitten)** *Lipema Melisa* P Brown (P Brown); **t (kitten)** *Lipema Muriel* P Brown (P Brown); **tl (adult)** *Adkrish Mary Contarie* C Andrews (P Brown);
• **17 bl kitten** *Rejuta Irrisistible* T & R Quick (T & R Quick); **bl kitten** *Rejuta Prize Guy* T & R Quick (T & R Quick); **bl kitten** *Rejuta Sacramentosam* T & R Quick (T & R Quick); **br Adult** *Sarouks Sweet William* W & J Benson (T & R Quick); **cl (kitten)** *Sargenta Blue Gismo* U Graves (U Graves); **cl (left kitten)** *Leolee Larnyen Poppy* (S Lee Soper); **cl (right kitten)** *Leolee Leetee* (S Lee Soper); **cr** *GrCh Wellmar Flamenco* J Martin (M Frew); **tc** *GrCh Miletree Masquerade* R K Towse (P Allen); **tl (kitten)** *Westways Jane Seemoor* A West (E Button); **tr** *Ch Leolee Sweet Song* (S Lee Soper); **tr (below)** *Indalo Knights Templar* B Pridham (B Pridham)
• **18 br** *GrPr Honeycharm Pandarella* B Patch (A Tonks); **tr** *Pr Shermese Elysium* C Simpson (F & D Powell)
• **19 bc** *Cobby Chops Kitten* M Tolliday (M Tolliday); **bc** *Cobby Chops Kitten* M Tolliday (M Tolliday); **bl** *Cobby Chops Kitten* M Tolliday (M Tolliday); **c** *Cobby Chops Clarida* M Tolliday (M Tolliday); **t** *Cobby Chops Confetti* M Tolliday (M Tolliday)
• **20 br** *Ch Watlove Windser* H Watson (H Watson)
• **21 tr (great grandfather)** *GrCh Fleic Chocolate Imperial* P & J Choppen (P & J Choppen); **step-by-step kitten** *Jasrobinka Annamonique* P & J Choppen (P & J Choppen); **step-by-step kitten** *Jasrobinka Dominique* P & J Choppen (P & J Choppen); **step-by-step kitten** *Jasrobinka Jade Princess* P & J Choppen (P & J Choppen); **step-by-step kitten** *Jasrobinka Jean Pierre* P & J Choppen (P & J Choppen)
• **22 all steps** *Picwick Puff Dragon* P Rogers (P Rogers); **br** *GrCh Miletree Masquerade* R K Towse (P Allen)
• **23 cr, bl, bc, & br** *GrCh Pannaduloa Yentantethra* Bred by J Hansson (J Hansson)
• **23 tc & tr** *GrCh Aerostar Spectre* J E D Mackie (S Callen & I Hotten)
• **26 bl** *Honeymist Blue Seastar* M Howes (M Howes);

br *Kaleetay Dextoniatoo* J Marshall (T Cornwall); **cr** *Lipema Shimazaki* P Brown (G Dean); **cr** *Jardinage Penny Royale* D Jardine (G Dean)
• **27 b** *Shaird Bare Essentials* A Rushbrook & J Plumb (A Rushbrook & J Plumb); **cr** *GrCh Maruja Samson* M Moorhead (M Moorhead); **tr** *Pr Bobire Justin Tyme* I E Longhurst (A Charlton)
• **30 bl** *Susian Just Judy* S Kempster (M Way); **tl** *GrCh Chermician Santa Fe* G & S Sanders (G & S Sanders); **tr** *Ch Bartania Pomme Frits* B Beck (B Beck)
• **31 cl** *Parthia Angelica* (M A Skelton); **cr** *Ch Sargenta Silver Dan* U Graves (U Graves); **tl** *Ch Leolee Sweet Song* S Lee Soper (S Lee Soper); **tr** *Ch Ballantyne Sadrazam* L Miles (L Miles)
• **32 b** *Shaird Bare Essentials* A Rushbrook & J Plumb (A Rushbrook & J Plumb); **c** *GrCh Aerostar Spectre* J E D Mackie (S Callen & I Hotten) **t** *Zultan Paquita Ballet* J Powell (B & B Raine)
• **35 cl (Somali)** *Sitah Orllando* M Harvey (M Harvey)
• **36 bc** *IntGrCh Gardenia du Vaumichon* G Bock (J Simonnet)

LONG-HAIRED CATS

• **40 all** *GrCh Adievo Ladydido* P Woodman (P Woodman)
• **41 bl &cr** *Annelida Shalom* A Ashford (M Butler Aust); **tl** *Ch Gleeway Iceberg* G Lee (G Lee); **tr** *Ch Lafrabella Queynote* I Bangs (G & S Sanders)
• **42 bl & br** *Picwick Puff Dragon* P Rogers (P Rogers); **tl** *Ch Chrysellus Cream Emperor* R Smith (G Miller)
• **43 bl** *Honeymist Blue Seastar* M Howes (M Howes); **br** *Ch Lollipop Blue Rascall* M Edwicker (G Miller); **t** *Bowmans Lilac Rhapsody* E Frankland (D Thompson)
• **44 bl & br** *Ch Honeymist Black Domino* M Howes (M Howes); **tl & tr** *Ch Bowmans Rose Dream* A L Frankland (A L Frankland)
• **45 bl** *GrCh Chermician Santa Fe* G & S Sanders (G & S Sanders); **br** *Ch Honeycharm Amanda* B Patch (B Patch); **tl & tr** *Ch & GrPr Cherub Hendel* A Cromton (A Bowman)
• **46 bl** *Chermician Teaseme* G & S Sanders (G & S Sanders); **tl & tr** *Crystaldee Bi Design* C & K Smith (E Baldwin)
• **47 bl** *Chermician Who Dundat* G & S Sanders (G & S Sanders); **br** *Pr Myway Beau Sabreur* I Witney (A Tonks); **tl & tr** *Adirtsa Choc Ice* D Tynan (C & K Smith)
• **48 bl & br** *SupGrCh Honeycharm*

Jasmine B Patch (B Patch); **tc & tr**
Honeymist Roxana M Howes
(M Howes)
• **49 tc** *Humdinga Heartsease* B Haigh
(C Evans); **tr** *Angieal Naughty Butnice*
A Mitchell (A Mitchell)
• **50 b** *Honeycharm Channell* B Patch
(B Patch); **cl** *Annelida Madonna*
A Ashford (A Ashford); **tr** *GrPr*
Honeycharm Pandarella B Patch
(A Tonks)
• **51 b** *Crystaldee Hope* C & K Smith
(C & K Smith); **tl & tr** *Casalina Dolly*
Mixture E Baldwin (E Baldwin)
• **52 bl & br** *Primabella Blueberry pie*
(C Gook); **t** *Watlove Hamish* H Watson
(H Watson)
• **53 bl & br** *Adraylo Silva Gabriella*
N Holt (M Harvey); **tl & c**
Ch Pieris Thomasina A & M Baker
(A & M Baker)
• **54 b** *Honeymist Taboo* M Howes
(M Howes); **cr** *Sarasamsan Honkytonk*
Angel S Corris (C Gook); **t (kitten)**
Rejuta Irrisistible T & R Quick (T & R
Quick); **t kitten** *Rejuta Prize Guy*
T & R Quick (T & R Quick);
t (kitten *Rejuta Sacramentosam* T & R
Quick (T & R); **tr (Adult)**
Sarouks Sweet William W & J Benson
(T & R Quick)
• **55 bl** *Celebrity Silver Bonbon* D Slater
(D Slater); **br** *GrCh Bellablanca*
Thumbelina S Greaves (S Greaves);
tl & tc *Mowbray Tanamera* D Cleford
(D Cleford)
• **56 bl & br** *Mandarin Halcyon*
D Thomson (D Thomson); **tc & tr**
Ch Diwenna Mandarin D Went
(D Thomson)
• **57 b** *Zultan Paquita Ballet* J Powell
(B & B Raine); **tc & tr** *Penumbra*
Samsons Secret J Palfreyman
(J Palfreyman)
• **58 bl & br** *Ch & GrPr Bessjet Silver*
Dollar J Smith (C Wall); **t** *Pickwick*
Exquisite Pixie P Rogers (P Rogers)
• **59 b** *Taloola Oopsadaisy* J Saunders
(J Saunders); **cl & tr (adult)** *Cashel*
Golden Yuppie A Curley (A Curley);
cr (kitten) *Cashel Golden Alice*
A Curley (A Curley)
• **60 b** *GrPr Bellrai Faberge* B & B
Raine (B & B Raine); **tl & tr**
Bellrai Creme Chanel B & B Raine
(B & B Raine)
• **61 cl** *Ch Ambergem Orlandos* A Burke
(A Burke); **cr & b** *Adhuilo*
Meadowlands Alias P Hurrell
(S Josling); **tr** *Klaxon Matterhorn* Mary
Harrington (M Harrington)
• **62 all** *Anneby Sunset* A Bailey
(A Bailey)
• **63 b** *Impeza Chokolotti* C Rowark
(E Baldwin); **t** *Ch Watlove Mollie-*
Mophead H Watson (H Watson)
• **64 b** *Amocasa Beau Brummel* I Elliott
(I Elliott); **tr & c** *GrCh Anneby*
Trendsetter A Bailey (A Bailey)
• **65 bl & br** *Ch Dermask Dolly*
Daydream J Bettany (M Allum);
tl & tr *GrCh Anneby Charisma*
A Bailey (A Bailey)

• **66 b** *Ch Watlove Windser* H Watson
(H Watson); **tl & tr** *Ch Jonalynn*
Munchkin J & L Wallett
(J & L Wallett)
• **67 bl & br** *Casaline Malteaser*
E. Baldwin (E Baldwin); **t** *Ch*
Crystaldee Frilly Knickers C & K Smith
(C & K Smith)
• **68 all** *Saybrianna Tomorrows Cream*
A Carritt (A Carritt)
• **69 bl & br** *Schwenthe Kisca*
F E Brigliadori (F E Brigliadori &
K Robson); **tl & tr** *Panjandrum*
Bestman A Madden (E Leach)
• **70 bc & br** *Ch & GrPr Panjandrum*
April Suprice A Madden (A Madden);
t *GrCh Adivelo Anchantress* D Wedmore
(C Flynn)
• **71 all** *Shwechinthe Katha*
F Bridliadori (F Robinson)
• **72 bl & br** *Boemm Shantung Silk*
K Bairstairs (G Rankin); **t** *Aesthetikat*
Toty Temptress Mrs G Sharpe
(H Hewitt)
• **73 bc & br** *Panjandrum Pan Yan*
A Madden (A Madden); **c (kitten)**
Shandatal Yelena S Talboys
(S Talboys); **cl & tr** *Panjandrum*
Swansong Anne Madden (S Talboys)
• **74 bl** *Shanna's Snowy Fleur* M Harms
(M Harms); **br** *Shanna's Demiz Sayah*
M Harms (I Halewyck); **cr (Adult)**
Ch Yemin de Saint Glinglin H Den
Ouden (M Harms)
• **75 cr & b** *Shanna's Essen Demir*
M Harms (D Hondijk Zuuring);
t *Shanna's Tombis Hanta Yo* M Harms-
Moeskops (G Rebel van Kemenade)
• **76 b & cr** *Shanna's Boncuk Bertje*
M Harms (Ad Senders); **t** *Shanna's*
Yasmine Sevince M Harms (H Dieman)
• **77 b & cr** *Shanna's Yacinta-Sajida*
M Harms (M Harms); **tc & tr**
Kazibelli Kedi's Tamar M Bosch
(G Rebel van Kemenade)
• **78 all** *Ch Lady Lubna Leanne*
Chatkantarra T Boumeister
(J van der Werff)
• **79 all** *Ch Ballantyne Sadrazam*
L Miles (L Miles)
• **80 all** *Chantonel Snowball Express*
R Elliot (R Elliot)
• **81 b & cr** *Jardinage Penny Royale*
D Jardine (G Dean); **tc (adult)** *Ohope*
White Mischief C Andrews (P Brown);
tr & c (kitten) *Lipema Major*
Balmerino P Brown (P Brown)
• **82 b** *Lipema Shimazaki* P Brown
(G Dean); **t (kitten)** *Lipema Monty*
Moon P Brown (P Brown); **t (kitten)**
Lipema Melisa P Brown (P Brown);
t (kitten) *Lipema Muriel* P Brown
(P Brown); **tr (adult)** *Adkrish Mary*
Contarie C Andrews (P Brown)
• **83 all** *Quinkent Honey's*
Mi-Lei-Fo I A van der Reckweg
(I A van der Reckweg)
• **84 all** *Koonluv White Fury* A Rowsell
(T Cornwall)
• **85 cr & br** *Charlemma Blue Balco*
D Froud (D Gourd); **tl & tc** *USA GrCh*
Honeycoon Voodoo Boy K Muller
(T Cornwall)

• **86 bl & br** *Namrib Silvasand*
H Horton (J Lindsey); **c (kitten)**
Caprix Dinah T Cornwall (Mr and Mrs
Harley); **cl (adult)** *Caprix Marvellous*
Marvin T Cornwall (T Cornwall);
tr *Caprix Dynamite* T Cornwall
(T Cornwall)
• **87 bl & br** *Kaleetay Dextoniatoo*
J Marshall (T Cornwall); **tc & tr**
Purpuss Mainchance T & S A Morgan
(T Morgan)
• **88 b** *Caprix Silver Mist* T Cornwall
(T Cornwall); **c** *Charlemma Fire Dancer*
D Froud (Col. & E Stapleton);
tr *Koonluv Chevrolet* A Rowsell
(T Cornwall)
• **89 bc & br** *Bealltainn Cadillac*
Sheeman (T Cornwall); **cl & tr**
Adixillo Coon Laura C Evans
(H Horton)
• **90 all** *Skogens Modi* A S Watt
(G Elston & K Harvey)
• **91 br** *Skogens Volla* A S Watt (A Moss
& J Higgins); **cl & tc** *Skogens Magni*
A S Watt (K Garratt)
• **92 bc & cr** *Skogens Odin* M & M
Laine (A S Watt); **tc & tr** *Skogens SF*
Eddan Romeo A S Watt (S Garrett)
• **93 all** *Olocha* A Danveef
(H von Groneburg)
• **94 all** *Ladibyrd Ragadam* S Ward-
Smith (C M Carter & M Sumpter)
• **95 all** *Pandapaws Blue Flash* S Ward-
Smith (C M Carter & M Sumpter);
bc *Pandapaws Mr Biggs* S Ward-Smith
(J Varley & Jon Dicks)
• **96 all** *Adhuish Alefeles Topaz*
R J Allen (P G & M Frayne)
• **97 br** *Sitah Kissamayo* M Harvey
(M Harvey); **tl & tc** *Sir Duncan Van*
Manja M Van Zweden (L Warwick)
• **98 bc & cr** *Vestisler Risingstar*
L Warwick (L Warwick); **tl & tr** *Bonzer*
Fandango J Ponsford (L Warwick)
• **99 bl & bc** *Melody Von*
Haimhaurschloss N Reiger (J Holderer-
Hortensius); **cr** *Bealltainn Bezique*
T Stracstone (T Stracstone);
tr *Kelmscott Falcon* T Stracstone
(T Stracstone)
• **100 all** *Frafadi's Silver Aurora*
D Hondijk Zuuring (D Hondijk
Zuuring)
• **101 bc** *Uptomalian Forgetmenot*
F Upton (F Upton); **c & tr** *Uptomalian*
Jessica Rabbit F Upton (L Warwick)
• **102 all** *Palvjia Pennyfromheaven*
J Buroughs (T Tidey)
• **103 b** *Pr Pandai Feargal* E Corps
(B V Rickwood); **tc & tr** *Blancsanglier*
Rosensoleil A Bird (A Bird)
• **104 bc & cr** *Pr Blancsanglier Beau*
Brummel A Bird (A Bird); **t** *Ronsline*
Whistfull Spirit R Farthing
(R Farthing)
• **105 bc & cr** *Jeuphi Golden Girl*
J Phillips (L Cory); **tr & tc** *Dasilva*
Tasha J St. John (C Russel &
P Scrivener)
• **106 b** *Ch Apricat Silvercascade*
R Smyth (E & J Robinson); **tr & c**
GrCh Soleil Imperial Rufus L Howard
(L Howard)

- **107 b** *Mossgems Sheik Shimizu*
M Mosscrop (H Grenney); **tc & tr**
GrPr Nighteyes Cinderfella J Pell (J Pell)
- **108 all** *Favagello Hamlet* J Bryson
(R I Bryson)
- **109 b & cr** *Kennbury Dulcienea*
C Lovell (K Harmon); **c & tr** *Favagello
Brown Whispa* J Bryson (J Bryson)
- **110 all** *Polar Star* L Price
(L Williams)
- **111 all** *Shilley Wilderbras*
C M Balemans (Family Wouters)
- **114 all** *Maggie* (Bethlehem Cat
Sanctuary)
- **115 bl & bc** *Dumpling* (Bethlehem
Cat Sanctuary); **tc** *Dan-I-Lion*
(V Warriner)
- **116 cl & tr** *Dan* (D & C Ellis)
- **117 cr & br** *Mr Beau* (V Warriner);
tc & tr *Stardust* (V Warriner)

SHORT-HAIRED CATS

- **118 all** *Ch & SupGrPr Welquest
Snowman* A Welsh (A Welsh)
- **119 b** *Ch Lancendel Girl Friday*
P Ross (J Bradley); **tl & tr** *GrCh
Miletree Twinkle* R Towse (R Towse)
- **120 bc (adult)** *Adixish Talisman*
M Acton (M Acton); **c (kitten)** *Kavida
Primetime* L Berry (L Berry);
cr (kitten) *Kavida Amethyst* L Berry
(L Berry); **tc & tr** *GrCh Westways
Purfect Amee* A West (G B Ellins)
- **121 tc & tr** *GrCh Maruja Samson*
M Moorhead (M Moorhead);
bl (kitten) *Kavida Cadberry* L Berry
(L Berry); **br** *Satinmist Charlie Brown*
I Worsley-Waring (I Worsley-Waring)
- **122 bc & br** *GrCh Blakewood Tuteine*
G B Ellins (G B Ellins); **l** *Miletree Black
Rod* R Towse (R Towse); **tr** *Susian
Cara Mia* S Kempster (S Kempster)
- **123 bc & cr** *Ch Bartania Pomme
Frits* B Beck (B Beck); **tl (kitten)**
Sheephouse Tallullah J Bradley
(J Skinners); **tr** *Bradlesmere Nerine*
J Shaw (B Hollandt)
- **124 b** *Ch Sargenta Silver Dan*
U Graves (U Graves); **cr (kitten)**
Sargenta Blue Gismo U Graves
(U Graves); **tc** *GrCh Wellmar Flamenco*
J Martin (M Frew)
- **125 bc & br** *Tammeko Tamoshanter*
M Simon (R Taylor); **tr** *Ch Wellmar
Boson* J Martin (J Martin)
- **126 bc** *GrCh Tammeko Marmaduke*
M Simon (M Simon); **tl & tc**
Ch Tammeko Cappuccino M Simon
(M Simon)
- **127 cl & br** *Susian Just Judy*
S Kempster (M Way); **tc & tr**
GrCh Miletree Masquerade R K Towse
(P Allen)
- **128 b** *Miletree Magpie* R Towse
(M Le Monnier); **cr (adult)**
Ch Lancendel Santa Claw P Ross
(G Ellins & B Hollandt); **tc (kitten)**
Sheephouse Precious Pearl J Bradley
(J Bradley); **tr (kitten)** *Sheephouse
Diamond Lil* J Bradley (J Bradley)
- **129 bl & cr** *Wellmar Keziah* J Martin
(A M Gothard);

tr *GrCh Starfrost Dominic* E Conlin
(C Greenall)
- **130 bc & br** *Ch Adreesh Lotte*
J Bradley (K McKenna)
- **130 c & tr** *Ch Semra Smokeancoke*
M Sutton (J M Allison)
- **131 bc & cr** *GrCh (CA) Ch (GCCF)
Westways Dusty Miller* A West (A West)
- **131 cl & tr** *Ch Phykell Milliways*
M Sparshot (Mrs R K Towse)
- **132 all** *Kavida Hamilton* L Berry
(V Clerkin)
- **133 bc** *Boadicat Bertie* P Griffiths
(J Jones); **cr** *Cordelia Cassandra*
J Codling (C Excell); **l & tr** *Boadicat
Bizzie Lizzie* P Griffiths (L Berry)
- **134 bl & br** *Kavida Sweet Georgia
Brown* L Berry (L Berry); **cr** *Beeblebox
Plum Crazy* J Crafer (C Boyd);
tr *Adhuish Cattino* C Excell (C Excell)
- **135 bl & cr** *Boadicat Camilla*
P Griffiths (L Berry); **tc** *Adhuish
Carnival Queen* C Excell (C Excell);
tr *Kavida Misty Daydream* L Berry
(L Berry)
- **136 cl & cr** *Blondene Choochy chops*
G Butler (M Smith); **tl** *Tzarkesh Aint
Misbehavin* J Rogers (M Smith)
- **137 c & b** *Adqwesh Avra* Mrs Farmer
(S W McEwen); **tr** *Pennydown Penny
Black* S W McEwen (S W McEwen)
- **138 bl & bc** *IntCh Silvery Glow
Dwarrelhof* A P Groeneugen
(A P Groeneugen); **c** *French Can Can*
M Schuriderski (E Christian Tilli)
- **139 bc & cr** *EurCh None Such of the
Golden Rainbow* A P Groeneuegen
(A P Groeneuegen); **tc** *Pennydown
Touch of Class* S W McEwen
(S W McEwen)
- **140 all** *Myrneen Cloudy Man Sell*
L Price (L Williams)
- **141 bc & cr** *Myrneen Timmiswara*
L Williams (L Williams); **tr** *Minty*
L Williams (H Walker & K Bullin)
- **142 br** *Adrish Alenka* L Price
(L Williams); **tc & cr** *Tattleberry Signed*
J Hellman (L Williams)
- **143 all** *Ngkomo Ota* A Scruggs
(L Marcel)
- **144 all** *Delicious Panda Vanzechique*
M Wijers (M Wijers)
- **145 all** *Lucky Boy Wildebras*
C M Balemans (C M Balemans)
- **146 b** *Esmaralda Wildebras*
C M Balemans (C M Balemans);
cl & tc *Ambre de Brentwood Drive*
M Lisart (M Wijers)
- **147 bl & tr (kitten)** *Linkret Evie*
M Trompetto (J Swinyard); **br & cl**
Linkret Barclay Mews M Trompetto
(M Trompetto)
- **160 all** *IntCh & Pr Rimsky de
Santanoe* L Kenter (L Kenter)
- **161 bl & br** *Eldoria's Crazy Girl*
O van Beck and Aat Quast (O van
Beck and Aat Quast); **t** *Eldoria's
Graziana* O van Beck and Aat Quast
(O van Beck and Aat Quast)
- **162 bl & cr** *Eldoria's Goldfinger*
O van Beck and Aat Quast (O van
Beck and Aat Quast); **t** *Eldoria's
Yossarian* O van Beck and Aat Quast

(O van Beck and Aat Quast)
- **163 all** *IntCh Orions Guru* Lomaers
(Mulder-Hopma)
- **164 all** *Aurora de Santanoe* L Kenter
(L Kenter)
- **165 bc & tr** *IntGrCh Gardenia du
Vaumichon* G Bock (J Simonnet);
bl (kitten) *IntCh Giroflée du Bois de
Meudon* G Bock (G Bock)
- **166 all** *Pr Adkrish Samson*
P K Weissman (P K Weissman)
- **167 b** *Ch Adhuish Anak Barong*
P K Weisman (P K Weissman); **tc & tr**
Rastacat Yzella J Cross (J Cross)
- **168 bc & cr** *Amaska Fantasia*
S Luxford-Watts (S Luxford-Watts);
tl & tr *Leshocha Little Gem*
E Himmerston (E Himmerston)
- **169 bc & cr** *Amaska Tia Maria*
S Luxford-Watts (S Luxford-Watts);
cl & tr *Amaska Silver Cinnerama*
S Luxford-Watts (S Luxford-Watts)
- **170 br** *Leshocha Azure My Friend*
E Himmerston (E Himmerston);
tc & tr *Myowal Rudolph* J Cornish
(T Compton)
- **171 b** *Lohteyn Whispered Word*
L Heath (J Green); **tc & tr** *Ch Myowal
Moppers Blues* G Cornish (G Cornish)
- **172 all** *Capillatus White Simba*
J Cook (J Cook)
- **173 bl & cr** *Adhuish Grainne*
N Jarrett (J Burton); **tc & tr** *Adhuish
Happy Joker* M & H Benson (J Burton)
- **174 b** *GrCh Ikari Donna* S Davey
(J Plumb); **tc & tr** *Sailorman Horay
Henery* K Hardwick (K Hardwick)
- **175 bl & cr** *Washtog Oil Slick*
C Plumbly (C Plumbly); **tr** *Washtog
Intoeverything* C Plumbly (C Plumbly)
- **176 b** *GrPr Berilleon Dandi Lyon*
B Lyon (M Chitty); **cl & tr** *Myowal
Susie Sioux* G Cornish (J and B Archer)
- **177 br** *Pr Bobire Justin Tyme*
I E Longhurst (A Charlton); **tl & tc**
UK GrCh Nobilero Loric Vilesilensa
AE & RE Hobson (M Reed)
- **178 all** *Riahon Auda Bebare* Shana
Scanlin (A Rushbrook & J Plumb)
- **179 all** *Shaird Bare Essentials*
A Rushbrook & J Plumb
(A Rushbrook & J Plumb)
- **180 all** *Shearling Faerie Neem* Mary
Harrington (M Harrington)
- **181 bc (adult)** *Shearling Annie Smith
Peck* Mary Harrington (M Harrington);
bl (kitten) *Shearling Swiss Bliss* Mary
Harrington (M Harrington)
- **182 all** *Astahazy Zeffirelli* (M von
Kirchberg)
- **183 all** *GrCh Aerostar Spectre*
J E D Mackie (S Callen & I Hotten)
- **184 all** *GrCh Pannaduloa Yentantethra*
J Hansson (J Hansson)
- **185 bl & br** *Ch Willowbreeze Goinsolo*
Mr & Mrs Robinson (T K Hull-
Williams); **tr** *Dawnus Caruso*
A Douglas (A Douglas)
- **186 bl** *Leolee Sweet Song* S Lee Soper
(S Lee Soper); **cr** *Leolee Larnyen Poppy*
S Lee Soper (S Lee Soper); **tc & tr**
Ch Pannaduloa Phaedra J Hansson
(J Hansson)

• **187 b & cr** *GrCh Dawnus Primadonna* A Douglas (A Douglas); **tl & tr** *Pr Parthia Black Watch* M Skelton (O Watson)
• **188 b** *Midamist Shynal* J Bright (C Bone); **tc & tr** *Rocamadour Heightofashion* K Holder (K Holder)
• **189 b** *Midamist Taffetalace* J Bright (J Bright); **tc & tr** *Ch Darling Copper Kingdom* I George (S Mauchline)
• **190 bc & cr** *Ch Sisar Brie* L Pummell (L Pummell); **tc & tr** *GrPr Bluecroft Sunsationallad* P Mapes (M Brazier)
• **191 bc & cr** *Indalo Knights Templar* B Pridham (B Pridham); **t** *Parthia Giselle* M Skelton (S Johnson & P Norman);
• **192 b** *Peryorsia Casandra* L E Martin (L E Martin); **tc & tr** *Jophas Mysticetti* J Reed (M Saunders)
• **193 b** *Ch Bosan Carmen* S Bell (L E Martin); **t** *Ch Rondell Christmas Cracker* F Jackson (F Jackson)
• **194 all** *Braeside Moonflower* H Hewitt (H Hewitt)
• **195 bc & cr** *Ch Hobberdy Hokey Cokey* A Virtue (A Virtue); **tl & tr** *Braeside Red Sensation* H Hewitt (H Hewitt)
• **196 bc & cr** *GrCh Bambino Alice Bugown* B Boizard-Neil (B Boizard-Neil); **t** *Ch Bambino Seawitch* B Boizard-Neil (B Boizard-Neil)
• **197 b & cr** *Kamehahd Pecious Purrdy* D Tomlinson (D Tomlinson); **tc & tr** *Ch Mootam Flyaway Peter* S Fearon (S Hillman)
• **198 all** *Ch Bambino Dreamy* B Boizard-Neil (B Boizard-Neil)
• **199 b & br** *Impromptu Crystal* M Garrod (M Garrod); **tc & tr** *Oakenshield Blue Willow* C Kemp (C Kemp)
• **200 br** *Adhuish Atlas* T J H Bishop (M S Hodgekinson); **cl & tr** *Adonis* D Bishop (D Bartlett)
• **201 bl** *Yanazen Birmanie* D Bartlett (M Harvey); **br** *Tajens Rula Girl* T Jenkinson (D Bartlett); **cr (kitten)** *Tajens Irridescent Opal* T Jenkinson (T Jenkinson); **tc** *Pearls Princess* M Martin (T Jenkinson)
• **202 bc** *Tajens Isabella* T Jenkinson (T Jenkinson); **bl (kitten)** *Tajens Oliver* T Jenkinson (T Jenkinson); **cr** *Yanazen Bonnechance* D Bartlett (M Harvey); **tc** *Yankie Doodle Dandy* J Elkington (S Klein)
• **203 bc & cr** *Adhuish Plumtree* N J A C Young (M S Hodgekinson); **t** *Amber* H Foreshaw (A Crowther)
• **204 all** *Lasiesta Miss Puddleduck* G W Dyson (G W Dyson)
• **205 br & cr** *Ballego Betty Boo* J Gillies (J Gillies); **tl & tr** *Lasiesta Nutcracker* J P Dyson (D Boad)
• **206 bc & cr** *Kartush Benifer* C & T Clark (C & T Clark); **tc & tr** *Kartush Cyberleh* C & T Clark (C & T Clark)
• **207 all** *Favagello Tabitha* J Bryson (J Bryson)
• **208 b** *Astahazy Zoltan* (M von

Kirchberg); **cl (kitten)** *Braeside Sunsukinyasohn* H Hewitt (H Hewitt); **tc** *Yolanda Maple Zuzi* Late Y Symes (H Hewitt)
• **209 b & cr** *Lasiesta Blackberry Girl* G W Dyson (G W Dyson); **cl & tc** *Vatan Mimi* D Beech & J Chalmers (J Moore)
• **210 all** *Boronga Black Savahra* P Impson (R Stanbrook)
• **211 (kittens)** *Silvaner Pollyanna & Un-named kitten* C Thompson (C Thompson); **c (adult)** *Silvaner Kuan* C Thompson (C Thompson)
• **212 all** *GrCh Sukinfer Samari* J O'Boyle (J O'Boyle)
• **213 bl & bc** *Ch Pr Adixish Minos Mercury* A Concanon (A Concanon); **t** *Patrican Palomino* S Humphris (G Ford)
• **214 bl** *Adhuish Champignon Sattin* N Williams (N Williams); **cr** *Adhuish Tuwhit Tuwhoo* N Williams (N Williams); **t** *Marilane Bryony* G Ford (G Ford)
• **215 b & cr** *Sunjade Brandy Snap* E Wildon (E Tomlinson); **t** *Scilouette Angzhi* C & T Clark (C & T Clark)
• **216 b & cr** *GrPr Jasrobinka Jeronimo* P & J Choppen (B & T Plumb); **cl & tr** *Shelemay Logan* B Castle (L Flint)
• **217 bl & cr** *Simonski Sylvester Sneakly* S Cosgrove (S Cosgrove); **tl & tr** *Tenaj Blue Max* J Tonkinson (K Iremonger)
• **218 bl & br** *Sayonora Cinnamon Specs* G Worthy (C Harrison); **t** *Salste Mr Mistoffelees* S Franklin (S Franklin)
• **219 b** *Bosskats Jenny Anydots* G Hemmings (G Hemmings); **tc & tr** *Ercit Diadem Chelone* K & L Spencer-Mills (K & L Spencer-Mills)
• **220 b** *Joysewel Ernisteminway* J Stevens (L Muffett); **tl & tr** *Ch Jasrobinka Angelique* (P & J Choppen)
• **221 b** *Felides Vivres Purr-sé* Y C Kleyn (A P Groeneuegen); **tc & tr** *Myomah Madelaine* K Toft (S Elliot)
• **222 b** *Siaforebur Black Marketeer* L Muffett (L Muffett); **tl (adult)** *Salste Kaneelbusterboy* S Franklin (K McGrath); **tc (kitten)** *Salste Kaneelbobby* S Franklin (S Franklin); **tr (kitten)** *Salste Kaneelbusterboy* S Franklin (S Franklin)
• **223 bc & cr** *Parthia Angelica* M A Skelton (M A Skelton); **cl & tc** *Lynfield New Moon* E Morse (L Muffett)
• **224 all** *Salste Edwin* S Franklin (D & A Popham)
• **225 bc & br** *Scintilla Silver Whirligig* P Turner (D Walker); **t** *Greysbrook Polly Doodle* M Hornet (P R Wilkinson)
• **228 br (kitten)** *Karthwine Elven*

Moonstalk* R Clayton (M Crane); **cl & cr (adult)** *Kingcup Lilac Wine* M Cook (P Gillison); **tr (kitten)** *Karthwine Elven Moonstalk* R Clayton (M Crane)
• **229 cl & br** *Giselle Chocolate Ceres* C Bachellier (V Spragg); **tc & cr** *GrCh Emarelle Milos* M R Lyall (R Hopkins)
• **230 bl** *Charriet Cupid* H & C Patey (H & C Patey); **cr (kitten)** *Satusai Fawn Amy* I Reid (I Reid); **tc** *Giselle Silver Spirit* C Bachelier (E & S Hoyle); **tr (kitten)** *Braeside Marimba* H Hewitt (H Hewitt)
• **231 bc & cr** *Ch Anera Ula* C Macaulay (C Symonds); **tc & tr** *Lionelle Rupert Bear* C Bailey (C Tencor)
• **232 all** *Adqwesh Chi Chi Chablis* A Cooper (A Cooper)
• **234 all** *Gogees Jungle Jim* G Johnson (M Hornett)
• **235 b & cr** *Thickthorn Carroway* G Johnson (S Sweeny); **t** *Gogees Firespot* G Johnson (M Hornett)
• **236 all** *Carragato Lassik* T Edwards (V Maria Tatti)
• **238 bc & cr** *Carragato Kotaki* T Edwards (V Maria Tatti);
• **239 bl** *Jungle Spirit* F Wagner (G Pascoe & B Street); **cl** *Jezabel Jamberee* F Wagner (G Pascoe & B Street); **cr & tr (adult)** *Gogees Warhawk* G Johnson (G Pascoe & B Street)
• **240 bl (kitten)** *Misty* (P Pickering); **cl & br** *Sinbad Sailor Blue* (V Lew)
• **241 bl & br** *Crumpet* (Bethlehem Cat Sanctuary); **tl** *Esther* (D & C Ellis); **tr** *Peanut* (P Pickering)
• **242 b** *Vikivashti* (D Fagg); **tc & tr** *Dreamy Woman* (Bethlehem Cat Sanctuary); **tl & tr** *Thomson* (D & C Ellis)
• **243 bl & br** *Truffles* (V Warriner)
• **244 bc & cr** *Tiger* (D & C Ellis); **t** *Friskie* (Bethlehem Cat Sanctuary)
• **245 bl & br** *Rosie* (V Warriner); **tc & tr** *Nigel* (D & C Ellis)
• **249 tr** *Grimswald de Shiva Devale* M & S Gubbel-Noens (M & S Gubbel-Noens)
• **252 b** *Eldoria's Crazy Girl* O van Beck and Aat Quast (O van Beck & A Quast)
• **254 tl & tr** *Braeside Pikilo* H Hewitt (H Hewitt)
• **256 b** *GrCh Starfrost Dominic* E Conlin (C Greenall)

GLOSSARY

• **AGOUTI**
Combination of light and dark banding along length of individual hairs, notably in tabbies.
• **ALBINO**
Cat with no color pigment whatsoever, appearing pure white with pinkish eyes.
• **ASIAN**
Cat of Burmese **type**, but not showing Burmese coloration, patterning, or coat length.
• **AWN HAIRS**
Coarser form of secondary hair, with thickened tips.
• **BARRING**
Striped patterning, associated with tabbies but considered to be a fault in selfcolored cats.
• **BICOLOR**
Coat showing areas of one solid color and patches of white.
• **BLAZE**
Marking, usually white, between eyes extending from forehead down to nose.
• **BLOODLINE**
Group of cats related to each other through several generations or by their **pedigrees**.
• **BLUE**
Blue-gray coloration.
• **BREAK**
Alteration to nose profile; also known as a stop.
• **BREED**
Cats having similar, defined appearance and related ancestry.
• **BREED STANDARD**
Criteria against which cats of particular breed are judged.
• **BRINDLING**
Scattered hairs of wrong color apparent in coat.
• **BRUSH**
Describes profuse covering of hair on tail, typical of long-haired cats.
• **CALICO**
American description for Tortoiseshell and White.
• **CALLING**
Distinctive vocalization of female cat when in **estrus.**
• **CAMEO**
Hair with cream or red **tipping**, referring to Chinchilla, Shaded, or Smoke cats.
• **CARNIVORE**
Animal feeding mainly on food of animal origin.

• **CARPAL PAD**
Pads present at level of carpus on both front feet.
• **CAT FANCY**
Organized, selective breeding and exhibiting of cats.
• **CATTERY**
Where cats are kept and bred, with cattery's name included as part of **pedigree** name.
• **CHAMPAGNE**
American description for Lilac form of Tonkinese and Chocolate Burmese.
• **CHAMPION**
Title accorded to cat after a number of wins at shows.
• **CHINCHILLA**
Tip of fur colored, with remainder pale or white.
• **CHOCOLATE**
Medium to pale brown. Lighter than Seal in **pointed** cats.
• **CHROMOSOME**
Threadlike paired structure present in cell nucleii, carrying genetic material encoded in genes.
• **COBBY**
Short, compact body shape, as exemplified by British Shorthair.
• **CONGENITAL**
Nonhereditary health problem arising before birth.
• **CROSS-BREEDING**
The mating together of two different breeds.
• **DILUTE**
Paler version of color, such as Cream (dilute form of Red).
• **DOMINANT**
Genetic term, describing characteristic inherited from one parent and appearing in offspring.
• **DOUBLE COAT**
Thick, longer **topcoat** over short, soft **undercoat.**
• **DOWN HAIR**
Soft, short, secondary hairs.
• **EAR FURNISHINGS**
Hair growing within ears.
• **ENTIRE**
Not **neutered.**
• **ESTRUS**
Breeding period in females.
• **FAMILY**
In taxonomy, grouping between order and individual genera.
• **FELINE**
Member of cat family.
• **FERAL**

Domestic cat that has reverted to living wild.
• **FOREIGN**
Cat with lithe, fine-boned appearance, such as Siamese.
• **FRILL**
Neck **ruff** of longer fur.
• **GENES**
Contain encoded information for all features of cat (or other organism).
• **G.C.C.F.**
Governing Council of the Cat Fancy (UK)
• **GHOST MARKINGS**
Traces of faint tabby markings often seen in kittens.
• **GLOVES**
White areas of fur on back of feet of Birmans.
• **GUARD HAIRS**
Longer hairs forming **topcoat.**
• **HARLEQUIN**
Description used in America for **Van patterning**.
• **HEAT**
Female's period of **estrus.**
• **HIMALAYAN PATTERNING**
Darker coloration at extremities of body, which can be affected by body temperature.
• **HYBRIDIZATION**
Production of offspring by mating different species or breeds.
• **IN-BREEDING**
Mating together of very closely related cats, such as the pairing of brother and sister.
• **JOWLS**
Cheek folds, prominent in mature, unneutered, male cats.
• **KINK**
Malformation, typically of tail, most commonly associated with Siamese and other breeds of Oriental origin.
• **LACES**
White fur extending from paws up hind legs in Birmans.
• **LAVENDER**
Pale pinkish gray coloration.
• **LEVEL BITE**
Jaws correctly aligned, and not with one overlapping other.
• **LITTER**
Kittens born to female at same time. (Also lining for dirt tray.)
• **LYNX POINT**
American term used to describe tabby **points.**
• **MACKEREL MARKINGS**
Distinctive pattern of striping on

body of tabbies, said to resemble fish's skeleton.
• **MANTLE**
Area of back, closest to head.
• **MASCARA LINES**
Dark lines connecting to eyes.
• **MASK**
Contrasting darker coloration present on face of **pointed** breeds such as Siamese.
• **MELANIN**
Black pigmentation.
• **MITTENS**
White fur on front feet, as seen in Ragdolls.
• **MOGGY**
Describes domestic cat of non-pedigree origins.
• **MOLT**
Shedding of coat, usually in response to seasonal changes.
• **MUTATION**
Change in genes, giving rise to unexpected alteration in appearance of kittens, compared with that of parents.
• **MUZZLE**
Comprises nose and jaws.
• **NATURAL MINK**
Color description for darkest form of Tonkinese, equivalent to Seal Point Siamese.
• **NECKLACE**
Darker markings encircling neck; not always complete.
• **NEUTER**
Cat that has been castrated (males) or spayed (females).
• **NICTITATING MEMBRANE**
Thin, transparent membrane that may become apparent at corner of eyes if cat is sick or malnourished. Otherwise known as the "haw" or the third eyelid.
• **NOSE LEATHER**
Area of colored skin on nose, not covered by fur.
• **ODD-EYED**
Eyes of different colors, typically blue and orange.
• **ORIENTAL**
Term used to describe cat of fine-boned, lithe, **foreign** appearance, such as the Siamese.
• **OUTCROSS**
Pairing with unrelated individual, possibly of different breed.
• **OUTER COAT**
Comprises longer **guard hairs**.
• **PADS**
Leathery areas without hair on feet.
• **PARTICOLORED**
Coat consisting of two or more colors, such as Black and White.

• **PATCHED TABBY**
Tortoiseshell Tabby.
• **PEDIGREE**
Line of descent of purebred cat, showing the ancestry over a number of generations.
• **PENCILING**
Thin, darker lines, resembling pencils, seen in tabbies.
• **PERSIAN**
Equivalent to Longhair in Britain.
• **PEWTER**
Describing Silver Shaded cat, with orange or coppery eyes.
• **POINTS**
Darker colored areas of body, on head, ears, legs, paws, and tail, associated with Siamese and similar pointed breeds.
• **POLYDACTYL**
Having extra digits on feet.
• **PREMIER**
Neutered champion.
• **PRICKED**
Describes ears held erect.
• **PRIMARY HAIRS**
Longer **guard hairs** of topcoat.
• **PUREBRED**
The result of controlled pairings over a number of generations.
• **QUEEN**
Unneutered female to be used for breeding purposes.
• **RECESSIVE**
Genetic feature passed from one generation to the next, but not always being evident.
• **RECOGNITION**
Acceptance of **standard** for new breed by cat association.
• **REGISTRATION**
Recording of kitten's birth and ancestry with cat association.
• **RUFF**
Longer hair around neck.
• **RUMPY**
Manx with no trace of tail.
• **RUMPY RISER**
Manx showing trace of tail.
• **RUSTINESS**
Trace of reddish brown fur apparent in coat of black cat.
• **SABLE**
American description of brown Burmese (the darkest form).
• **SCARAB MARKING**
M-shaped darker marking on the head of tabbies.
• **SEAL**
Dark brown coloration, typically describing **points** of Siamese.
• **SEX CHROMOSOMES**
Pair of chromosomes responsible for determining gender.

• **SEX LINEAGE**
Genetic trait associated with **sex** chromosomes.
• **SHADING**
Widespread darker area toning with basic coloration of coat.
• **SPAYING**
Neutering of female cat.
• **SPINA BIFIDA**
Congenital malformation of backbone.
• **SPRAYING**
Habit, especially of unaltered males, using urine to mark territory.
• **SQUINT**
Deformity causing eyes to stare at nose, giving cross-eyed impression.
• **STANDARD OF POINTS**
Description and scoring system used by show judges.
• **STIFLE**
Cat's knee joint on hind leg.
• **STUD**
Male cat kept for breeding.
• **STUD TAIL**
Accumulation of greasy secretion around tail area, especially in unneutered males.
• **STUMPY**
Manx with residual tail.
• **TABBY**
Coat markings that can be striped, blotched, spotted, or ticked **agouti**.
• **TICKING**
Bands of color seen on hairs.
• **TIPPED**
Colored ends to hairs.
• **TOM**
Intact or **unneutered** male cat.
• **TOPCOAT**
Comprises **guard hairs**.
• **TORBIE**
Tortoiseshell Tabby.
• **TORTOISESHELL**
Cat, usually female, showing black, and light and dark red areas in coat.
• **TRICOLORED**
Coat with three distinct colors apparent in coat.
• **TYPE**
Overall size and shape of cat.
• **UNDERCOAT**
Soft hairs beneath **guard hairs**, providing insulation.
• **VAN PATTERN**
Coat mainly white, with tail and head being colored.
• **WEDGE-SHAPED**
Describes head shape of Siamese and similar breeds.
• **WHIP TAIL**
Long, thin, tapering tail.
• **WILD TYPE**
Feral or wild cat appearance.

INDEX

A
Abyssinian 228
  Black Silver 230
  Blue 229
  Chocolate 229
  Fawn 230
  Lavender 228
  Ruddy 231
  Sorrel 231
  Sorrel Silver 232
American Curl Longhair 112
  Black 112
  Black and White 113
  Brown Mackerel Tabby and White
    113
American Curl Shorthair 158
  Black 159
  Brown Classic Torbie 158
  Seal Lynx Point 159
American Shorthair 148
  Black 148
  Black Smoke 149
  Blue-cream 153
  Blue Mackerel Tabby 152
  Brown Classic Tabby 150
  Brown Patched Tabby 151
  Chocolate Shaded 155
  Cream Classic Tabby 154
  Cream Mackerel Tabby 152
  Dilute Calico 153
  Odd-eyed White 149
  Red and White Van Tabby 151
  Red Classic Tabby 150
  Shaded Chocolate 155
  Shaded Silver 155
  Silver Classic Tabby 154
  Silver Shaded 155
American Wirehair 156
  Brown Mackerel Tabby 157
  Calico 156
  Calico Van 157
Angora 80
  Blue-eyed White 80

Chestnut 82
Cinnamon 82
Green-eyed White 81
Lavender 81
Asian 207
  Black Smoke 209
  Brown Mackerel Tabby 207
  Burmese-brown Smoke 208
  Chocolate Smoke 209
  Red (Cornelian) 208

B
Balinese 102
  Blue Point 103
  Chocolate Point 103
  Lilac Point 102
  Seal Point 104
Bengal 239
  Leopard 239
Birman 68
  Blue Lynx Point 73
  Blue Point 70
  Chocolate Point 71
  Cream Point 68
  Lilac Point 69
  Red Point 69
  Seal Lynx Point 73
  Seal Point 70
  Seal Tortie Lynx Point 72
  Seal Tortie Point 72
Black 28
  American Curl Longhair 112
  American Curl Shorthair 159
  American Shorthair 148
  Bombay 210
  British Shorthair 122
  Exotic 137
  Maine Coon 85
  Nonpedigree Longhair 115
  Persian 44
  Turkish Angora 75
Black and White
  American Curl Longhair 113
  British Shorthair 128
  Manx 141
  Nonpedigree Shorthair 241
  Norwegian Forest 90
  Persian 47
  Scottish Fold Shorthair 144
  Sphynx 179
Black Silver Abyssinian 230
Black Silver Spotted Oriental Shorthair
  225
Black Smoke
  American Shorthair 149
  Asian 209
  British Shorthair 130
  Devon Rex 176
  Egyptian Mau 227
  Oriental Shorthair 221
  Persian 57
Black Smoke and White
  Cornish Rex 171
  Maine Coon 89
  Norwegian Forest 92
  Oriental Shorthair 221
  Scottish Fold Shorthair 146
Black Tortie Smoke
  Selkirk Rex 181
  Turkish Angora 77

Blue 28
  Abyssinian 229
  British Shorthair 121
  California Spangled 237
  Devon Rex 173
  Exotic 136
  Korat 183
  Malayan 196
  Nonpedigree Longhair 114
  Oriental Shorthair 217
  Persian 43
  Russian Shorthair 182
  Somali 98
Blue and White
  British Shorthair 128
  Cornish Rex 167
  Maine Coon 85
  Nonpedigree Shorthair 240
  Persian 46
  Scottish Fold Shorthair 145
Blue Classic Tabby British
  Shorthair 129
Blue-cream
  American Shorthair 153
  British Shorthair 127
  Burmese 199
  Nonpedigree Shorthair 242
  Persian 48
  Selkirk Rex 180
  Somali 101
  Turkish Angora 75
Blue-cream Point
  Color Pointed British Shorthair 135
Blue-cream Smoke
  Cornish Rex 171
  Persian 49, 57
Blue-eyed White
  Angora 80
  British Shorthair 119
  Persian 41
Blue-gray Chartreux 165
Blue Lynx Point
  Birman 73
  Javanese 106
  Turkish Angora 77
Blue Mackerel Tabby and
  White Nonpedigree Shorthair 243
Blue Mink
  Tonkinese 201
Blue Point
  Balinese 103
  Birman 70
  Color Pointed British Shorthair 133
  Color Pointed European Shorthair
    164
  Himalayan 64
  Siamese 186
Blue Smoke
  Cornish Rex 170
  Persian 56
Blue Spotted British Shorthair 124
Blue Tabby and White Norwegian
  Forest 91
Blue Tabby Persian 52
Blue Tortie Lynx Point
  Himalayan 67
Blue Tortie Point
  Himalayan 65
Blue Tortie Lynx Point Colorpoint
  Shorthair 192
Blue Tortie Point Colorpoint Shorthair
  187
Bombay 210
  Black 210

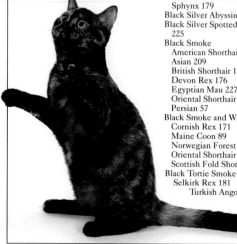

British Shorthair 118
  Black 122
  Black and White 128
  Black Smoke 130
  Black Tipped 131
  Blue 121
  Blue and White 128
  Blue Classic Tabby 129
  Blue-cream 127
  Blue-eyed White 119
  Blue Spotted 124
  Brown Classic Tabby 125
  Calico 123
  Chocolate 121
  Cream 120
  Cream and White 122
  Cream Spotted 126
  Dilute Calico 123
  Lilac 120
  Odd-eyed White 119
  Orange-eyed White 118
  Red Classic 129
  Red Mackerel Tabby 126
  Red Spotted 125
  Red Tipped 131
  Silver Spotted 124
  Tortie Smoke 130
  Tortoiseshell 127
Brown Classic Tabby
  American Shorthair 150
  British Shorthair 125
  Maine Coon 87
  Persian 54
Brown Mackerel Tabby
  American Wirehair 157
  Asian 207
  Nonpedigree Shorthair 245
Brown Patched Tabby American
  Shorthair 151
Brown Spotted and White
  Siberian Cat 93
Brown Spotted Exotic 139
Brown Tabby
  Devon Rex 177
  Nonpedigree Longhair 116
Brown Tabby and White
  Maine Coon 87
  Nonpedigree Shorthair 245
  Norwegian Forest 92
Burmilla 204
  Brown Tipped 206
  Chocolate Tipped 204
  Light Chocolate Tipped 206
  Lilac Shaded 205
  Lilac Silver Shaded 205

C
Calico
  American Wirehair 156
  British Shorthair 123
  Nonpedigree Longhair 117
  Nonpedigree Shorthair 242
  Persian 50
  Scottish Fold Shorthair 146
Calico Van
  American Wirehair 157
  Cornish Rex 168
  Persian 50
California Spangled 236
  Blue 237
  Brown 238
  Charcoal 238
  Gold 236
  Silver 237

Caramel Silver Ticked Tabby
  Oriental Shorthair 218
Caramel Ticked Tabby Oriental
  Shorthair 223
Champagne
  Burmese 195
Champagne Mink
  Tonkinese 202
Charcoal California Spangled 238
Chartreux 165
Chinchilla Persian 55
Chocolate
  Abyssinian 229
  Angora 82
  British Shorthair 121
  Ocicat 234
  Persian 44
Chocolate and White Persian 47
Chocolate Classic Tabby Oriental
  Shorthair 223
Chocolate Point
  Balinese 103
  Birman 71
  Color Pointed British Shorthair 134
  Himalayan 63
  Siamese 186
Chocolate Point Si-rex Cornish Rex
  169
Chocolate Shaded American Shorthair
  155
Chocolate Silver Somali 101
Chocolate Smoke Asian 209
Chocolate Lynx Point
  Balinese 107
  Colorpoint Shorthair 191
  Himalayan 67
Chocolate Torbie
  Persian 51
Chocolate Tortie
  Malayan 197
  Oriental Shorthair 219
  Persian 51
Chocolate Tortie Lynx Point
  Colorpoint Shorthair 193
Chocolate Tortie Point
  Colorpoint Shorthair 188
  Javanese 105
Cinnamon
  Angora 82
  Javanese (UK) 83
  Oriental Shorthair 215
Color Pointed British Shorthair 132
  Blue-cream Point 135
  Blue Point 133
  Chocolate Point 134
  Cream Point 132
  Red Point 134
  Seal Point 133
  Seal Tortie Point 135
Color Pointed European Shorthair 164
  Blue Point 164
Colorpoint Shorthair
  Blue Tabby Point 191
  Blue Tortie Point 187
  Blue Tortie Tabby Point 192
  Chocolate Tabby Point 191
  Chocolate Tortie Point 188
  Chocolate Tortie Tabby Point 193
  Cream Point 184
  Cream Tabby Point 190
  Lilac Tabby Point 190
  Lilac Tortie Tabby Point 192
  Red Point 185
  Red Tabby Point 189

Seal Tabby Point 189
  Seal Tortie Point 188
  Seal Tortie Tabby Point 193
Cornish Rex 166
  Black Smoke and White 171
  Blue and White 167
  Blue-cream Smoke 171
  Blue Smoke 170
  Chocolate Point Si-rex 169
  Cinnamon Silver 169
  Cream 167
  Red Smoke 170
  Tortie and White Van 168
  Tortoiseshell 168
  White 166
Cream 28
  British Shorthair 120
  Burmese 194
  Cornish Rex 167
  Devon Rex 173
  European Shorthair 160
  Oriental Shorthair 213
  Persian 42
  Tonkinese 200
  Turkish Van 78
Cream and White
  British Shorthair 122
  Devon Rex 175
  Nonpedigree Longhair 115
  Persian 45
Cream Classic American Shorthair 154
Cream Point
  Birman 68
  Color Pointed British Shorthair 132
  Colorpoint Shorthair 184
  Himalayan 62
Cream Shaded Cameo Persian 60
Cream Shaded Cameo Tabby
  European Shorthair 162
Cream Shell Cameo Persian 60
Cream Silver Somali 98
Cream Silver Tabby Maine Coon 86
Cream Smoke Himalayan 56
Cream Spotted British Shorthair 126
Cream Lynx Point Colorpoint
  Shorthair 190
Cymric 110
  Orange-eyed White 110

D
Devon Rex 172
  Black Smoke 176
  Blue 173
  Brown Tabby 177
  Cream 173
  Cream and White 175
  Cream Lynx Point Si-rex 174
  Dilute Calico 176
  Red Silver Tabby 177
  Silver Torbie 174
  White 172
  White and Black Smoke 175
Dilute Calico
  American Shorthair 153
  British Shorthair 123
  Devon Rex 176
  Persian 49
  Scottish Fold Longhair 111

E–F
Egyptian Mau 226
  Black Smoke 227
  Bronze 227
  Silver 226

European Shorthair 160
  Black Silver Tabby 163
  Cream 160
  Cream Shaded Cameo Tabby 162
  Red Shaded Cameo Mackerel Tabby
    161
  Red Silver Mackerel Tabby 162
  Tortie Smoke 161
Exotic 136
  Black 137
  Blue 136
  Blue Point Colorpoint 137
  Brown Spotted 139
  Lilac Lynx Point Colorpoint 139
  Shaded Golden 138
  Silver Torbie 138
Fawn 28
  Abyssinian 230
  Oriental Shorthair 214

G
Gold California Spangled 236
Golden-eyed White
  British Shorthair 118
  Maine Coon 84
Golden Persian 59

H
Havana Brown Oriental Shorthair 216
Himalayan 62
  Blue Point 64
  Blue Tortie Lynx Point 67
  Blue Tortie Point 65
  Chocolate Lynx Point 67
  Chocolate Point 63
  Cream Point 62
  Lilac Lynx Point 66
  Lilac Point 63
  Lilac Tortie Point 65
  Red Lynx Point 66
  Seal Point 64J

J–K
Japanese Bobtail 143
  Red and White 143
Javanese 102
  Blue Lynx Point 106
  Chocolate Lynx Point 107
  Chocolate Tortie Point 105
  Red Lynx Point 106
  Seal Lynx Point 107
  Seal Tortie Lynx Point
    105
  Seal Tortie Point 104
Javanese (UK) 83
  Cinnamon 83
Korat 183

L
Lavender
  Abyssinian 228
  Angora 81
  British Shorthair 120
  Oriental Shorthair 213
  Persian 43
  Somali 99
Lavender and White Persian
  46
Lavender Classic Tabby Oriental
  Shorthair 220
Lavender Ticked Tabby Oriental
  Shorthair 222
Leopard Bengal 239
Lilac-cream
  Malayan 198
Lilac Lynx Point
  Colorpoint Exotic 139
  Colorpoint Shorthair 190
  Himalayan 66
Lilac Point
  Birman 69
  Himalayan 63
  Siamese 185
Lilac Tabby Persian 52
Lilac Tortie
  Tonkinese 203
Lilac Tortie Lynx Point
  Colorpoint Shorthair 192

M
Maine Coon 84
  Black 85
  Black Smoke and White 89
  Blue and White 85
  Blue Silver Patched Tabby 89
  Brown Classic Tabby 87
  Brown Tabby and White 87
  Cream Silver Tabby 86
  Golden-eyed White 84
  Silver Patched Tabby 88
  Silver Tabby 86
  Torbie and White 88
Malayan 194
  Blue 196
  Blue-cream 199
  Brown Tortie 199
  Champagne 195
  Chocolate Tortie 197
  Cream 194
  Lilac-cream 198
  Platinum 196
  Red 195
Manx 140
  Black and White 141
  Red Classic Tabby 141
  Red Classic Tabby and White 142
  Tortoiseshell 142
  White 140

N
Natural Mink
  Tonkinese 202
Nonpedigree Longhair 114
  Black 115
  Blue 114
  Brown Classic Tabby 116
  Cream and White 115
  Red Spotted 116
  Silver and White 117
  Tortie and White 117
Nonpedigree Shorthair 240
  Black and White 241

Blue-cream 242
Blue Mackerel Tabby and White 243
Brown Classic Tabby and White 244
Brown Mackerel Tabby 245
Brown Spotted 244
Brown Tabby and White 245
Calico 242
Red Classic Tabby and White 243
White and Tortie 241
Norwegian Forest Cat 90
  Black and White 90
  Black Smoke and White 92
  Blue-cream Smoke and White 91
  Blue Tabby and White 91
  Brown Tabby and White 92

O
Ocicat 234
  Chocolate 234
  Silver 235
  Tawny 235
Odd-eyed White
  American Shorthair 149
  British Shorthair 119
  Persian 41
Orange-eyed White
  Cymric 110
  Persian Longhair 40
Oriental Shorthair 212
  Black Silver Spotted 225
  Black Smoke 221
  Black Smoke and White 221
  Blue 217
  Caramel 216
  Caramel Silver Ticked Tabby 218
  Caramel Ticked Tabby 223
  Chestnut Silver Classic Tabby 225
  Chestnut Spotted 220
  Chestnut Ticked Tabby 224
  Chestnut Tortie 219
  Chocolate Classic Tabby 223
  Cinnamon 215
  Cinnamon Tortie 218
  Cream 213
  Ebony 217
  Havana Brown 216
  Lavender 213
  Lavender Classic Tabby 220
  Lavender Ticked Tabby 222Red 214
  Red and White 215
  Red Ticked Tabby 222
  Tortie Black Silver Spotted 219
  White 212

P
Persian 40
  Black 44
  Black and White 47
  Black Smoke 57
  Blue 43
  Blue and White 46
  Blue-cream 48
  Blue-cream Smoke 57
  Blue-eyed White 41
  Blue Smoke 56
  Blue Tabby 52
  Blue Tortie Smoke 49
  Brown Classic Tabby 54
  Chinchilla 55
  Chocolate 44
  Chocolate and White 47
  Chocolate Torbie 51
  Chocolate Tortie 51
  Cream 42

Cream and White 45
Cream Shaded Cameo 60
Cream Shell Cameo 60
Cream Smoke 56
Dilute Calico 49
Golden Persian 59
Lavender 43
Lavender and White 46
Lilac Tabby 52
Odd-eyed White 41
Pewter 58
Red 42
Red and White 45
Red Shaded Cameo 61
Red Tabby 53
Shaded Silver 55
Silver Tabby 53
Torbie 54
Tortie and White 50
Tortie and White Van 50
Tortie Cameo 59
Tortie Smoke 58
Tortoiseshell 48
Pewter Persian 58
Platinum
  Malayan 196
Platinum Mink
  Tonkinese 201

R
Ragdoll 94
  Blue Mitted 95
  Seal Bicolor 95
  Seal Point 94
Red
  Malayan 195
  Oriental Shorthair 214
Red and White
  Japanese Bobtail 143
  Oriental Shorthair 215
  Persian 45
Red and White Van Tabby
  American Shorthair 151
  Red Classic British Shorthair 129
Red Classic Tabby
  American Shorthair 150
  Manx 141
Red Classic Tabby and White
  Manx 142
  Nonpedigree Shorthair 243
Red Lynx Point
  Javanese 106
  Himalayan 66
  Colorpoint Shorthair 189
Red Point
  Birman 69
  Color Pointed British
    Shorthair 134
  Colorpoint Shorthair 185
Red Shaded Cameo Persian 61
Red Silver Mackerel Tabby European
  Shorthair 162
Red Silver Tabby Devon Rex 177
Red Smoke Cornish Rex 170
Red Spotted
  British Shorthair 125
  Nonpedigree Longhair 116
Red Tabby Persian 53
Red Tipped British Shorthair 131
Ruddy
  Abyssinian 231
  Somali 97
  Wild Abyssinian 233
Russian Shorthair 182

S
Sable Burmese 197
Scottish Fold Longhair
  Dilute Calico 111
Scottish Fold Shorthair 144
  Black and White 144
  Black Smoke and White 146
  Blue and White 145
  Calico 146
Seal Bicolor Ragdoll 95
Seal Point
  Balinese 104
  Birman 70
  Color Pointed British Shorthair 133
  Himalayan 64
  Ragdoll 94
  Siamese 187
Seal Lynx Point
  American Curl Shorthair 159
  Birman 70
  Colorpoint Shorthair 189
  Javanese 107
Seal Tortie Lynx Point
  Birman 72
  Colorpoint Shorthair 193
  Javanese 105
Seal Tortie Point
  Birman 72
  Color Pointed British Shorthair 135
  Colorpoint Shorthair 188
  Javanese 104
Selkirk Rex 180
  Black Tortie Smoke 181
  Blue-cream 180
Sepia Agouti Singapura 211
Shaded Golden Exotic 138
Shaded Silver American Shorthair 155
Shaded Silver Persian 55
Siamese 184
  Blue Point 186
  Chocolate Point 186
  Lilac Point 185
  Seal Point 187
Siberian Cat 93
  Brown Spotted and White 93
Silver
  California Spangled 237
  Egyptian Mau 226
  Ocicat 235
  Somali 100
Silver Classic Tabby American
  Shorthair 154
Silver Patched Tabby Maine Coon 88
Silver Spotted British Shorthair 124
Silver Tabby
  Maine Coon 86
  Persian 53
Silver Tortie Classic Tabby Exotic 138
Singapura
  Sepia Agouti 211
Snowshoe Seal and White Point 147
Somali 96
  Blue 98
  Blue-cream 101
  Blue Silver 99
  Chocolate Silver 101
  Cream Silver 98
  Lavender 99
  Ruddy 97
  Ruddy Silver 100
  Sorrel 97
  Sorrel Silver 96
Sorrel
  Abyssinian 231

Somali 97
Sorrel Silver
  Abyssinian 232
  Somali 96
Sphynx 178
  Black and White 179
  Brown and White 178

T
Tawny
  Ocicat 235
Tiffany 108
  Blue Tipped Silver 109
  Brown 109
  Red 108
Tonkinese 200
  Blue Mink 201
  Brown Tortie 203
  Champagne Mink 202
  Honey Mink 200
  Natural Mink 202
  Lilac Tortie 203
  Platinum Mink 201
Torbie and White Maine Coon 88
Tortie Smoke
  British Shorthair 130
  European Shorthair 161
  Persian 58
Tortoiseshell
  British Shorthair 127
  Cornish Rex 168
  Manx 142
  Persian 48
  Selkirk Rex 181
Turkish Angora
  Black 75
  Black Tortie Smoke 77
  Blue-cream 75
  Blue Mackerel Tabby 77
  Cream Classic Tabby 76
  Cream Classic Tabby and White 76
  White 74
Turkish Van 78
  Auburn 79
  Cream 78

W
White 28
  Cornish Rex 166
  Devon Rex 172
  Manx 140
  Oriental Shorthair 212
  Turkish Angora 74
White and Black Smoke Devon
  Rex 175
White and Tortie Nonpedigree
  Shorthair 241
Wild Abyssinian
  Ruddy 233

USEFUL ADDRESSES

American Cat Association
8101 Katherine Avenue,
Panorama City, CA 91402

American Cat Fanciers' Association
PO Box 203, Point Lookout, MO 65726

Canadian Cat Association
52 Dean Street, Brampton, Ontario,
Canada L6W 1M6

The Cat Fanciers' Association Inc.
PO Box 1005, Manasquan,
NJ 08736-1005

Cat Fanciers' Federation, Inc.
9509 Montgomery Road, Cincinnati, OH 45242

The International Cat Association
PO Box 2684, Harlingen, TX 78551

Best Friends Animal Sanctuary
PO Box G, Kanab UT 84741

Cat Fancy
PO Box 6050, Mission Viejo, CA92690

Cat World™ International
PO Box 35635, Phoenix, AZ 85069

ACKNOWLEDGMENTS

THE AUTHOR would like to thank the many kind cat fanciers who allowed their cats to be photographed for the book. Particular thanks are due to Fiona Henrie and Phyllis Choppen for co-ordinating this process, and to Marga Harms and Marijke Wijers who helped to organize cats for photography in the Netherlands. The author would also like to thank: Marc Henrie, with whom it is always a pleasure to work; Colin Walton and Irene Lyford for their care and expertise in designing and editing the book; and Jane Laing, Mary-Clare Jerram, and Gill Della Casa at Dorling Kindersley for their valuable input. He would like to thank Rita Hemsley for her typing skills and, last but not least, the consultants Therese Clarke, Daphne Negus, and Baroness Miranda von Kirchberg for their invaluable advice and contributions.

DORLING KINDERSLEY would like to thank: Paul Casey for information on the California Spangled; Phyllis and John Choppen for their hospitality when photographing the four generations of Orientals; Andrea Fair for help with Grooming and Choosing a Kitten photography; Jan Osborne of *Purrsonal Touch* for use of equipment, and the co-operation of her Persian *Rapunzel Cherokee Chief* in photography; Ruta and Peter Towse for their help with photography of Shorthairs and Foreigns.
We would also like to thank Dr A.W. Gentry of the Natural History Museum for advice on the cat family, and Dr Andrew S. Nash of Glasgow University Veterinary School for advice on fur types.
We are indebted to: Michael Allaby for proof-reading and the Index; Mike Darton for proof-reading; Alison Edmunds, Angeles Gavira, Carol McGlynn, and Bella Pringle for editorial assistance; Steve Tilling for help with the Identification Key; Alastair Wardle for invaluable technical assistance.

PICTURE CREDITS
All specially commissioned photographs by Marc Henrie, except those on *pp.14-15* by Jane Burton.

The publishers would like to thank the following photographers and organizations for their permission to reproduce the photographs indicated below:
Bridgeman Art Library 7 bl; Stephe Bruin 9 all; 36 bc; 165 all; Chanan Photography 7 t; 31 bl; 36 tcl; 149 b; 149 tl; 149 tr; 151 t; 152 b; 152 tl; 152 tr; 153 t; 157 b; 157 t; 237 c; 237 bl; 237 br; 237 t; 238 t; Michael Holford 6 tl; Johnson Photography 25 tr; Dr Andrew S. Nash, University of Glasgow Veterinary School 26 t; Science Photo Library 8 tr; Through the Cat's Eye 153 b; Tony Stone Worldwide 8 c; Tetsu Yamazaki 27 cl; 31 br; 49 b; 112 b; 112 t; 113 bl; 113 br; 113 t; 148 l; 148 r; 150 bl; 150 tl; 150 br; 150 tr; 154 bl; 154 br; 154 tl; 154 tr; 155 bl; 155 br; 155 tl; 155 tr; 156 l; 156 r; 158 ; 159 bl; 159 tl; 159 br; 159tr; 181 c; 226 br; 226 c; 226 tr; 227 bl; 227 br; 227 tl; 227 tr; 233 r; 233 l; Dave King 7 br; 116 bc; 116 cr; 151 bl; 151 cr;
The black and white photographs on *p.6* and *p.18* were taken from *The Book of the Cat*, by Frances Simpson (Cassell and Co. Ltd; 1903).

Endpapers by Caroline Church
All other artwork by Janos Marffy
Picture research: Julia Pashley